OWLS
OF THE WORLD

Great horned owl *Bubo virginianus*. From a series of
engravings published in London by G. Kearsley in 1808.

OWLS OF THE WORLD

their evolution, structure and ecology

Illustrated by John Rignall

Edited by John A. Burton

PHILIP BURTON
MICHAEL FOGDEN
HOWARD GINN
DAVID GLUE
COLIN HARRISON
G. P. HEKSTRA
HEIMO MIKKOLA
RONALD MURTON
IAN PRESTT
JOHN SPARKS
BERNARD STONEHOUSE
REGINALD WAGSTAFFE
C. A. WALKER
W. VAN DER WEYDEN

E. P. DUTTON & CO., INC.

NEW YORK 1973

EDITOR'S NOTE

In this book we have attempted to write about and to illustrate every known species of owl. The type of information available about owls varies widely. A few of the common species have been well studied but many others are still largely unknown. The explanation for this is quite simple: not only are most species nocturnal, but most also live in forests, particularly in tropical forests where observation is difficult.

Each chapter has been written by a different author and inevitably there are differences of approach and style. Generally we have aimed at an ecological rather than a taxonomic account, though in one chapter, on the Barn owls, the subspecies of *Tyto alba* – one of the most variable of the owl species – have been treated in detail.

We have illustrated as many owls as possible with colour photographs; many, however, have rarely been photographed, and these have been specially painted by John Rignall. Though it has not been possible to reproduce these to scale, we have tried to give some sense of size differences.

The basic framework for any book of this kind is the check list. The one we have used is based on that of J. L. Peters (*Birds of the World*, Vol. IV (1940) Harvard University Press). This appears on page 198.

John A. Burton

The publisher gratefully acknowledges the advice and assistance
given by many people in producing this book.
Particular thanks are due to the following:
C W Benson, Robert Burton, Michael and Patricia Fogden,
Dr G F Mees and the Rijksmuseum van Natuurlijke Historie, Leiden, the Netherlands,
The Academy of Natural Science, Philadelphia, USA,
The British Museum (Natural History), Tring, England,
the Koninklijk Museum voor Midden-Afrika, Tervuren, Belgium
and the Institut voor Taxonomische Zoölogie, Zoölogisch Museum,
Amsterdam, the Netherlands.

Index compiled by M O'Hanlon

Maps by Geographical Projects

Copyright © 1973 by Eurobook Limited

Published simultaneously in Canada by
Clarke, Irwin & Company Limited, Toronto and Vancouver

SBN 0-525-17432-X

Library of Congress Catalog Card Number: 73-8271

Printed in the Netherlands by Smeets Offset, Weert

Preface

Owls are one of the groups of birds most subject to prejudice, both malevolent and to a lesser extent benevolent, and to misunderstanding. All over the world those concerned with shooting pheasant or hunting other game birds tend to view owls with much the same suspicion as they do hawks and falcons: with curiously conflicting emotions of love or hate. This book aims to clear people's minds of such prejudices, and will go some way towards helping them to understand the place of nocturnal birds of prey in the ecology of a habitat. Although written by scientists who are experts in their own field, it describes the known behaviour of owls with exactness, in non-technical language suitable for the many thousands of people who have recently taken to birdwatching.

Owls have fascinated men for thousands of years. The Greek and Roman goddesses of wisdom, Pallas Athene and Minerva, were both particularly associated with them and one can only assume that the unmoving calm of an owl in daylight gave it the appearance of wisdom while its mournful hooting at night perhaps added to its charisma. Though nowadays it is clear to naturalists that the owl is no more or less wise than other birds, its reputation persists. In the fifth century BC a Greek coin appeared with a picture of an owl on one side and of Pallas Athene on the other: some 2,500 years later the fifty dollar gold piece struck for the Panama-Pacific Expedition in 1915 carried the same two figures.

Whatever the cause of their fascination, there are still remarkable and tantalizing gaps in our knowledge of owl behaviour and ecology, as the authors of this book freely admit. This is a heartening state of affairs, particularly to the keen young bird student 'willing to travel'. Knowledge is badly needed to combat the prejudices of those hunters and gamekeepers throughout the world who persecute owls needlessly, often using inhuman and illegal traps, which kill indiscriminately. Books like this can play a valuable part in spreading knowledge and understanding of the owl's true character, and of its place in nature.

Peter Conder
Director
Royal Society for the Protection of Birds

THE INTERNATIONAL COUNCIL FOR BIRD PRESERVATION
Like many animals today, birds of prey are increasingly
at risk. Some owls are already very rare indeed, known
perhaps from only a single specimen or, like the
laughing owl of New Zealand, thought to be already
extinct. As habitats are changed, often destroyed by
man, other species are likely to be affected, while the
increasing use of pesticides threatens the food supply of
many more.

At the forefront of efforts to ensure a continued place
in the world for owls and other birds, the work of the
International Council for Bird Preservation stands out.
As an example, the Caen Conference on Birds of Prey
and Owls, sponsored by ICBP in 1964, was the first
international conference devoted to the subject of protection of these birds, at which scientists, conservationists, sportsmen, falconers, foresters and agriculturists
alike, representing 11 nations, passed recommenda-
tions calling for more adequate protection of all birds
of prey, including owls.

The International Council for Bird Preservation was
founded in 1922 by Dr T. Gilbert Pearson, President
of the National Association of Audubon Societies of
the USA. His aim was to effect an international
organization which would stimulate the growing
interest in bird protection by the interchange of
publications and by occasional conventions where
representatives of different countries could meet. Such
a council could also tackle a number of problems that
were by their nature international: oil pollution of the
seas, for example, and the export and import of birds
or their feathers.

Originally consisting of eminent conservationists
from Britain, Holland, France and America, the
Association has since expanded to include members
from 61 nations, in every continent of the world.
Together, these national sections and their many
constituent societies work to generate interest and
provide information about bird preservation at home,
and to effect co-operative conservation internationally.

The achievements of the ICPB have been considerable, and in many cases its concern has been far in
advance of world opinion – which is only now coming
to recognize dangers that the ICPB have been fighting
for years. Pollutants, for example, have been of
particular concern to the Council ever since Dr
Pearson brought members' attention to the problem
of oil pollution of the ocean in 1922; and as early as

1950 the Council was calling on governments to
prevent the indiscriminate use of pesticides.

The protection of birds is, of course, the primary aim
of the Council, and it has achieved a number of
successes in this field. 1963 saw a significant milestone
in international co-operation when after a long-
standing ICPB campaign, a greatly improved
International Convention for the Protection of Birds
came into effect. Migratory birds come under the
special protection of the ICPB, as the Council has long
argued that they are not the property of one country
alone, but a matter of international responsibility.
ICPB-inspired schemes include a plan for a series of
reserves along European migration routes where birds
are often massacred in their millions, and international
censuses to establish the population and demography of
endangered species. Finally, the Council works to
preserve rare bird species through advising governments and conducting research projects. *Owls of the
World* is warmly welcomed by the International
Council for Bird Preservation.

Introduction

Like penguins or pelicans, owls are easy birds to identify. With few exceptions they look like nothing but owls, and the most inexperienced ornithologist among us knows very well when he is looking at one. Their distinctive appearance – huge head, large, forward-looking eyes, concentrated expression, chunky body and sober habit – has made us notice them, and owls have insinuated themselves to an extraordinary degree into human affairs. Children the world over meet them in legends and storybooks, humanized and endowed with solemn wisdom – pompous like archetypal headmasters, but on the whole benign. Without owls, advertisers would have to find a new symbol for sound scholarly judgement, and horn-rimmed executives a new professional image.

Small birds, too, react strongly to owls, though their response is inborn, not taught: on sighting an owl, many Passerine birds break off whatever they are doing to 'mob' the bird, making aerial attacks with an elaborate display of alarm and concern. These displays alert the community to the presence of the owl, effectively robbing it of any chance of surprising them. What is there about owls that fascinates humans and small birds alike?

Superficially, owls as a group show several striking qualities which distinguish them from other birds. Many are adaptations to night hunting. Where most birds are strongly diurnal, owls have specialized in hunting in poor evening light and at night. Not all are nocturnal: some hunt by day and by night. But about two-thirds of the 130 or more species of owls are busiest in late evening and during the dark hours, when they become the nocturnal counterpart of eagles, harriers and falcons.

Their prey includes small birds, which as diurnal foragers are ill-adapted for poor light, and at a disadvantage after sunset. A few species hunt actively on the wing, taking moths and other small creatures in flight. This is not a role for which most owls are especially well adapted: far better at catching nocturnal insects on the wing are frogmouths and nightjars (Caprimulgiformes) which are among their closest kin. Some owls are highly skilled fishermen, catching fish in their talons from the surface of rivers; others hunt crabs on shores and river shallows. But most quarter the ground in silent flight, or scan it from a convenient perch, waiting – often listening intently – for ground-living insects and small mammals.

Birds which hunt mainly in poor light or darkness need excellent, specialized eyesight capable of using every scrap of light to the best advantage. The huge owl eyes set forward in the skull, to provide overlapping binocular vision have, like expensive cameras, a combination of qualities which render them unusually efficient – perhaps fifty to one hundred times more efficient than our own – at distinguishing small objects in dull light. Wide open, the owl's eyes are alert and perceptive, especially at night when the circular curtains of irides are drawn back and the dark pupils distended. Half-hooded by heavy eyelids during the day, they remain watchful and efficient, like the eyes of sleepy invigilators: owls see well in daylight, accommodating rapidly from day to night conditions.

The eyeballs, shaped like tapering cylinders to provide the largest possible expanse of retina, lack even the small mobility of most birds' eyes; they cannot rotate up, down or sideways. Alerted to some object or movement in its foreground, an owl cannot swivel its eyes like a mammal. Instead it turns its whole head, mounted on unusually flexible bearings, and stares directly with a curiously human intensity. Contrasting with the sideways glance of most birds, this conveys an air of concentrated attention. Owls often spoil this effect by bobbing the head up and down or craning sideways at an alarming angle, behaviour which probably helps them to judge distance.

Many species of owls have flexible tufts of feathers above the eyes, usually held obliquely or vertically, which look like ears or eccentric eyebrows, but are in fact neither. Their movements, under the control of scalp muscles, alter the outline of the head and add a range of expression to the face, which may be an important aid to identification and communication between individual birds at close quarters. Whether owls use their ear tufts and expressions to convey information about their emotional state, as other birds use crests and vivid patches of feathers, is not known. Owls certainly express themselves vocally during their nightly activity. Throughout the world they have an extraordinary repertoire of shrieks, hoots and caterwaulings, in a range of frequencies which carry far on the night air. These announce their presence and the existence of occupied territories; like the songs of blackbirds and the drumming of snipe they convey to wanderers of the same species that the area is occupied. Calls are completely diagnostic of species, and owls are as likely to recognize other individuals by voice as by sight during their travels in the dark. Apart from territorial calls, owls have an additional vocabulary of softer conversational calls for use at short range between partners and between parent and offspring.

Like other birds, owls have dense, soft plumage which makes them look much bigger than they are and helps to keep them warm during long periods of inactivity between hunting forays. Apart from facial discs and ear tufts, they have few decorations — unadorned by crests or curliques, their plumage is usually a delicate, drab colour, matching their background by day and blending readily with the darkness of night. Some are colourful indeed, as the portraits in this book show, but there is a collective sobriety about their appearance. The plumage is unusually soft, lacking the hard sheen of many birds' feathers, and the leading quills on the wings have a soft, serrated edge. These qualities, combined with lightness and large wing area, help owls to move silently through the air — to hear other sounds while they are in flight, and to avoid giving alarm to their prey. Small birds which mob owls seem to respond especially to their shape, colour and texture. Tests with models have shown that to a songbird owlness is a chunky, rounded shape without neck or protrusions, matt in texture and drab in colour, sitting upright on a perch.

Apart from their eyes, owls have other superlative aids for night hunting. Where vision fails, hearing grows in importance, and many of the truly nocturnal owls have ears of extraordinary efficiency. The saucer-shaped discs of feathers surrounding the eyes of most nocturnal species, which look as though they should be concerned with sight, are in fact reflectors. Their rear surfaces, lifting slightly from the face by muscular action, help to deflect sound into the vast openings of the ears which lie beneath. In several species with especially acute hearing, the ear openings are placed asymmetrically on the skull, one higher than the other, and guarded by feathered flaps of skin which probably serve as additional sound deflectors. Barn owls, tawny owls and other night-hunting species hear sounds well below the threshold of human hearing. They are especially sensitive to sounds with a component of high frequencies – the squeals of small rodents, the rustle of dry leaves – and the asymmetry of their head helps them to locate the source of the sound with precision. Centres of the brain associated with hearing are correspondingly well developed, containing more cells and linkages than are found in auditory centres of less gifted species.

With this enviable apparatus of sight and hearing, packed neatly and unobtrusively in a moderately oversized skull, night hunting owls scan the ground from their perch or sweeping flight. Ears and eyes together detect and locate each source of sound, and the experienced bird swoops precisely to strike with its talons. Under experimental conditions barn owls have shown their ability to strike successfully mouse-sized prey in complete darkness – a combination of sensory and muscular skills.

Owls occupy all kinds of habitats, though many prefer woodland or forest edge. A few, like the Arctic Snowy owl and the desert-living species of North America, live in situations where trees cannot grow. Woodland species nest in trees, roost in them during the day, and use them as convenient bases for their hunting sorties at night. Many small owls of old, well-established forests are hole-nesters, often taking over cavities previously occupied by woodpeckers or other species. Newly planted woodlands with few old trees generally lack suitable holes to attract them, but foresters who provide nestboxes find that owls take readily to them, and help their hosts by keeping down stocks of woodland rodents. Larger owls nest untidily in open sites, often in the abandoned nest of a raptor or corvid high in the treetops. Owls of desert, taiga and tundra nest on open ground or in low vegetation; species of tropical deserts tend to live underground taking over abandoned rodent burrows to escape the heat of the sun.

Whether nesting in the open or deep in cavities, owls are not houseproud and do not include homebuilding among their skills. Some add lining material to existing nests, providing at least a minimum of protection for their eggs and young. The eggs are white and undecorated; most are rounded, some almost spherical, and clutches of two, three or four are characteristic. Burrowing owls and other ground-nesting species tend to lay more, and clutches of ten to thirteen have been recorded when food is abundant. Chicks wear a thick down of grey, brown, or white, warm and serviceable but characteristically drab. Incubation and care of young tends to be the responsibility of females, while the males – which are usually smaller – forage and bring food home to the family group.

Many but not all species of owls adopt a family planning measure common to other groups of predatory birds. Eggs laid at intervals of two or three days hatch asynchronously at similar intervals, because incubation begins with first egg laid, providing a brood in which the oldest may be over a week in advance of the youngest. When food is plentiful, all survive: when it is scarce, competition between nestlings is biased heavily in favour of the one or two oldest chicks, which survive at the expense of the others. Investing the available food in this way ensures that one or two well endowed chicks, rather than three or four starvelings, are launched to face the rigours of the following winter, and increases the chance that one at least will survive to maturity.

Like other birds, owls have light, flimsy bones which make poor fossils, and the record of their evolution is meagre. The oldest owl remains so far discovered appear in Eocene rocks of the mid-Western United States, probably dating from about sixty million years ago. Fossils from the mid and late Tertiary are more plentiful, and include recognizable ancestors of living genera. In time the history of the group will probably be traced back into the Palaeocene and late Cretaceous. However, at present it seems likely that the major diversification of owls and their spread across the world occurred during the early to middle Tertiary.

This was the time when the recently established families of modern mammals were beginning to diversify, and many new forms of small mammal were occupying new niches in newly-established grasslands and forests. Both the diurnal and the nocturnal predators of small mammals would be seizing opportunities to exploit these new food reserves; hence the development and diversification of the owl pattern of living.

The fossil record tells us little about ancestral links between owls and other groups of birds. Bones of the earliest owls are good owl bones, but not halfway stages between owls and some other ancestral groups, and nothing in the later record suggests that other groups of birds have arisen by diverging from the mainstream of owl evolution. Similarities of way of life, and basic anatomy have suggested to bird taxonomists for well over a century that owls are mostly closely related to diurnal birds of prey, especially to hawks and falcons. Some taxonomists placed owls and hawks together in the same order. Others ascribed them to separate orders, but grouped them closely under the general title of 'raptors'. Today there is general agreement that owls merit an order of their own (Strigiformes), hawks, falcons and vultures another (Falconiformes), and there is perhaps less certainty that the two orders as a whole are closely linked.

Recent opinion based on a new taxonomic indicator – the distribution of proteins in egg white – confirms that owls form a closely knit group and suggests that their closest kin are the Caprimulgiformes – the oilbirds of the Caribbean (which eat seeds and live in caves) and the nocturnal, insect-feeding potoos, nightjars and frogmouths which are highly adapted for catching their food on the wing, and show many superficial and anatomical similarities to owls. Egg-white proteins also support small anatomical characters in suggesting affinities between barn owls and true falcons – two slightly maverick families of their respective orders which have often been linked also on minor points of anatomical similarity. Until further evidence is forthcoming we can only say that the owls are most clearly akin to the Caprimulgiformes and show affinities also with the Falconiformes – especially with the true falcons themselves.

Within their order Strigiformes living owls fall readily into two clear-cut groups – the barn owls (Tytonidae) and the others (Strigidae). The most obvious character distinguishing the two is the shape of the face; barn owls have a heart-shaped face, strigid owls a round or oval face without a prominent dip in the upper border between the eyes. The barn owl's tail usually ends in a shallow V, its second and third toes are roughly equal in length, the claw of the middle toe has a comb-like serrated edge and the wishbone and breastbone are fixed together for strength. Strigid owls have a round tail, second toe shorter than the third, no comb on the middle claw, and separate wishbone and keel. Apart from some further small but constant differences in feathering and skeletal structure, barn owls and strigid owls are very similar. More than one author has suggested that classifying them in separate families over-emphasizes the differences between them, and that the two should be no more than subdivisions of a single family. Two further families of extinct owls, known only from fossil remains, have also been described.

The Tytonid owls include eight species of barn owl (genus *Tyto*) and two of bay owls (*Phodilus*). *Tyto alba*, the common barn owl, is one of the world's most widespread species, appearing on every inhabited continent. A skilled hunter of rodents, for hundreds, even thousands of years it has profited from living in rural areas close to man. Clearing forest and cultivating the land, combined with wasteful methods of sowing, reaping and storing grain, encouraged the development of large local populations of rats and mice. As its name implies, the barn owl found farm buildings an acceptable alternative to trees and cliffs for roosting, and has for long paid rent in kind by ratting and mousing.

Recent changes in agricultural practice – including use of chemical insecticides and dressings, have upset this happy relationship and decimated populations of common barn owls in civilized countries: less civilized communities continue to enjoy the company and help of these engaging birds. Other species of barn owls are found in Africa, on islands in the Indian Ocean and East Indies, and in Australasia. Bay owls are an anomalous pair of species respectively from Central Africa and the Oriental region, which have puzzled several generations of taxonomists. Included by most in the Tytonidae, they have also been linked with *Asio* (the long-eared and short-eared strigid owls) and, by a recent reviewer even ascribed to a family of their own.

The very much larger family of strigid owls includes about 120 species, of wide-ranging habitats and ways of life. There is no general agreement as to how the two dozen genera should be grouped. Traditionally they are divided into two subfamilies, mainly according to the complexity of their ear flaps. Owls of the subfamily Buboninae including screech, scops, eagle, fishing, pygmy, hawk and burrowing owls, among many others, in general have relatively simple external ears; those of the subfamily Striginae, including tawny, wood, long-eared, short-eared, and snowy owls, have larger, more complex ear apertures, with correspondingly elaborate flaps. Though the justification for this division is in doubt, the traditional subfamilies tend to be retained for want of a better arrangement.

Large or small, diurnal or nocturnal, pursuing fish, flesh or fowl in their various professional ways, owls have practised their skills as avian master-predators with little regard for the presence of man. Throughout their long co-existence the world has always been broad enough to contain both ancient birds and modern man without enmity – without even rivalry, for their paths have seldom crossed. Owls first caught man's imagination simply by being owls – wide-eyed birds of the night. Then they caught his interest, as creatures endowed with unusual skills and adaptations to support their way of life. Now they must command his attention, his respect, and his protection; like so many other animals of outstanding quality, they stand in twin jeopardy from his ruthless destruction of habitat and his mindless spreading of poisons across their world.

PART I

CHAPTER ONE

Owls and men

These are they which ye shall have in abomination among fowls; they shall not be eaten . . . the eagle, and the owl, and the nighthawk, and the cuckow . . .
And the little owl, and the cormorant, and the great owl.

This quotation, from Leviticus Chapter 11, verses 13–17, must be one of the first recorded natural history lessons: these birds were judged unwholesome, not for superstitious reasons but because of their preference for feeding on carrion and choosing to inhabit derelict and desolate places.

The paths of men and owls had, however, crossed long before the Jewish law was formulated. The pictorial legacy of the Palaeolithic people of Europe includes representations of owls. At Trois Frères, in France, the unmistakable outline of a pair of snowy owls and their chicks is etched into a rock face. The artist lived at a time when the Arctic climate extended farther south than today, and rendered much of France suitable as a breeding ground for these large white owls. Snowy owls were not only considered as birds worthy of an artist's attention, but also appealed to the palate: the presence of their scraped bones on Neolithic dwelling sites proves that many a plump owlet was taken for the pot, as snowy owls are today by Eskimos.

From very early days to the present, owls and men have had a continuous relationship, and owls are prominent in myth, superstition and folklore. Myths and superstitions are often based upon the animal's real habits which, by association, become linked with happy or fearful events. Or they may be founded upon the fact that we see animals as projections of ourselves. Furthermore, we envy their qualities which would enhance our own performance in certain situations – in battle for instance, or in the dark. The evidence suggests that owls have generated strong passions in us. Though we cannot feel indifferent to them, our emotions are clearly ambivalent. On one side, to see or hear an owl is an omen of bad news; a message of doom and gloom. On the other, owls are wise old birds, and enough toy owls are sold over the counters every year to support the view that we also look on owls with a certain amount of affection.

What evidence is there of a love-fear relationship between us and these predatory birds, and what facets of the owl's appearance and character arouse such powerful feelings in us? Normally the answers to such questions would be mere conjecture, but fortunately a recent British television survey into the public's attitudes towards wildlife programmes provides some very

A cave painting at Balu-Uru, in northern Australia demonstrates that owls have fascinated men for thousands of years. The 'owl-man' probably represents one of the half-human spirits that Aborigines believed existed at the Creation of the world. In other parts of Australia owls were thought to guard the souls of women—a belief that gave them a measure of protection.

revealing information about owls. Over 300 people above the age of 15 were carefully and methodically interviewed about their animal likes and dislikes. In the list of favourite animals, headed by dolphins, owls came a long way down, at twenty-seventh. Penguins, 'tropical birds', flamingos, pelicans, robins, swallows and ostriches were all judged to be more appealing than owls. One-third of the people would have made a point of watching a television programme about owls; one-sixth would have avoided being exposed to them on their television screens. Owls were clearly not in the same class as penguins, the universal favourite, but were much more favourably considered than vultures. Ambivalence towards owls was clearly reflected in the way the panel described these birds. The consensus was that owls were *cruel* as opposed to *kind*, *strong* as opposed to *weak*, *not cuddly* as opposed to *cuddly*, and *unapproachable* as opposed to *approachable*. These could all be said to be characteristics causing us to dislike owls. However, owls were also thought to be *clever*, *sad*, *fascinating*, and – surprisingly – *beautiful*. In view of the balance between likeable and dislikeable features, it was interesting that when given a choice between the terms *frightening* and *non-frightening*, 39 per cent of the people found it frightening, 35 per cent did not, and 26 per cent preferred to view owls as neither. This modern survey confirms the owl as a Jekyll and Hyde character, worthy of our respect for its cleverness and beauty but at the same time evil and sinister.

Why do we hold these conflicting views? It is

not difficult to see why we should find owls unedifying. They are killers, superbly adapted for finding prey and despatching it quickly and efficiently. With a few notable exceptions, predators have never been popular with us, although in certain cases we have through sympathetic magical rites attempted to acquire their strength and ferocity. It is no accident for instance that armies such as the Romans and the Germans have marched behind eagle-adorned banners. Whatever else we may feel for them, we have no love for eagles; and yet they are not so very different from owls. An owl, too, is equipped with cruel talons, and has a large beak curved like a meat hook. However, because of their design for nocturnal hunting, they also present us with signals to which we react favourably, if unconsciously. It is a truism that, for an animal, the way to our hearts is to look as human as possible, and owls display so many anthropomorphic characteristics, while at the same time managing to hide the tools of their killing trade, that we cannot help seeing them as endearing caricatures of ourselves.

An owl has enormous eyes set at the front of its head to enhance visual acuity and provide stereoscopic vision. These are set in cheek-like facial discs. The head is broad like ours to accommodate widely spaced and highly developed ears. The beak is all but hidden by feathers; what little of it shows, projects just where we would expect a nose. A vertical body posture adds to the 'human' illusion, and the soft, billowing plumage produces an attractive shape while hiding murderous talons. Ear tufts

Left: Athene, the Greek goddess of wisdom is traditionally associated with the little owl, the sacred owl of Athens, which bears her name, *Athene noctua*.

Anthropomorphic owls are common in children's literature in many parts of the world. Usually they are endowed with wisdom: the owl that set sail with the pussy-cat in Edward Lear's song was perhaps a less sober bird.

on some species, a voice of human quality and eyes that blink with upper eyelids, reinforce the human image.

It should come as no surprise that we think of owls as learned. The truth is, of course, that owls are no more or less intelligent than other predatory birds. However, looking like us, they have been credited with some of our own cleverness. Owls appear to be highly perceptive, their large eyes seeming to penetrate even darkness. This may be responsible for the association between owls and deities; the best known of these is between the little owl (*Athene noctua*) and the Greek goddess of wisdom, Pallas Athene. The origin of Athene is obscure. She may have evolved from a pre-Hellenic rock goddess from Anatolia and the owl, as a crevice inhabitant, may have become linked with her. Lilith, the goddess of death, is depicted with two lions and owls on a Sumerian tablet dating back to 2300–2000 B.C. Whatever her history, Athene became associated with the sacred owl of Athens, which now bears her name. Little owls were also shown on the city's coins.

The tradition of the wise old owl appears later, in the legends of King Arthur, where Merlin is described as having an owl perched on his shoulder. Owls generally became widely accepted as symbols of learning and scholarship and, as in the Middle Ages knowledge was largely vested in the clergy and alchemists, the owl became the companion of the wise. In the thirteenth century allegory *The Owl and the Nightingale*, owls represented the clergy. The myth has persisted and has been reinforced by another of the owl's features: its stony reticence when observed during the daytime. Someone who speaks nothing must surely be contemplating deeply. Are not scholars given to long bouts of silence?

A wise old owl sat in an oak,
The more he saw the less he spoke,
The less he spoke, the more he heard,
Why can't we all be like that wise old bird.

Anon.

Nursery tales, cartoon films, advertisements of all kinds still project the scholar owl – sometimes wearing a mortar board and gown, usually sporting spectacles, often holding a book. Perhaps the most famous of the wise old owls of the nursery is 'Wol' created by A. A. Milne to solve the problems of Pooh, Piglet and Eeyore.

Owls have very large eyes, the irides of which are often bright yellow or orange. They are probably the most conspicuous and compelling eyes in the world. The sudden exposure of roundels has a startling effect on animals and has formed the basis of many defence displays by insects. We can also be frightened by powerful eye patterns and owls have been employed for intimidation, on the basis that what can startle us can also be used to scare our real and imaginary enemies. The Carthaginians are said to have been routed in 310 B.C. by Agathokles, who released owls which settled on the helmets and shields of his men. Their self confidence was thereby increased. Representations of owls were used by the Romans to combat 'the evil eye'. In many places throughout the world, owls have been used to counteract demonic powers or to ward off evil spirits. The Ainu peoples of Japan, for example, made wooden models of eagle owls during famines and nailed them to their houses in the hope of bringing better fortunes. At such time, conditions could only improve, so the owls frequently proved to be powerful magic! Storms and lightning have also been combated with owls' carcasses.

Many of the myths and superstitions that concern owls stem from the fact that many of these birds are crepuscular or nocturnal. Their relatively large eyes are adaptations for collecting as much light as possible in the dim night world. To us, night is full of mysteries. When the glare of the sun is replaced at best by the silver glow of the moon, vision on which we so much depend is of relatively little use. Where our eyes cannot penetrate, we think strange things may be lurking; and the noises and voices we hear could be the sounds of a whole gamut of sinister underground spooks and demons. Furthermore the night is dark and, by association, like the grave and death. It is therefore little wonder that our nocturnal fears and fantasies are heaped on the shoulders of the owl. Apart from the fact that they are night birds, owls fly on silenced pinions – moving through the dim landscape like ghosts, without a rustle or whisper. Their voices have a mournful human quality and barn owls can produce screams worthy of the tortured souls in hell. Churchyards and derelict ruins often tend to provide roosting and hunting grounds for barn and tawny owls, and the sight and sound of these birds in such places has done nothing to allay traditional fears. Pliny the Elder wrote of the owl '. . . when it appears [it] foretells nothing but evil, and if auspices which import

Right: With cats and occasionally dogs, owls were recognized as witch's 'familiar spirits', given them by the devil to help them to carry out their evil deeds.

Below: With their silent flight and eerie calls, owls have become universal messengers of ill-tidings. The barn owl's preference for using churchyards and deserted ruins as roosting places has only added to its supernatural reputation.

the public weal are being taken at the time, is more to be dreaded than any other bird . . . whenever it shows itself in cities or at all by daylight, it prognosticates dire misfortunes.'

The relationship between owls and death is widespread. To the Chinese, owls snatched away souls, and their calls were referred to as 'digging the grave'. In some parts of the world, it was believed that the soul became united with an owl after death. In southern Australia, for example, tribal life was much bound up with animals, but men were especially represented by bats, and women by owls. Since no one knew exactly which owl guarded a particular soul, all owls were effectively protected – 'if my sister Mary's life is an owl, then the owl is my sister and Mary is an owl'. The Kirwa Indians believed that, after dying, their medicine men became owls. Owls themselves were less lucky: they were reincarnated as crickets.

Owls are universally acknowledged messengers of ill tidings. To hear the hoot of an owl is to know of an imminent death. If the cry is dull and indistinct, a near neighbour will die, if clear and distinct, then a person far away. Spenser referred to the owl as 'Death's dreadful messenger' – a superstition still adhered to in many rural areas. In Sicily, scops owls are especially feared. Should one call near to the house of a sick man, he will die three days later. If there are no ailing people around, then it announces that someone will be struck down with tonsil trouble.

Poets and playwrights have used the image of wailing owls to arouse emotions of foreboding in their readers and audiences. The murder of

Julius Caesar was preceded by screeching owls:

> And yesterday the bird of night did sit
> Even at noonday, upon the market place,
> Hooting and shrieking.
>
> *Julius Caesar*

And the ambitious Lady Macbeth, listening and waiting while her husband murders his king, exclaims:

> Hark! – Peace! It was the owl that shriek'd,
> The fatal bellman which gives the stern'st
> goodnight.
>
> *Macbeth*

One verse, clearly about the tawny owl, combines natural and unnatural history:

> Te whit, te whoo, te whit, to whit.
> Thy note, that forth so freely rolls,
> With shrill command the mouse controls,
> And sings a dirge for dying souls,
> Te whit, te whoo, te whit, to whit.
>
> *Anon.*

Even today the calls of tawny owls are used by radio, television and film producers when they wish to add a hint of evil and mischief.

Whether rich or poor, weak or powerful, no one could escape from the owl's prophetic course. The fate of Julius Caesar has already been referred to. Agrippa's death was precipitated by an owl. Having fallen into disfavour with Tiberius Caesar, he was arrested at Capreae and was tied to a tree in which an eagle owl was sitting. A German augur, who was present, prophesied that he would be released and would become king of the Jews – adding however that when he saw that owl again his death would be near. And so it was; for when sitting on his throne in state at Caesarea, he looked upwards and saw an owl perched on one of the cords which ran across the theatre. Recognizing the portent of ill, he fell back smitten with disease, and in five days was dead. A variation of this belief was found in Ethiopia. When the Ethiopians wished to pronounce sentence of death on a criminal, they carried the condemned prisoner to a table on which an owl was painted. Seeing it the guilty man was expected to do the honourable thing and kill himself.

Death, particularly an untimely one, is the ultimate in bad luck. There are, however, other misfortunes which owls are said to foretell. In Wales, the loss of virginity is foretold by the hooting of owls. An owl presiding at one's birth is generally thought to be an evil sign. In France, the shrieking of an owl indicates to a pregnant woman that she will shortly produce a girl and not a son to till the fields.

At various times the word 'owl' has been incorporated into our language as slang. Now obsolete, the meanings were inspired by the bird's nocturnal habits. Thus a harlot could be referred to as an owl in the nineteenth century. If she had been engaged in *owling* (i.e. smuggling sheep or wool from England to France), she might have to *walk by owl light* (i.e. in fear from being arrested). As a result of her calling, she would have regularly had *to owl* (to sit up at night), and should any of her clients refuse to pay then it would have been reasonable for her to have *taken the owl* (to have become angry). Should love have intervened and kindled her enthusiasm for a more permanent relationship, then she would have had to set about *turning a night owl into a homing pigeon*.

The association between owls and witchcraft probably stems from the birds' way of life, particularly its mysterious ability to find its way about in the dark. Owls also figured regularly in black magic recipes – in *Macbeth* a lizard's leg and owlet's wing were part of the witches' bubbling hell-broth.

It is easy to see how, through sympathetic magic, the eating of owls' eyes could help one to see in the dark or restore one's eyesight. An English version of this Indian treatment required the eating of owls' eggs charred and powdered. Cherokee Indians bathed their children's eyes in water containing owls' feathers so that they would be able to keep awake all night. There is also a Yorkshire belief that owl soup will help to cure whooping cough. This is based on the idea that these birds hoot and whoop so much without coming to any harm that a broth made from their bodies should cure the disease. Other recipes are less easy to understand. If the heart and right foot of an owl are laid on a sleeping person, then he will confess all. Feathers placed beneath a pillow can produce a peaceful slumber. Soup made from owls' eggs while the moon is waning can cure epilepsy or, in many parts of Europe, is said to be a sure remedy for drunkenness. To give a child an owl's egg would by the same token ensure that he would never become a drunkard. There are many variations on this belief.

Owls roosting by daytime are often bedevilled by persistent mobbing attacks of smaller birds. It is a common response to certain predators that pose some degree of threat. Presumably this behaviour has survival value to the mobbers by drawing everyone's attention to the where-abouts of the killer. For many centuries, hunters have made use of the innate reaction of other birds to owls. By tethering an owl, otherwise wary species can be lured within the range of guns, nets, or snares. Eagle owls have always been a favourite decoy, and countless thousands or millions of crows, jays, and magpies have died as a result of meeting a far more devious enemy than the one on which their attention had been rivetted. There is a report of 120 jays being caught during a single day. Smaller birds were once lured for the pot by the strategic placing of cleft sticks or perches smeared with sticky bird lime around the owl. A woodcut in Petrus von Crescens' *Opus ruralium* (1493) shows this method very clearly and testifies to the antiquity of the practice. Sometimes a portable hide was used, bedecked with perches

Right: Chinese bronze wine vessel, eleventh or twelfth century BC.

'Owl and full moon', a Japanese brush painting by Isen-In Hogen Fude, 1775–1825.

and owl. The operator sat inside and, by calling, could tempt flocks of song birds close enough to see the owl. The method was so profitable that the sticky perches would often have to be cleared several times during each sitting. The basic method is still used today in Italy to lure migrating song birds to the ground. Once there they are trapped or shot. More often than not, living owls have given way to stylized rotating models equipped with supernormal eyes and flashing plates – a substitute which is just as effective and deadly.

Owls have been used to entice birds in other kinds of hunting. An eagle owl, tethered to a fox's brush to make it more conspicuous, was an indispensable part of the team for hunting buoyant-winged kites. While these fine birds of prey were busy mobbing the owl at low altitude, speedy-winged peregrine or lanner falcons were loosed. Their aim was to ground the kite, which was afterwards released. Sometimes, however, the hawks or falcons did not return to the fist and the falconers, always eager to make good their losses, took the opportunity to snare goshawks which also came to parry at the jessed and tethered owl. Today the technique has been brought up to date by bird photographers interested in snapping hosts of angry, mobbing birds which are aroused by a stuffed owl. In North America, the bird catching techniques of the Middle Ages have come in useful for capturing birds of prey for ringing (banding). A great horned owl tethered near a nest has been successfully employed for catching hen harriers (marsh hawks). As the parents swoop onto the trespassing owl, they collide with nets strategically placed round it. Even ospreys have been caught by this technique, using a captive great horned owl, on a floating timber platform.

Many species of owl are rodent eaters, and so should be among the farmer's best friends. In Europe the creation of meadows and pastures, and the growing of cereals, have favoured the spread of barn owls at the expense of the woodland-living tawny owl. The remains of barn owls have certainly been found on the site of the Iron Age lake village of Glastonbury in Somerset, which flourished in pre-Roman times. Rats, mice and voles which lived off the rich pickings from grain farmers must have formed a healthy supply of food for barn owls, and ramshackle buildings provided the roosting and nesting sites. The very name testifies to the close association between farmer and owl, and some barns even had built-in nest boxes. In the Netherlands, the Friesland farmers have for a long time encouraged these silent white hunters of the hated rats and mice, by providing them with access into the lofts and roof spaces. Some of the large farmhouses so characteristic of the Friesland landscape often show a decorative complex called an 'owl board' (oeleboerd) on the front of the roof ridge, with a round opening in the centre – 'the owl hole' (oelegat).

In the British Isles, changes in agricultural practice, the cleaning up of farm buildings and country churches, and the introduction of poisonous pesticides have decimated the barn owl population, despite its total protection by law. The tawny owl, which suffered a decline in the eighteenth and nineteenth centuries, due to the contraction of woodlands and the indiscriminating campaign of extermination carried out by gamekeepers, is now the most common bird of prey in the British Isles, with a population estimated at one hundred thousand pairs. An adaptable species, it has come to populate even towns and cities, where it thrives by snatching small birds from their roosts rather than by catching rodents. A survey carried out in London revealed that no less than 48 pairs were living within twenty miles of St Paul's cathedral. A pair was also once found nesting in a tower of the Smithsonian Institution building in Washington. Alexander Sprunt records that the 200 pellets collected from the nest contained 454 mammal skulls – 225 meadow mice, 179 house mice, 20 rats and 20 shrews – 'an amazing collection for a pair of owls living in the heart of America's capital city'.

Because of their nature and habits, owls have undoubtedly aroused dread in us and have therefore spawned more superstitions than any other family of birds. Despite this, we have retained a place in our hearts for them. We have enlisted them as allies against the powers of evil, and, on a more mundane level, protected them for rodent catching around the sheaves and hayricks. It is consequently satisfying to recall that, with only a few exceptions, owls have not fared badly, and some are even making a good living in our own city strongholds. Nevertheless, when the territorial hooting of tawny owls stirs us in our snug suburban bedrooms, it is difficult to suppress that spinal shiver and to exclude all superstitions from the mind.

CHAPTER TWO

The origins of owls

Palaeornithology remains one of the most neglected of natural history subjects. There are two main reasons for this: firstly, bird bones are extremely difficult to identify, and secondly the study of fossil vertebrates has been closely associated with evolution from primitive forms to higher mammals, birds being regarded only as an interesting diversion from the main line. The majority of scientific workers now agree that birds evolved from one of two groups of dinosaurs (Ornithischia or Saurischia) during the early part of the Jurassic period. Unfortunately, as so often happens, the fossil record is incomplete and one cannot trace all the steps between birds and their reptilian ancestors.

Opinions differ as to the nature of the 'pre-avis'. Some say it was a tree-dwelling reptile which began flight by gliding from one branch to another; others claim that it was a running, leaping, terrestrial animal which gradually increased the length of its leaps by the use of elongated forelimbs. Both sides have put forward good arguments and the truth is probably to be found somewhere between the two.

Compared with fish, reptiles and mammals, birds are poorly represented as fossils, partly because bird bones are thin-walled, hollow, very fragile and easily destroyed by predators or scavengers. Often they are so badly damaged during the process of fossilization that they cannot be identified. The best medium for preservation of fossils is probably silt, which forms a matrix that preserves fine details of bones so necessary for critical analysis. Rather a high proportion of the best avian fossil material comes from large aquatic or semi-aquatic birds – the kinds which stood the best chance of having at least part of their skeleton preserved.

In evaluating the record of fossil birds, it is important to understand the conditions under which the palaeornithologist distinguished a particular species. In most cases fossil species are known not from whole skeletons but from a few dis-articulated bones. Even today the two living owl families (Strigidae and Tytonidae) are not always clearly defined osteologically, and it is obviously very difficult to place extinct species within these families on the evidence of an odd bone. When a whole fossil bird is available it is easy to see the difficulties involved. The bird may have lived during the time when birds were still experimenting with the numerous ecological niches open to them and may show characteristics now associated with several different modern families; the skull may be like one family, the pelvis or tibiotarsus like another. If the bones become separated then they may easily be described as belonging to different species – even to different orders. However, naming a species on the basis of a solitary bone is often justified, if only because it can provide a guide for subsequent workers.

Some of the confusion which still surrounds the relationships of ancient birds has been caused by the conservatism of some of the earlier scientists. Bird bones themselves are conservative and in most cases if there is any slight consistent variation it usually indicates at least a new species. The earlier workers often noted these differences but, either because modern bird bones

An artist's reconstruction of a scene from the Eocene Period of North America, showing a sample of the extinct owl family *Protostrigides*. Other animals depicted include two pond tortoises, a crocodile, *Uintotherium* (an extinct ungulate about the size of an African rhinoceros) and two small primitive horses.

were insufficiently known, or because they wanted to show the relationships of their fossil birds, they more often than not placed them within extant genera. At the other extreme, some workers have felt that if a specimen comes from a different geological age it must automatically be a different species and as a result some forms have been described with little reference to their distinguishing characters.

OWLS AS FOSSILS

In 1971 Brodkorb published the fourth volume of his *Catalogue of Fossil Birds* in which he lists some 41 extinct species of owl, 5 of which belong to the Protostrigidae, 25 to the Strigidae and 11 to the Tytonidae. Much of the up-to-date information in this chapter is extracted from this work.

In geological terms birds are relative newcomers to the earth's fauna. *Archaeopteryx lithographica*, the first known bird, appeared in the Upper Jurassic, but it is not possible to say how soon after this the owls evolved. The first reliable records of owls date from the Eocene, some 60 to 40 million years ago. Two distinct strigiform families (Protostrigidae and Strigidae) are known to have existed during this period, and it is reasonable to assume that the order must have evolved much earlier – in the Palaeocene (70 to 60 million years ago) or even earlier, in the latter half of the Mesozoic era. It is impossible to draw any evolutionary lines from Mesozoic birds to the earliest owls. *Archaeopteryx* was so primitive that it retained many of the characters (teeth and

---

Table I   Fossil owls from the Upper Eocene to Lower Oligocene Periods

PROTOSTRIGIDAE

Eostrix mimica (WETMORE)	Lower Eocene	Wyoming, U.S.A.
Protostrix lydekkeri (SHUFELDT)	Middle Eocene	Wyoming, U.S.A.
Protostrix leptosteus (MARSH)	Middle Eocene	Wyoming, U.S.A.
Protostrix saurodosis (WETMORE)	Middle Eocene	Wyoming, U.S.A.
Protostrix californiensis HOWARD	Upper Eocene	California, U.S.A.

STRIGIDAE

Bubo incertus MILNE-EDWARDS	Upper-Eocene–Lower Oligocene	Quercy, France
Necrobyas harpax MILNE-EDWARDS	Upper Eocene–Lower Oligocene	Quercy, France
Necrobyas rossignoli MILNE-EDWARDS	Upper Eocene–Lower Oligocene	Quercy, France
Necrobyas edwardsi GAILLARD	Upper Eocene–Lower Oligocene	Quercy, France
Strigogyps dubius GAILLARD	Upper Eocene–Lower Oligocene	Quercy, France
Strigogyps minor GAILLARD	Upper Eocene–Lower Oligocene	Quercy, France
Asio henrici (MILNE-EDWARDS)	Upper Eocene–Lower Oligocene	Quercy, France

---

Table II   Fossil owls from the Miocene Period

STRIGIDAE

Bubo poirreiri MILNE-EDWARDS	Lower Miocene	France
Otus wintershofensis BALLMANN	Middle Miocene	Germany
Strix dakota MILLER	Lower Miocene	South Dakota, U.S.A.
Strix brevis BALLMANN	Middle Miocene	Germany

TYTONIDAE

subfamily Tytoninae		
Prosbybris antiqua (MILNE-EDWARDS)	Lower Miocene	France
Tyto ignota (PARIS)	Middle Miocene	France
Tyto sancti-albani (LYDEKKER)	Upper Middle Miocene	France
Tyto edwardsi (ENNOUCHI)	Upper Middle Miocene	France
subfamily Phodilinae		
Paratyto arvernensis (MILNE-EDWARDS)	Lower Miocene	France

long, bony tail) normally associated with reptiles, and if the feather impressions had not been preserved it would almost certainly have been described as a lightly-built dinosaur. The remaining Mesozoic forms all appear to be birds normally found in or around an aquatic environment, and none of these seems to be related in any way to owls. Although it is still not clear from which group the owls evolved, it is generally thought that the Strigiformes and Caprimulgiformes (nightjars and frogmouths) are in some way related. Unfortunately, the fossil record of the nightjars is non-existent, so it does not help us in our search for owl ancestors.

MESOZOIC ERA
Cretaceous Period (135 to 70 million years ago)

During this period the environment consisted of large seas, lakes and deltas with deserts, coal-forming swamps and occasional glaciers. The evidence of the flora suggests that a mild climate was widespread. In the early stages, the vegetation was very much like that of the Jurassic and included cycads, ferns and conifers, but towards the end the flowering plants became a dominant part of the flora. The land fauna was still dominated by the great 'dinosaurs' which were to become extinct before the period ended.

As yet no fossil owl has been described from the Cretaceous, but it was probably towards the end of this period, when the last of the dinosaurs were dying out, that the first primitive owls evolved. A species of bird found in the Upper Cretaceous deposits of Romania, and originally identified in 1913 by Andrews as belonging to the Pelecaniformes (pelicans, cormorants, tropic birds etc.) has recently been re-examined. The femur, on which the identification was based appears to be correctly assigned, but the other elements, two tarso-metatarsi, have strigiform characters; if the new diagnosis is accepted, this will prove to be the earliest known owl.

CAENOZOIC ERA
Palaeocene and Eocene Epochs
(70 to 40 million years ago)

The first ten million years of the Eocene are now referred to as the Palaeocene, but for convenience they will be dealt with here as part of the Eocene. Geographically, the Palaeocene and Eocene were periods of great change, with considerable volcanic activity and geological unrest. Tropical and temperate conditions were more widespread than they are today. Southern England and parts of France were covered with sub-tropical or tropical forests, and temperate plants grew in what is now the Arctic. Mammals were evolving and spreading, and the ancestors of many modern forms were recognizable. The radiation of birds into the complex variety of modern types also took place at this time; all but ten of the recognized orders are represented in the record by the end of the Eocene. Of the once-dominant reptiles only a small fragment – crocodiles, turtles, snakes, and lizards – remained alive and active.

No fossil owl has yet been described from the Palaeocene, but two tarso-metatarsi, as yet undescribed, from the phosphorite deposits of Cernay (France) appear to belong to the Strigiformes. These are leg bones of a large owl similar to and about the size of the eagle owl (*Bubo bubo*). There are five recorded occurrences of owls from Eocene deposits of the United States. Included in two genera, *Eostrix* and *Protostrix*, they belong to the extinct Protostrigidae of Wetmore (1933) which at present has a recorded range from the Lower to Upper Eocene of the U.S.A. Seven further species were recorded from phosphorite deposits in Quercy (France). Originally considered to date from the Eocene, these deposits are now known to range between Upper Eocene and Lower Oligocene. The exact horizon was not noted when the specimens were collected, and their precise age remains in doubt. For convenience, they are all listed here under this period. (See Table I.)

Oligocene Period (40 to 25 million years ago)

Disturbances in the earth's crust continued during the Oligocene and started the formation of great mountain ranges, including the Alps. Uplift caused some former marine basins to be cut off from the sea, turning them into brackish lagoons or freshwater lakes. Europe was at one stage joined to Asia (which was still linked to North America). Temperate conditions were wide-spread, though certain continents had cooler areas, and grasslands increased at the expense of forested regions. About one quarter of the present-day families of birds were represented.

The Protostrigidae probably died out before the Oligocene began, although it is possible that when a critical analysis has been carried out, some of the European genera from the Quercy deposits may be found to have closer links with the North American family than their present arrangement indicates.

Miocene Period (25 to 12 million years ago)

During the Miocene period movements of the earth's crust continued, and the upheaval of the Alps and Himalayas was completed. Asia became finally joined to Europe and for a short time was still connected to North America. The climate became cooler, and temperate floras replaced the sub-tropical ones; grassy plains spread even further as the forests retreated. Most of the mammals of this period belonged to families which have persisted to the present-day; they included elephants, rhinoceroses, pigs and antlered deer. Birds followed the same pattern, and over a third of them are sufficiently close to living species to be placed in the same genera.

Two groups of owl make their appearance during this period, represented by the sub-families Tytoninae (barn owls) and Phodilinae (bay owls). The Phodilinae were found in the Lower Miocene deposits of France, while the Tytoninae are known from two genera (one extinct) which have been reported from deposits in France and North America, of Lower and Middle Miocene age. It is probable that the species placed in extant genera (*Bubo, Otus, Strix,* and *Tyto*) are the first true examples of their type. Earlier specimens described from Upper Eocene/ Lower Oligocene deposits have been ascribed to the genera *Bubo* and *Asio* but they need to be re-examined before either genus can be accepted as having existed before the Miocene. (Table II.)

Pliocene Period (12 to 3 million years ago)

The Pliocene period was one of greater stability, though the land continued to rise. Continents and oceans were assuming their present-day form, and towards the end of the period ice-caps began to develop in the northern hemisphere. The climate was cooler than the preceding periods, but not as cool as those prevailing today. The mammal fauna was less varied than in the Miocene, but more diverse than at present. The first man-like apes were to be found in South Africa, while elephant, wild horses (*Hipparion*) and deer of many different types roamed the grasslands and forests respectively. Three-quarters of the avifauna described from this time have been assigned to living genera.

Owls are known from six Pliocene localities, four in North America and two in Europe. *Bubo* and *Asio* are represented, also the genus *Lechusa* (now extinct). *Speotyto megalopeza*, related to the modern burrowing owl, has been recovered from the Hagerman lake deposits of Idaho which some authorities believe to be early Pleistocene in age, so *Speotyto megalopeza* could range from Upper Pliocene to Lower Pleistocene. (Table III.)

QUATERNARY ERA
Pleistocene Period (3 million to 10,000 years ago)

The Pleistocene period is sometimes referred to as the Great Ice Age because of the ice-sheets and

---

Table III   Fossil owls from the Pliocene Period

STRIGIDAE

Bubo florianae KRETZOI	Lower Pliocene	Hungary
Speotyto megalopeza FORD	Upper Pliocene and Lower Pliocene	Kansas & Idaho, U.S.A.
Asio pigmaeus SEREBROVSKY	Lower Pliocene	Ukraine
Asio brevipes FORD AND MURRAY	Upper Pliocene– ?Lower Pleistocene	Idaho, U.S.A.

TYTONIDAE

Lechusa stirtoni MILLER	Middle Pliocene	California, U.S.A.

glaciers which spread across the northern continents. Many people believe that Arctic conditions prevailed throughout the world at this time, but in fact many parts of the earth were never affected by glaciation. Even the areas affected by the ice had alternating cold and warm conditions. There were also important land movements and volcanic activity in Africa and the Middle East and changes of sea level.

The record of fossil birds is much more extensive than for earlier periods. A total of 44 species of owls have been recorded from many parts of the world. There are 39 species of Strigidae, of which 10 are now extinct, and 6 species of Tytonidae, of which 5 are now extinct. (See Table IV.)

Holocene Period (10,000 years ago to the present day)

Numerous species of owls have been recorded from prehistoric sites all over the world; all except one (*Rhinoptynx clamator*, Venezuela) appear in the list for the Pleistocene below.

Table IV   Fossil owls from the Quaternary Era

STRIGIDAE

Bubo binagadensis BURCHAK-ABRAMOVICH	Middle Upper Pleistocene	Azerbaijan
Bubo sincliari MILLER	Upper Pleistocene	California, U.S.A.
Bubo leguati ROTHSCHILD	Quaternary	Rodriguez Is.
Otus providentiae BRODKORB	Upper Pleistocene	Bahamas
Athene murivora (MILNE-EDWARDS)	Quaternary	Rodriguez Is.
Ornimegalonyx oteroi ARREDONDO	Upper Pleistocene	Cuba
Glaucidium dickinsoni BRODKORB	Upper Pleistocene	Bahamas
Pulsatrix arredoi BRODKORB	Upper Pleistocene	Cuba
Asio priscus HOWARD	Upper Pleistocene	California, U.S.A.
Strix brea HOWARD	Upper Pleistocene	California, U.S.A.

Neospecies (still living) of Strigidae from Pleistocene sites

Otus scops	Europe, Asia and Middle East
Otus flammeolus	Central and North America
Otus asio	Central and North America
Otus trichopsis	Mexico
Otus nudipes	West Indies
Bubo virginianus	Central and North America
Bubo bubo	America
Bubo bubo	Europe, Asia and Middle East
Bubo africanus	Sardinia
Ketupa zeylonensis	India
Nyctea scandiaca	Europe and Asia
Surnia ulula	Europe
Glaucidium passerinum	Europe
Glaucidium gnoma	Central and North America
Glaucidium brasilianum	Central and South America
Ninox novaeseelandiae	New Zealand
Sceloglaux albifacies	New Zealand (may now be extinct)
Athene noctua	Europe, Asia and Middle East
Speotyto cunicularia	North and South America, West Indies
Ciccaba virgata	Mexico
Slrix aluco	Europe
Strix occidentalis	Central and North America
Strix varia	Central and North America
Strix uralensis	Europe
Strix nebulosa	Romania
Asio otus	Europe, Asia, North and Central America
Asio stygius	Dominican Republic and Brazil
Asio flammeus	Europe, Asia, North and Central America
Aegolius funereus	Europe and North America
Aegolius acadicus	North America

TYTONIDAE

Tyto ostologa WETMORE	Upper Pleistocene	Haiti
Tyto pollens	Upper Pleistocene	Bahamas
Tyto cavatica WETMORE	Quaternary	Puerto Rico
Tyto melitensis (LYDEKKER)	Upper Pleistocene	Malta
Tyto sauzieri (NEWTON AND GADOW)	Quaternary	Mauritius

Neospecies of Tytonidae from Pleistocene sites

Tyto alba	Europe, Middle East, West Indies and America

CHAPTER THREE

What makes an owl

To operate efficiently as nocturnal predators, owls have evolved extensive modifications; their distinctive appearance is largely a consequence of these. This is obvious above all in the anatomy of the head. The large forward facing eyes, surrounded by broad facial discs, give owls a semi-human appearance, in which lies much of their appeal to man but these features are primarily an indication of the great refinement of the senses of sight and hearing, essential for hunting in the dark. It seems appropriate, therefore, to begin this account of owl anatomy by dealing with the structure of eyes and ears.

Sight is of vital importance to all birds; this is reflected in the relatively enormous size of the eyes, which take up a huge amount of space in the head; in most birds the two eyes are separated only by a thin bony sheet in the mid-line of the skull. The eyeballs of some large hawks and owls are in fact, bigger than our own. Underlying this disproportionate size is a basic design limitation in the structure of eyes. This limitation is imposed by the light-sensitive cells of the retina, the rear part of the eye on which the image is thrown. The resolution of the eye – that is, its capacity to discern detail – depends on the number of retinal cells over which the image is spread, a greater number giving more detailed perception. Since the size of these cells is roughly constant, it follows that a larger eye will generally provide higher resolution than a smaller one of the same basic shape. This limitation is a particularly acute problem for owls, since their eyes are also

modified for extreme sensitivity under poor lighting conditions and, in many respects, adaptations for high sensitivity run counter to those for high resolution.

The light-sensitive cells of the retina are of two types, named, from their shape, rods and cones. The rods are more sensitive to low light, but they achieve this sensitivity partly by functioning in small groups, each group stimulating only a single nerve cell, whereas cones generally each have their own nerve cell to conduct their response to the brain. The result of this is that image details falling on a group of rods are merged and lost, whereas, had they fallen on cones, they might have been separately perceived.

A retina with many rods, as found in the eyes of owls and other nocturnal animals, has thus sacrificed some of its capacity for resolution. Many nocturnal animals also possess a reflecting layer – the tapetum – inside the eye, to use more fully the light which enters, but the presence of such a layer in the eyes of owls has yet to be conclusively shown.

A further adaptation to low light intensities is to bring the lens and retina closer together, so that the image itself is less dispersed and consequently brighter. In consequence it is also smaller, and hence spread over fewer retinal cells, thus further worsening the capacity for resolution. Enlarging the eyes to the maximum has helped owls to overcome these disadvantages, but to do this they have had to accept a sacrifice in field of view, so that, although the image is spread over an adequate

Spotted eagle owl *Bubo africanus*. Though specially constructed to see well in poor light, owl eyes are also useful in daylight, for they have an exceptional range of pupil size, controlled by the iris. In bright sunlight the retina is further protected by a nictitating membrane, or 'third eyelid'.

area of retina for purposes of resolution, it covers a smaller proportion of the owl's surroundings than in other birds. This has led to the evolution of the 'tubular' eye, with a relatively abbreviated retina, and a huge, highly convex lens. As in all birds, the eyeball is protected by a ring of small bony plates (scleral ossicles), and in owls these form a long bony tube which is one of the most striking features of a prepared skull specimen. In many hawks the eye is superficially similar, but lengthening has taken place without any proportionate enlargement of the lens, or reduction of retinal area. The object in their case is to spread the image over as many retinal cells as possible, to give maximum resolution.

The forward-facing arrangement of the eyes of owls is partly a means of accommodating them in the head, but also makes possible a considerable degree of binocular vision – that is, vision in which both eyes view the same scene from slightly different aspects, an aid to depth perception. The total visual field in owls is some 110°, of which about 60° to 70° is overlapping; man in comparison sees a total field of 180°, of which about 140° is covered by both eyes. These figures may be compared with, for example, a total field of about 340° in a homing pigeon, of which only 24° is covered by both eyes. Compensating for their rather narrow field of view, owls have an exceptional ability to rotate the head. Even a diurnal bird of prey can turn the head through about 180°, and, in owls, this figure reaches 270°. Many owls are able to hunt in daylight, and none are helpless during the day. This is made possible

by an exceptional range of aperture – pupil size – controlled by the iris.

Experiments have shown for three species of owls (*Strix varia*, *Asio otus* and *Tyto alba*) that they could see and approach dead prey from six feet or more under illumination as low as 0.00000073 foot candle. This is between one hundredth and one tenth the minimum intensity that man requires. Despite this extreme sensitivity, owls supplement their vision with hearing of equal refinement, and it has been demonstrated that a barn owl can capture living prey in the total absence of light. This is made possible by adaptations in ear structure which have modified the skull as profoundly as those of the eyes. The most obvious of these adaptations is the sheer size of the ear openings. Instead of fairly small round openings, as in most birds, owls have long vertical slits, nearly as deep as the head itself. The facial discs, so characteristic of owls, are an indication of their presence, for the edges of the discs are fringed by stiff short feathers bordering the openings, and carried upon flaps, front and back, which can move to control the size of the ear opening. This control enables owls to scan different parts of their environment for sounds in the same way that many mammals can move their external ears. (The 'ear tufts' which many species possess, are in fact nothing to do with the sense of hearing.)

The skulls of owls are proportionately much wider than in most birds. This is partly a consequence of their large eyes and binocular vision, but it also helps them in locating the

ANATOMY OF A TYPICAL OWL

Owls show a number of adaptations which enable them to operate with outstanding efficiency as nocturnal predators. Large, forward-facing eyes give them a considerable degree of binocular vision; wide skulls and assymetrical ear openings are thought to help in pinpointing the source of sound more accurately; softened flight feathers make silent flight possible, while bill and claws are obviously suited to their predatory way of life.

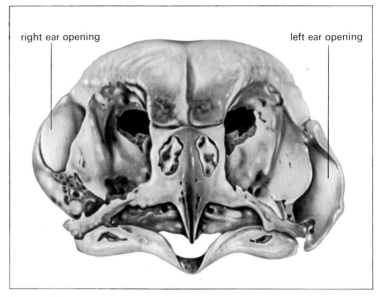

Skull of Tengmalm's owl *Aegolius funereus* showing the assymetrical ear openings.

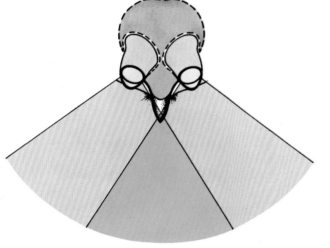

Diagram to show visual field and extent of binocular vision in an owl.

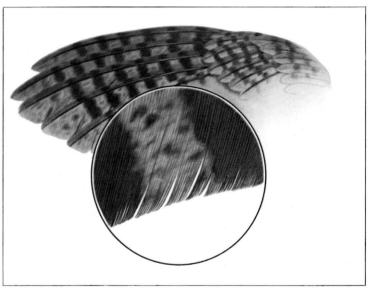

The wing of a tawny owl *Strix aluco*. The enlarged detail shows the softened edges of the flight feathers – an aid to silent flight.

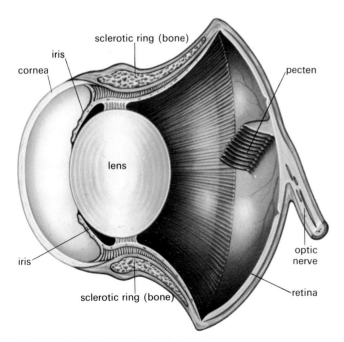

Cross section of the eye of an eagle owl.

Right: Tawny owl *Strix aluco*. The skeleton shows that a tawny owl is actually considerably smaller than its soft, loose feathers make it appear. Found mainly in deciduous woodland and among scattered groups of trees, it has rather shorter wings than owls of more open country. An owl's eyes are forward facing, and the bird must turn its whole head to look sideways. Its exceptionally long and flexible neck enables it to turn its head a full 180 degrees.

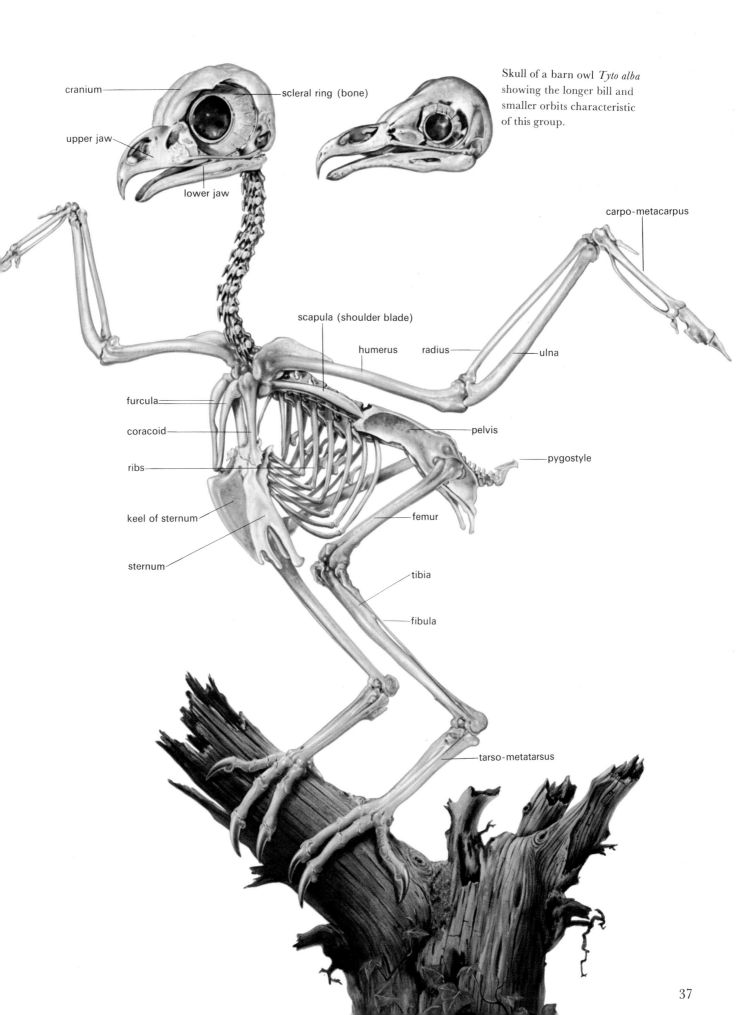

cranium

scleral ring (bone)

upper jaw

Skull of a barn owl *Tyto alba* showing the longer bill and smaller orbits characteristic of this group.

lower jaw

carpo-metacarpus

scapula (shoulder blade)

humerus   radius   ulna

furcula

coracoid

pelvis

ribs

pygostyle

keel of sternum

femur

sternum

tibia

fibula

tarso-metatarsus

37

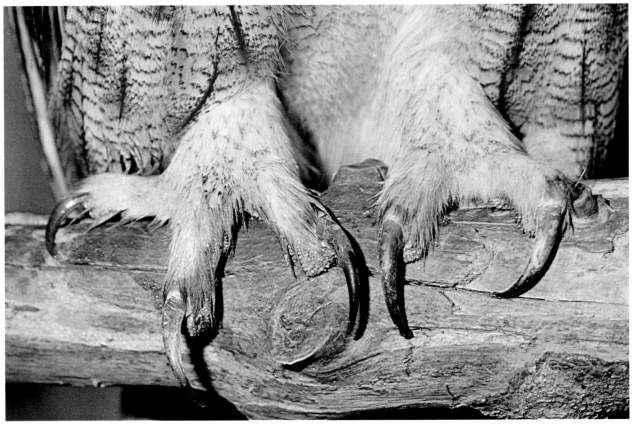

Claws of eagle owl *Bubo bubo* (above) and snowy owl *Nyctea scandiaca*
Most owls have fairly short legs, though terrestrial species
such as the burrowing owl *Speotyto cunicularia* are exceptions.

Legs and toes are usually feathered: the snowy owl's
abundant covering provides useful insulation against the
cold, Arctic climate.

direction of a sound. This is because a sound made to one side will be perceived by one ear fractionally before the other; the tiny time difference, some 0.00003 seconds, is sufficient to be perceived and to indicate on which side the sound source lies. The sound will also be louder in the ear nearer the sound source, at least for sounds with wavelength equivalent to or shorter than the width of the head. Another factor, which is clearly important in many species, though not fully understood, is the asymmetrical placing of the ear openings. The right hand opening is higher, and it is thought that this exaggerates the effect of displacement of the sound to one side or the other, permitting more rapid readjustment. The inner ear of owls is also large, and the auditory region of the brain is provided with many more nerve cells than in other birds of comparable size. The range of frequencies which they can detect is, if anything, more limited than our own, particularly at the lower end of the scale. Nevertheless, the region of maximum sensitivity is relatively high in most species, and ideal for locating the high pitched squeaks of rodents. For the tawny owl, the region of greatest sensitivity lies between 3000 and 6000 cycles per second. In the great horned owl, as in ourselves, it is around 1000 cycles.

Not all owls have the ears so highly developed. In general, eagle owls and scops owls have relatively small openings, with little asymmetry, while large openings and asymmetry are marked in *Strix*, *Asio* and others. However, recent studies have shown that, in regard to size, the ear flaps are best developed in northern species, and smallest in tropical forms. This may be connected with the fact that northern nights are more silent, and in winter very much longer, than those of tropical areas, with their chorus of frogs and cicadas.

Keen hearing would be almost useless if the owl itself made a great deal of confusing noise, to say nothing of the warning this would give to potential prey. Owls have consequently evolved the ability to fly in nearly complete silence. This faculty results in part from the structure of the feathers, which have markedly softened edges compared with those of other birds. In addition, owls have a low wing loading, that is to say, they are light in relation to their wing area. This gives them a buoyant effortless flight, which eliminates much of the need for noisy

flapping. The usual descent of an owl to its prey is, in fact, a glide.

In most other features of their anatomy, owls show obvious adaptations for a predatory way of life, many of them paralleling those of the diurnal birds of prey. The hooked bill, with a soft cere at the base, around the nostrils, is common to both owls and hawks, but in owls the bill is more sharply deflected downwards – a modification to reduce obstruction of the already limited visual field. The claws are extremely long and sharp in both groups, but in owls the outer toe is reversible, and can be pointed backwards alongside the hind toe – a faculty which only the osprey possesses among diurnal birds of prey. The legs and toes are feathered, as in many hawks and eagles, a protection against possible bites from prey. An exception to this is shown by the fishing owls, which catch their prey, fish, in the water; they have bare legs and feet with rough spiny soles, as in the osprey and other fishing species. Most owls have fairly short legs, like mammal-eating hawks, but unlike the hawks of the genus *Accipiter*, which prey on small birds. An exception is the burrowing owl (*Speotyto cunicularia*) of South America, whose terrestrial habits have led to a noticeable increase in leg length. Unlike diurnal birds of prey, owls have no crop, and their intestines are provided with long caeca (blind ending tubes), an unusual feature among carnivores.

As a group, owls show much more uniformity of structure than the diurnal birds of prey. This is partly because their primary adaptations to nocturnal life have restricted their capacity to exploit daytime niches; thus, carrion feeding owls are unknown, and bird-catching adaptations are much less in evidence. There are no soaring forms, and no real equivalent of the falcons – probably the hawk owl (*Surnia ulula*), with its pointed wings and long tail, is the nearest approach. Wings are in general rounded amongst the owls, shorter in forest forms which have to manoeuvre between trees, and relatively longer in open country and migratory species. The size range of owls, though considerable, is less than that shown by the hawks and falcons. The largest are some eagle owls (*Bubo*), reaching 710 mm in length, and the smallest the least pygmy owl, (*Glaucidium minutissimum*) 120 to 140 mm long. Anatomically, the most distinctive owls are the barn owls, usually separated as a subfamily (Tytonidae) from the remainder (Strigidae). The barn owls are distinguished by their smaller orbits, and rather longer skulls; in life, the distinctive feature of the head is the heart-shaped rather than round facial disc. They are distinguished also by their inner toes, which equal the middle in length. The claw of the middle toe is provided with serrations, absent in typical owls.

The anatomy of owls provides little clear cut evidence about their relationships, but there are some suggestive similarities to the Caprimulgiformes (nightjars and others) e.g. in the curious form of the intestinal caeca, which have swollen ends in both groups, a feature not seen in other orders. The Caprimulgiformes are linked to the owls by other evidence as well, and seem very likely to be their closest relatives. It is of interest that both groups are more or less nocturnal, although the Caprimulgiformes have specialized more in the capture of insects, especially on the wing. They include a curious family, the Aegothelidae, known as owlet nightjars. These are surprisingly owl-like in many features of their structure and habits, and seem to fill a niche rather like that of *Glaucidium* owls.

Comparison of the size of an eagle owlet *Bubo bubo* (right) and a tawny owlet *Strix aluco* gives some idea of the variety of owl species. In fact the size range, though considerable, is less than that shown by such other birds of prey as hawks and falcons.

PART II

CHAPTER FOUR

Barn and Bay owls

Tyto, Phodilus

The ten species of owls described in this chapter belong to the family Tytonidae, a group of owls that, because of a series of minor differences, particularly in bone structure, have been classified separately from the typical owls (the Strigidae). All but two of the species are included in the subfamily Tytoninae, and belong to the genus *Tyto*. They are usually called barn owls, though two species which live in open grassland are popularly known as grass owls.

Barn owls are typified by heart-shaped facial discs, relatively small, uniformly dark eyes, long slender legs covered with narrow feathers, bristled feet, a comb-like middle claw and, without exception, no ear tufts. The two indentations in the breast bone characteristic of most owls, are either very small or absent,

and while the opening to the ear is very long it has an extremely small orifice covered by a large flap (the operculum). In total length the different species range from 270 to 530 mm.

The remaining two species in the Tytonidae family belong to the subfamily Phodilinae, and to the genus *Phodilus*: they are commonly called bay owls. They are smaller than the barn owls (from 230 to 330 mm), but superficially resemble them. In particular they have a facial disc rather like the barn owl's, though it is incomplete above the eyes. Unlike the strongly hooked bill of the barn owl, the bay owl's bill is weak and compressed; they have no ear flaps.

The outstanding feature of the distribution of the barn and bay owls is the very wide dispersal of the barn owl (*Tyto alba*). It is found in North

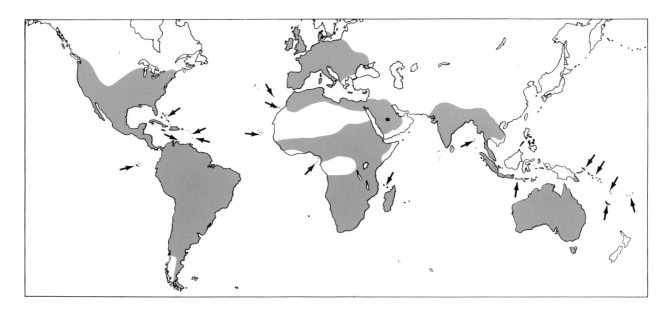

European farmers recognize the barn owl *Tyto alba* (330 to 430 mm) as an important predator of rats and mice and often build special 'owl doors' into their barns to encourage the birds to use them as roosts and nest-sites. This individual belongs to the dark-breasted race *T. a. guttata* of Scandinavia and central and eastern Europe.

Tyto alba: open habitats including moors, cultivated grassland, desert and parkland.

and South America, Europe, western Russia, Africa, southern Asia and Australia. Though it is often described as 'cosmopolitan', this is rather misleading, as with the exception of parts of Europe and the U.S.A. it is rarely found outside tropical regions, and is essentially restricted within latitudes 40° N and 40° S of the equator. In western Europe its most northerly locality is in Britain, but even here it is uncommon in the northern parts of the country. The greatest number of species of the Tytonidae occurs in the Australasian region. The bay owls are primarily oriental, occurring in Burma, India and Malaysia.

Because of its wide distribution, the barn owl must be one of the best known owls in the world. Geographical distances have produced many local races, the nominate race being the common or white-breasted barn owl (*T. a. alba*). This race was first described in 1769 from specimens collected in Italy. Now, however, it is known that the race extends from the British Isles, through the Channel Isles, western France, Spain, Portugal, Italy and countries bordering the Mediterranean.

Its nocturnal habits, relatively large size and white appearance make the common barn owl an easy bird to identify. It is about 400 mm long, has a wing span of 760 mm and a shortish tail. The upperparts are orange-buff, spotted with dark grey and white, the face is white and the underparts white, sometimes speckled with a few black spots with an occasional tinge on the breast. The sexes are more or less alike, though females have a tendency to be bigger and greyer on the upperparts. The beak is very pale yellow and the eyes and claws black. Apparently reliable reports of barn owls glowing in the dark are possibly explained by luminous bacteria, from decayed wood, adhering to the plumage.

The barn owl's long wings and buoyant flight are adaptations to hunting in open habitats, such as heaths, moors, deserts, cultivated land, grasslands, coastal plains and open parkland. Apart from exceptional circumstances, such as during periods of severe weather or when feeding young, it is only normally active in the evening or at night. During the daytime it roosts in dark places in ruins, churches, barns and lofts, in hollow trees or in crevices and caves in cliffs. In spite of its light colouration it can be surprisingly difficult to find a roosting barn owl as it stands bolt upright and motionless in a dark corner. Often its presence is first indicated by droppings on the walls or the beams, or by a pile of firm, black, glossy pellets under a favourite roost. The barn owl usually roosts singly or in pairs, but small groups roosting together have been recorded. A roosting site may also be used for nesting or be near the site eventually selected for breeding. If disturbed when roosting this owl usually flies only a short distance before it alights again. As with most owls abroad during the day, it is frequently mobbed by small birds.

The common barn owl is an active hunter, searching diligently on the wing for its prey. It must cover a total of many miles during a single night as it sweeps backwards and forwards over the ground, especially when it is feeding young. When hunting it rarely rises more than a few metres in the air except when it has to pass over bushes, walls and hedges. The buoyant flight is almost noiseless and is typically a series of slow flaps with alternating glides and occasional short spells of clumsy hovering. This owl often seems to follow regular routes, particularly along the sides of ditches, hedges or fence lines. In farmland it prefers the rough, uncultivated field edges and margins of woods where prey is more abundant.

The barn owl catches its prey in flight by suddenly dropping or diving onto it in the vegetation and grasping it with its claws, then swiftly crushing the head in its bill. Alternatively it may sit on a post or stump watching for prey in the nearby undergrowth and then catch it by suddenly dropping or gliding onto it. The extremely well-developed eyes and ears of the

barn owl enable it to take advantage of even faint light and slight sounds and so to hunt during the hours of darkness. Laboratory experiments have demonstrated that even in complete darkness the barn owl is able to intercept live prey by fixing on its calls or noises of movement. How much of the barn owl's hunting is in fact carried out during total darkness, how dependent they are on the faint light of dawn and dusk or how far they take advantage of moonlight, has yet to be established. Their silent flight enables them both to hear the movements and calls of their prey and to approach within striking distance without themselves being heard. It has been suggested that their sudden silent appearance and their shriek may make their prey too terrified to move.

After capture the prey is often devoured at once, or carried only a short distance to a more sheltered position before being swallowed. If it is feeding young, the owl will take the prey direct to the nest site, flying close to the ground, with the prey hanging from its claws. If the nest is in a church near a village centre, for example, the owl will fly low until it nears the outskirts of the village then gain height and continue on its course over the roof tops.

Like most owls, the barn owl generally swallows its prey whole only dismembering it if the prey is too large. The undigested portions, such as bones, fur and feathers, are regurgitated in the form of pellets. Apparently at least two pellets are produced during a twenty-four hour period. They are firm, large, more or less oval in shape (50 × 25 mm) and varnished glossy black.

Very resistant to decay, they can last many years, so considerable numbers may accumulate in the vicinity of a regularly used roosting or nesting site, providing a valuable clue to the prey that has been taken. (See p. 193.)

The barn owl's main food is small nocturnal rodents, and a wide variety of these have been recorded as prey. The particular species taken depends largely on which ones are most common near the nesting site. In Europe shrews, mice and voles generally form the major portion of the diet, but rats and even small rabbits have been recorded. Small birds, particularly sparrows, can also form an important part of the diet. They are snatched from their roosting places or sometimes flushed by the owl beating the bushes with its wings. Bats, frogs and large insects may

The African barn owl *T. a. affinis* is distributed throughout the lightly wooded parts of Africa and its ecology is similar to that of other races.

Barn owls have taken to nesting in barns, churches, ruins and other man-made structures, wherever they are available, in preference to hollow trees, rock crevices and other natural sites.

also be captured and a barn owl has been seen plunging into a pool like an osprey to seize a fish.

Breeding starts early in the year and may continue into the late summer or even autumn. Indeed in Britain it is claimed that egg-laying has been recorded in every month of the year except January. Little is known of this owl's mating rituals, but wing clapping in flight (presumably by the male) has been noted and accumulation of food at the nesting site just before egg-laying starts suggests presentation of food by the males to the females. No nest is built, although the owl's castings often form a compact surround for the eggs. The site is usually the floor of a dark crevice or hollow although old jackdaw nests are occasionally used. The owls will also use artificial sites, such as baskets or barrels.

When first laid barn owl eggs are pure white with little or no gloss, but later they often become stained yellowish. They are not quite so round as owl eggs usually are. The average size is 40 by 32 mm. The clutch usually varies from three to seven, but as many as 11 eggs have been found in one clutch. The eggs are laid at 48 hour intervals and incubation, principally by the female, usually starts with the first egg. Hatching occurs after 33 days and throughout the incubation period the female is fed by the male. Later both parents take part in feeding the young.

The newly-hatched young are clothed with a short white down, which is more plentiful on the upperparts than beneath. This first down is gradually replaced by a second longer and more plentiful creamy-buff down, which persists until juvenile plumage is complete. The young vacate the nest site after 9 to 12 weeks, by which time they are practically indistinguishable from their parents, except for the occasional remnants of down that still adhere to some of their feathers. If disturbed at the nest site the young are usually docile and can be handled with ease, while the parent birds quickly fly to safety. On occasions, however, the adult birds will take up a distinctive defensive posture. The bird crouches, or even becomes almost prone, with its wings widely spread. The head may be swung from side to side while the bird hisses and snaps its bill. Both parent and nestling owls can make an audible 'snap' with their bills, together with hissing and snoring noises.

While it is known that the common barn owl is widely distributed, little detailed information is available about its density in any particular area. In 1932 the Royal Society for the Protection of Birds surveyed the barn owl population of England and Wales and concluded that there were about 25,000 pairs. A further enquiry in 1964 conducted by the British Trust for Ornithology showed that the barn owl had recently decreased in many areas, notably in southern and eastern England. These declines were attributed to poisoning by certain chlorine-based pesticides (notably aldrin, dieldrin and heptachlor), by the replacement of old barns with modern farm buildings, and by the clearing of old trees and hedges. Strangely, though similar conditions are found in the U.S., barn owl populations are not noticeably declining there.

It is assumed that the common barn owl is probably territorial, at least in Britain, because of the separation of the pairs comprising a local population. The shriek it utters in flight, its whitish colouration, its obvious presence when hunting over an area or when perched bolt upright on a post or branch, have all had territorial significance attributed to them. Whether or not the population density is related to availability of prey has not yet been established, but what is apparent is that an abundance of prey is reflected in the breeding success in a particular season. In years when food is readily available it has been noted that more young are fledged and second broods are undertaken. The very protracted breeding season and the staggered or 'asynchronous' hatching of the eggs, resulting in young of very different ages, are almost certainly adaptations made in response to the availability of food.

In view of the extremely wide distribution of the common barn owl it is hardly surprising to find that it has evolved into a large number of geographical races. Much work has yet to be done to establish the relationship between them, for while some are quite distinct and immediately acceptable as a good stable subspecies, others differ only in minor details and their status is still a subject for discussion.

In an evolutionary sense the barn owls are a relatively recent member of the Strigiformes, the fossil evidence suggesting that they probably had their origin sometime during the Miocene period over 12 million years ago (see p. 32). Their subsequent spread and the resultant different forms that now exist in different geographical regions of the world are a matter of considerable biological interest. Colouration, for

Young barn owls moult from their fluffy nestling down directly into adult plumage.

This English barn owl, which has brought a vole to its nestlings, has chosen a most unusual nest site in the open among bracken-covered rocks.

example, varies from specimens with pure white underparts to those of a deep reddish brown. In general the lighter-coloured forms, some almost white above and below, are more common in the Australian, Mediterranean and Middle Eastern Regions.

The races vary in size from about 330 to 430 mm, with the smaller races being found nearer to the equator contrasting with those found to the north and south. There are also, as might be expected, indications of change in wing size and leg size associated with different hunting habits, but more data are required before these can be fully appreciated.

J. L. Peters in his authoritative *Birds of the World* includes 34 different races of *Tyto alba*, although additional races have been claimed. To compile the following notes on the different races all the original descriptions have been read. The features selected are those by which they mainly differ from the nominate race and which seem to typify their subspecific characteristics. In addition an examination has been made of specimens of many of the races.

For convenience the races have been grouped geographically, starting with those occurring in Europe in the northern part of the distribution.

If a well established popular name exists this is given, but many races are still only known by their scientific name. After the scientific name the name of the describer is given, with the date on which the description was first published. (Where the describer's name is given in brackets it indicates that the bird was placed in a different genus to the one now used, which in the case of the barn owls was usually *Strix*.)

I EUROPE

1 *T. a. alba* (Scopoli) 1769.
THE COMMON OR WHITE-BREASTED BARN OWL
This is the nominate or typical race, that is the first barn owl to be described. A general description is given on page 43. Its detailed measurements as given in the *Handbook of British Birds* are: wing 265 to 295 mm, tail 110 to 125 mm, tarsus 55 to 62 mm, bill from base of feathers 23 to 29 mm.

2 *T. a. guttata* (C. L. Brehm) 1831.
THE DARK-BREASTED BARN OWL
Upperparts grey with little yellow, and with black spots and whitish tips to feathers. Facial discs vinous or white with a distinct black spot

The barn owls inhabiting Britain and parts of western and southern Europe belong to the very pale, white-breasted race *T. a. alba*.

HOSKING

The races of *Tyto alba*. The widely distributed common barn owl has evolved into a large number of geographical races, varying in size from 330 to 430 mm. The figures on this map refer to the figures in the text on pages 47 to 51.

in front of the eye; facial ruff brownish chestnut with black tips. Head, neck and underparts rufous. The wing is slightly larger (275 to 305 mm) than in the nominate race.

Its distribution extends from southern Sweden through Germany to the Alps in the south. Eastwards it is found in Poland, western Russia and to the south in Austria, Hungary, Bulgaria and the Crimea. Along the western edge of its distribution, in eastern France and western Germany, intermediates between this race and *T. a. alba* occur.

The ecology of the common and dark-breasted barn owls appears to be similar. A recent study in Holland showed the population there to be in the order of 3000 pairs. The numbers of owls fluctuated rhythmically with the population cycles of small rodents, with peaks about every third year. Individual pairs of owls occupied a territory of about 25 to 30 hectares and in good years raised up to nine young in two broods. When food became scarce the birds emigrated to other parts of Europe with many perishing from starvation.

3 *T. a. ernesti* (Kleinschmidt) 1901
Similar to *alba* but with upperparts distinctly pale and pure silvery underparts rarely spotted. Found in Corsica and Sardinia.

II AFRICA AND THE MIDDLE EAST

4 *T. a. affinis* (Blyth) 1862. THE AFRICAN BARN OWL
Slightly larger than the dark-breasted barn owl with the general colouring deeper. Upperparts more ashy, lower parts more intensely rufous and primaries and tail more distinctly banded.

Widely distributed throughout South Africa and in Tropical Africa from the west coast to the Sudan. Its ecology is similar to its European counterpart, but it has been recorded nesting in old eagle and hammerkop nests.

5 *T. a. schmitzi* (Hartert) 1900.
THE MADEIRAN BARN OWL
Paler above than the African barn owl and with noticeably large spots on slightly suffused rufous underparts. Well marked reddish-brown spot in front of the eye. Confined to Madeira.

6 *T. a. gracilirostris* (Hartert) 1905.
THE CANARY ISLANDS BARN OWL
Similar to Madeiran barn owl, but bill and legs more slender and spots on underparts noticeably smaller. Confined to Fuertaventura and Lanzarote.

7 *T. a. detorta* (Hartert) 1913.
THE CAPE VERDE ISLAND BARN OWL
Generally larger than previous race (wing 287 to 300 mm). Closely allied to the dark-breasted barn owl but has larger black and white spots on the upperparts, more thinly feathered legs and consistently darker orange underparts with smaller spots. Confined to Santiago and St. Vincent.

8 *T. a. thomensis* (Hartlaub) 1852.
THE SÃO THOMÉ BARN OWL
A noticeably dark race with dark grey upperparts

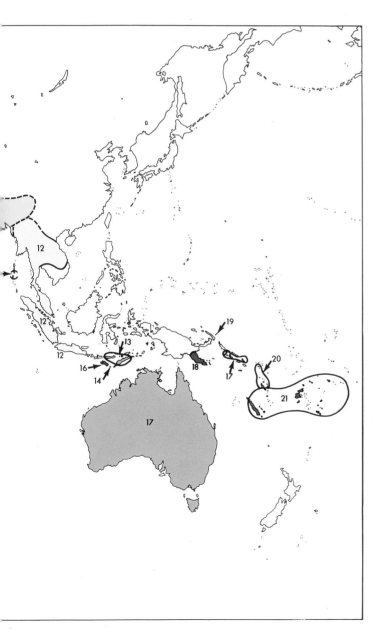

and conspicuous black and white spots. Facial disc very brown and underparts golden brown often with very large black and white spots. Wing 250 to 260 mm and feet large and powerful. Confined to the island São Thomé in the Gulf of Guinea.

9 *T. a. hypermetra* (Grote) 1928.
THE MADAGASCAR BARN OWL
A race confined to Madagascar and the Comoro Islands, only differing from the African barn owl by its slightly larger size. While the wing of the mainland form rarely exceeds 300 mm, 10 specimens of the Madagascar race ranged from 300 to 320 mm.

10 *T. a. erlangeri* (W. L. Sclater) 1921
A very pale race closely resembling the nominate form, but distinguished by the whole of the tarsus and toes being bare or covered with only a few hair-like feathers. Principal locality is Arabia, probably extends north into Iraq.

III SOUTH AND EAST ASIA AND AUSTRALASIA

11 *T. a. stertens* (Hartert) 1929.
THE INDIAN BARN OWL

12 *T. a. javanica* (Gmelin) 1788
These two races are similar in appearance and are found over a vast area extending from India, through south-eastern Asia into Indonesia. Of the two the Indian race is generally lighter in colouration with its upperparts being a pale grey rather than the golden buff of *javanica* and the underparts white or only pale yellow with smaller brown spots. It also occurs in Ceylon (where it is rare and restricted in its range) and in Assam, but it is displaced by *javanica* in Burma (the disposition of the two has yet to be worked out). *Javanica* also occurs throughout Thailand, Indo-China and throughout south-eastern Asia to Java and probably also on islands further east, up to and including Timor (but see *T. a. kuehni*). Both races have been frequently recorded in residential areas in gardens near temples and houses.

13 *T. a. kuehni* (Hartert) 1929

14 *T. a. everetti* (Hartert) 1929. THE SAVU BARN OWL
It is suggested that the barn owl of the Lesser Sunda islands from Flores to Timor is not *javanica* but a distinct race *kuehni*. Also that there is another race *everetti* on the island of Savu 100 miles west of Timor. These two races are extremely similar to *javanica* and can only be separated from each other by the smaller size of *everetti* compared to *kuehni* (wing of male 247 mm cf 253 mm and of female 265 mm cf 382 mm).

15 *T. a. deroepstorffi* (Hume) 1875.
THE ANDAMAN BARN OWL
A darker bird than the Indian barn owl being dark brown rather than grey above, with a rufescent face and deep brownish rufous underparts. Confined to the south Andaman Islands and considered to be extremely rare.

16 *T. a. sumbaensis* (Hartert) 1897.
THE SUMBA BARN OWL
A slightly bigger bird with larger bill and almost white tail with narrow black bars. Found only on Sumba Island.

17 *T. a. delicatula* (Gould) 1837.
THE AUSTRALIAN BARN OWL
It is suggested that the Australian race originated in India and came by way of the Malay Peninsula, Java and the Lesser Sunda Islands. It is now found throughout Australia and on some of the Solomon Islands. It has been recorded in New Zealand on three occasions in 1947, 1955 and 1960, but there is no evidence of breeding. In appearance it differs little from *T. a. alba* except that the upperparts are a light brownish grey rather than orange buff.

18 *T. a. meeki* (Rothschild and Hartert) 1907.
NEW GUINEA BARN OWL
Distinguished from the Australian barn owl by the pure white outer two tail feathers, sometimes with a few tiny spots. Remainder of tail pale buff with faint spots and bars. Most closely resembles *sumbaensis* which also has a light coloured tail, the outer feathers sometimes being white, but the barring on the tail of *sumbaensis* is always much darker and also its bill is thicker, higher and more arched than *meeki*. The dusky spots on the silvery white underparts of *meeki* are almost arrow-shaped. Found only in south-eastern New Guinea.

19 *T. a. crassirostris* (Mayr) 1935
Differs from the Australian barn owl by its

stronger bill and feet and darker colouration. Known only from the type locality of Boaing Island, Tanga Group, Bismark Archipelago.

20 *T. a. interposita* (Mayr) 1935
Mainly distinguished from neighbouring races by prevalence of orange-ochre colour present throughout plumage. Restricted to Santa Cruz Islands, Banks Islands and northern New Hebrides.

21 *T. a. lulu* (Peale) 1848
Upperparts light grey, mottled pale brown, with slight tawny tinge. Each dorsal feather has a black tip with a white centre and there are four brown bars on the tail. Underparts white. Present on New Caledonia, southern New Hebrides, Loyalty, Fiji, Tonga, Samoa and Society Islands. It has frequently been recorded hunting during the daytime.

IV NORTH AND SOUTH AMERICA

22 *T. a. pratincola* (Bonaparte) 1838.
THE NORTH AMERICAN BARN OWL
Widely distributed in North and Central America and south to the Gulf States, possibly as far as eastern Nicaragua. Generally similar to the European races, including both light and dark forms. The upperparts vary from pale orange buff to darker specimens in which grey is mixed with same, the underparts from white to pale orange spotted or 'V'-marked with brown.

23 *T. a. lucayana* (Riley) 1913.
THE BAHAMA BARN OWL
Similar to *pratincola* but with less of the greyish black-vermiculated tipped feathers of upperparts.

24 *T. a. furcata* (Temminck) 1827.
THE CUBA BARN OWL
More robust than the nominate race, with much stronger claws and larger legs. Upperparts pale orange buff with greyish-brown tips to feathers and a golden orange crown. Face, primaries, tail and underparts pure white with a few spots on flanks.

25 *T. a. glaucops* (Kaup) 1852
Race found on the West Indian islands of Tortuga and Hispaniola and characterized by a silver grey facial disc.

26 *T. a. nigrescens* (Lawrence) 1878

27 *T. a. insularis* (Pelzeln) 1872
Two races described from the Lesser Antilles Islands, the former from the Isle of Dominica and the latter from the southern Lesser Antilles. These owls are principally found in the mountains and higher valleys. Their colouration is dark, with the upperparts a fine blackish-brown rather sparsely marked with small white spots and the underparts light reddish-ochre with small round black spots.

28 *T. a. guatemalae* (Ridgway) 1873
In colouration resembles *guttata* of Europe more than the North American barn owl, but is more uniform above and more coarsely speckled below. Found in Central America from Panama to Guatemala.

29 *T. a. contempta* (Hartert) 1898
Upperparts black with fine pale grey mottling and small black tips with a white spot at the extremity of feathers, underparts pale rusty brown with black irregular cross-markings. Facial ruff very pale brown, tips of feathers black and a large black spot in front of the eye. Feet yellow, claws brown, bill greenish white. Found in parts of Columbia, Ecuador, Peru and Venezuela.

30 *T. a. subandeana* (L. Kelso) 1938
A race found in the tropical zone of Columbia and Ecuador. It differs from *T. a. contempta* by markings on underparts.

31 *T. a. tuidara* (J. E. Gray) 1829
Present in Brazil south of the Amazon to Chile and Argentina. Resembles *T. a. guttata* of Europe but the legs are longer.

32 *T. a. hellmayri* (Griscom and Greenway) 1937
Similar to *T. a. tuidara* in colouration, but considerably larger (wing of type 335 mm). Ranges from Guianas to the Amazon valley.

33 *T. a. bargei* (Hartert) 1892
A very small insular form, confined to the Island of Curaçao. Totally unlike the races of the barn owl of the West Indies, it is more like the European races but is much smaller and has shorter wings.

34 *T. a. punctatissima* (G. R. Gray) 1838

One of the smallest barn owls, found only on James Island of the Galapagos. Total length 330 mm, wing 234 mm, tail 41 mm, tarsus 59 mm. Above dull brown with a few dusky white spots. Face vinous rufous inclining to black round eye, underparts barred with brown.

In addition to *T. alba* and its large number of associated races, there are a further seven species of barn owl. Six of these are found in the Australasian region and two of them, the common grass owl and the masked owl, have been sub-divided into a number of races. Compared to *T. alba*, however, they are relatively restricted in their distribution, with the exception of the common grass owl *T. capensis*, which is found in Africa and from India to Australia.

After the common barn owl, the common grass owl is the most widely distributed of the barn owl species. It occurs in parts of India, China and southern Australia, and in Africa, although some people consider the African birds to be a distinct species. In appearance this owl resembles a slightly large, dark, long-legged common barn owl. Above, it is typically dark chocolate brown with varying amounts of buff or orange and a noticeable buff or white spot at the tip of the feathers. In the daylight it often appears greyish. The facial disc is pinkish-white or buff and the underparts vary from white-tinged orange to brownish yellow. In size, it is roughly similar to the common barn owl, but most specimens come at the larger end of the range.

Named because of its habitat, the grass owl roosts during the daylight hours in hollows or tunnels in long grass and lays its eggs in grass or sedge clumps. When disturbed in the daytime it typically flies only a short distance before dropping suddenly into the vegetation. Their prey is principally small mammals, but birds and beetles are also taken. In Australia remnants of the following have been found in pellets: yellow-footed marsupial mouse (*Antechinus flavipes*), pygmy marsupial mouse (*A. maculatus*), eastern swamp rat (*Rattus lutreolus*) and pretty sugar glider (*Pretaurus breviceps*).

The long almost bare legs of the grass owl are obvious adaptations to its open ground dwelling habits, enabling it to alight, rise and catch prey more easily. It does not build a nest, although the trampled vegetation may provide a bed for the eggs and the nest site is often linked to runs

LINDGREN/ARDEA

Above and right: though superficially similar to the barn owl, the grass owl *Tyto capensis* (380 to 420 mm) is easily distinguished by its much darker chocolate brown back. It is a variable species and the Asian and Australasian forms are sometimes considered to be distinct from the geographically isolated African form, in which case they are named *T. longimembris*. Grass owls differ from barn owls in having longer, almost unfeathered legs which are presumably better suited to their more terrestrial life in grassland habitats.

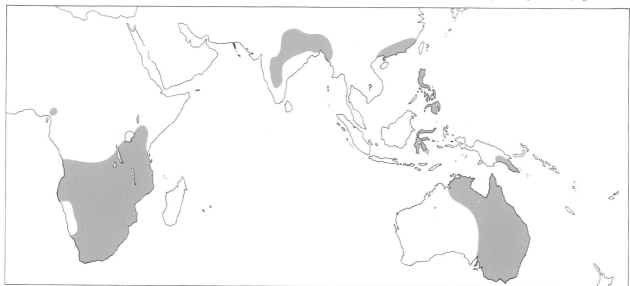

Tyto capensis (including *T. longimembris*): grassland.

formed under the vegetation. The clutch is usually about 4, but up to 6 eggs have been recorded and despite its ground nesting habits the eggs are conspicuously white. Although it is found over a very wide area, it is not generally common and is more aptly described as local. In Australia it has been most frequently recorded within 70 kilometres of the coast, but as it is very secretive in its habitats and difficult to see in the vegetation it may often be overlooked.

When the common grass owl is considered as a single species, the name *T. capensis* is applied throughout its range. If it is divided into two species, this name is confined to the African birds and the name *T. longimembris* is used for the birds in the remaining parts of its distribution. *T. longimembris* has itself been divided into several subspecies corresponding to the different parts of its range. Closely allied forms are found in Australia, the Philippines, Celebes, Kalidupa and the Fiji Islands and have been collectively termed *T. l. walleri*. A form confined to mountain grassland at 5000 to 6000 metres in south-east New Guinea is named *T. l. papuensis*. Two races have been described from south-eastern China. Both are more fawn in general colouring and one of them *T. l. melli* is further distinguished by its white, not rosy, facial disc, while the other *T. l. chinensis* has a very dark rosy facial disc. The nominate rate is widely distributed in India.

The sooty owl, *T. tenebricosa*, is in appearance the most exceptional of the barn owl species. It is relatively small (total length 330 to 380 mm) has the largest eyes of them all, probably the smallest tail, and in colouration lacks the familiar yellow-orange. The facial disc is sooty grey (more defined round the eyes), the upperparts are brownish black, with purple reflections and white spots at the tips of the feathers. Beneath it can be almost entirely brownish black, or white spotted with brown, particularly on the breast. The female is much larger than the male.

In Australia it has been recorded from Queensland, New South Wales, Victoria and South Australia, usually in coastal regions, and it is considered rare. The northern sooty owls have sometimes been claimed, on grounds of their smaller size, to be a separate race *T. t. multipunctata*.

The sooty owl is also found throughout New Guinea, below 200 metres elevation. Here they

LINDGREN/ARDEA

Though it is the most distinctive member of the genus, the sooty owl *Tyto tenebricosa* (330 to 380 mm) of Australia and New Guinea is probably one of the least known, for it is confined to dense forests and is seldom seen.

Tyto tenebricosa: dense forest.
T. inexpectata: confined to northern peninsula of Celebes.

The Australian masked owl *Tyto novaehollandiae* (490 to 530 mm) is the largest member of the genus and gets its name from its dark facial disc. This individual is in full threat display, snapping its bill and making itself appear as large and formidable as possible.

	Tyto inexpectata
	Tyto tenebricosa

are smaller than in Australia, have larger white spots on the back and are dark beneath.

Little is known of the sooty owl's ecology, but it is evidently an owl of dense forests, including rainforests, particularly in mountainous areas. It preys at night on smallish mammals such as possums and gliders. It is usually silent, but when it is breeding it may utter a drawn-out whistle and insect-like chirrupings. The breeding season is very extended and eggs are laid in hollows of high trees, with only one of the clutch of two usually hatching.

Another member of the barn owl genus, the masked or chestnut-faced owl, *T. novaehollandiae*, is also found in Australia, parts of Tasmania and New Guinea. With a total length of over 500 mm, it is the largest of the barn owls. The Tasmanian race is the largest, and is so much bigger than the others that some ornithologists consider it as a separate species. There is a considerable difference in size between the sexes, the female being bigger and darker.

The masked owl lives in forest and scattered woodland adjoining open country, but it is probably not common in any area. Nocturnal in habits, it roosts during the day in hollow trees or thick foliage, preying at night on rabbits (often taken from traps) small mammals, reptiles and birds. The pellets produced are huge, sometimes measuring 90 mm. These owls nest in hollows in high trees, and lay two to four eggs.

This species has been divided into seven subspecies, many of which contain both light

Tyto aurantia: confined to the island of New Britain.
T. rosenbergii: rainforest (includes islands marked A).
Tyto novaehollandiae: forest and scattered woodland near open country.

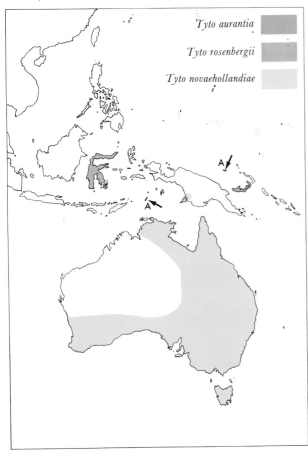

Tyto aurantia

Tyto rosenbergii

Tyto novaehollandiae

The barn owls have speciated to a greater extent in Australasia than anywhere else in the world. Two of the eight species of *Tyto* – the Celebes barn owl *Tyto rosenbergii* (410 to 510 mm) and, below, the Minahassa barn owl *Tyto inexpectata* (270 to 330 mm) – are confined to the island of Celebes and three other species are confined to the Australasian region.

and dark forms. The nominate race, from eastern and southern Australia, has a reddish-buff facial disc edged with black, dark-grey and rusty yellow upperparts, speckled with light grey and pale buff underparts spotted with brown. The Tasmanian race *T. n. castinops* includes the darkest form yet found, with dark brown speckled grey upperparts and rufous brown underparts covered with large and plentiful brownish spots. *T. n. perplexa*, a doubtful race from south-west Australia, has also been claimed on the grounds of being darker and larger than the nominate race. The New Guinea race *T. n. kimberli*, *T. n. manusi* confined to the Isle of Manus, *T. n. cayelii* to the Isle of Baru and *T. n. sorocula* to Tenimber Island, are all smaller than the mainland race.

Two species of barn owl occur on Celebes. The first, the Celebes barn owl (*T. rosenbergii*) is known from rainforests in a number of localities. It is a large owl (410 to 510 mm) with grey-brown upperparts, very obviously spotted – the white feathers have dark brown centres. The second, the Minahassa barn owl, (*T. inexpectata*) is restricted to the northern peninsula. Together with the New Britain Island barn owl (*T. aurantia*) it is smaller than *rosenbergii* and has yellow-orange patchwork on the dark brown.

The remaining species, the Madagascar grass owl (*T. soumagnei*) is an isolated species found throughout Madagascar. It is a small (about 270 mm) brown bird and is readily distinguished from the Madagascar barn owl.

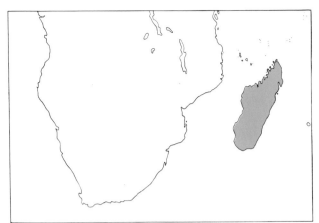

Tyto soumagnei: grassland.

The New Britain Island barn owl *Tyto aurantia* (270 to 330 mm) is confined to the Australasian island of its name.

The Madagascar grass owl *Tyto soumagnei* (about 270 mm) is an island representative of the widely distributed common grass owl.

Phodilus badius: forest, often near water.

Though superficially similar and related to the barn owls, the Oriental bay owl *Phodilus badius* (230 to 330 mm) is sufficiently distinct to be placed in a separate subfamily. It is a thoroughly nocturnal forest species but little else is known of its ecology and behaviour.

The bay owls are little known and information about their general ecology is sparse. They appear to be strictly nocturnal forest dwellers, and probably feed on small mammals, birds, lizards, frogs, insects and also (from their frequent association with water when hunting) possibly on fish. The short wings and tail enable them to hunt through dense young trees. A typical clutch of three or four white oval eggs is laid in hollows in trees which are also used for daytime roosting. Young of very different sizes have been found, suggesting that incubation starts with the first egg and is followed by asynchronous hatching. Their call is a soft hoot, but they can become very vociferous during the breeding season. Until comparatively recently only a single species (*Phodilus badius*) was known. However, what is claimed as a new species (*P. prigoginei*) was described from a single specimen obtained in March 1951 in the Congo.

The common bay owl has a wide distribution extending from northern India to Indonesia and has been sub-divided into five races. The nominate race *P. b. badius* (Horsfield) is found at the east of its range from eastern and central Burma through to Borneo and Java. Its total length is between 230 and 280 mm, which is smaller than the races at the western end of its distribution which go up to 330 mm. The upperparts are a rich chestnut and gold, spotted with black and white and the tail is heavily barred black. The top of its head is vineaceous, the facial disc white and the underparts creamy, spotted with black. A second, little known race, *P. b. saturatus*, extends from

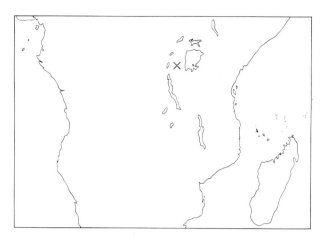

Phodilus prigoginei: the X shows the area in which the only known specimen was found.

The African bay owl *Phodilus prigoginei* (230 to 330 mm) is known from only a single specimen collected in mountain forest in the eastern Congo. Surprisingly, it hardly differs from the Oriental bay owl, in spite of being isolated from the latter by thousands of kilometres.

northern Burma into the northern part of India and the third race, *P. b. assimilis*, the Ceylon bay owl, is considered a rare inhabitant of wet forests in Ceylon up to an altitude of about 1500 metres. The remaining two races are each restricted to an Indonesian island. *P. b. parvus*, distinguished by the smaller feet, short bill and smaller wings (172 to 180 mm compared with 180 to 196 mm of Java specimens) is confined to Belitung Island and *P. b. arixuthus*, a slightly larger and lighter coloured bird, is known only from the unique type taken on Bunguran Island.

The specimen of *P. prigoginei* collected at 2500 metres north-west of Lake Tanganyika is described as being darker than the nominate race, with a more compressed beak and smaller feet and claws. This recent discovery is remarkable as it represents the first discovery of a bay owl on the continent of Africa, far removed from all its previous known localities.

CHAPTER FIVE

Fishing owls, Eagle owls and the Snowy owl

Ketupa, Scotopelia, Bubo, Nyctea

The little known fish owls in the genus *Ketupa* are a group of four large, powerful species that between them range over much of Asia. Together with the three African fish owls in the genus *Scotopelia*, they can be regarded as the nocturnal counterparts of the osprey and fish eagles. It is perhaps surprising that there are no fish owls in the New World, but one must remember that at least in tropical America there are two species of specialized fish-eating bats. It is possible that fish owls and fish bats fill niches so similar that they are prevented from living in the same geographical areas by direct competition.

In the past, the Asian fish owls were sometimes included together with eagle owls in the genus *Bubo*, but nowadays they are usually regarded as warranting separate status, mainly because they have specializations for feeding on fish. Nevertheless, they strongly resemble eagle owls in appearance, having similar prominent ear tufts, colouring, size and heavy build. In fact, they are often mistaken for eagle owls, although they differ in three main respects. Firstly, their feet are devoid of feathers and adapted for gripping slippery fish; secondly, they have even less prominent facial discs, presumably because their sense of hearing is a relatively unimportant aid in locating fish; thirdly, they lack soft plumage and silent flight, no doubt because their prey, being under water, is unable to hear them no matter how much noise they make in their approach.

The four Asian fish owls live in a wide range of environments, from hot, humid, equatorial forests to cold, boreal forests close to the Arctic Circle, but nevertheless have similar basic ecological requirements. All four species live by lakes, rivers and streams with well-wooded banks, and feed mainly on relatively large fish and other aquatic animals. They would almost certainly compete if they lived together in the same area, but this is largely avoided by there being little overlap in their distribution.

The range of Blakiston's fish owl (*K. blakistoni*) is completely exclusive, for it is separated by about 800 km from the nearest definitely known population of another species. It lives in wooded river valleys and, despite the fact that its range is so far to the north, it is apparently resident throughout the year. This species is rare everywhere, perhaps because it is dependent on streams and rivers which are sufficiently fast-flowing to remain partially unfrozen throughout the winter.

The ranges of the brown fish owl (*K. zeylonensis*), Malaysian fish owl (*K. ketupa*) and tawny fish owl (*K. flavipes*) are also largely exclusive. The brown fish owl has a tropical distribution, and is replaced by the Malaysian fish owl in the high rainfall, equatorial region of southern Indo-China and Malaysia. Both species are common throughout most of their range, although the brown fish owl is rare in the arid areas to the west of India. Both species are most numerous along sluggish streams and rivers meandering through forest or woodland, but occupy a wide range of other waterside habitats, including mangrove swamps, beach forests by the seashore, and even clumps of large trees by flooded rice-fields, fish-ponds and reservoirs. The tawny fish owl has a mainly montane distribution in the Himalayas and the mountains of southern China and Indo-China. Much less catholic in its choice of habitats than the other species, it is more or less confined to precipitous mountain streams flowing through dense forest. It appears to be rather rare throughout its range, or at any rate it has rarely been recorded.

The ranges of the brown, Malaysian and tawny fish owls overlap to some extent in parts of Indo-China. There is little information about their ecology in this region, but what there is suggests that they segregate into different habitats. In Burma, for example, the Malaysian fish owl is more or less confined to coastal regions and the courses of the larger rivers, particularly the Irrawaddy delta, while the brown fish owl occurs mainly along the wooded rivers and streams of the interior. It is also notable that both species are absent from mountain streams in Indo-China, where their place is taken by the tawny fish owl, though both occur at higher altitudes elsewhere in their range. The Malaysian fish owl, for example, occurs up to at least 1300 metres in Borneo, and the brown fish owl to 2000 metres in Ceylon. Much more ecological information is needed, but it appears probable that the different fish owls seldom come into contact with each other, even when the edges of their ranges overlap.

Blakiston's fish owl *Ketupa blakistoni* (510 to 610 mm) is an inhabitant of eastern Siberia and north-eastern China and the only fish owl to have fully feathered legs. Apparently it has the habit of wading in shallow water hunting for crayfish.

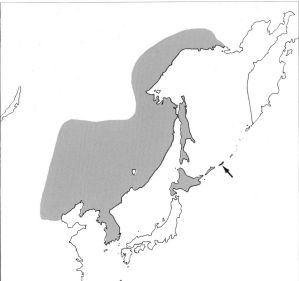

Ketupa blakistoni: wooded river valleys.

The Malaysian fish owl *Ketupa ketupa* (380 to 439 mm) is extremely similar to the brown fish owl, differing only in being smaller and in lacking faint horizontal barring on its underparts. It is a common species over most of its range.

In such circumstances, the evidence suggests that the different species share out the available habitats, or occur at different altitudes, each being more restricted in areas where it overlaps with other species than in areas that it occupies exclusively.

Like most owls, the fish owls are strongly territorial and tend to be evenly spaced in suitable habitats. Travelling along small rivers in the interior of Borneo, for example, it is normal to see or disturb a pair of Malaysian fish owls at regular intervals of 1 to 2 km. In one especially favoured area I saw nine pairs in less than 7 km of river. Fish owls usually roost in waterside trees with dense foliage, mangoes being particularly popular in tropical areas. Sometimes a pair roost together, but more often they roost in separate trees a short distance apart. They occasionally emerge from their roosts in the late afternoon, and this has earned them the reputation of being semi-diurnal. In fact, they rarely hunt before dusk, and are hardly more diurnal than eagle owls or other species that are generally regarded as thoroughly nocturnal. I have watched Malaysian and brown fish owls hunting on numerous occasions, but only once

Ketupa ketupa: streams and rivers through forest and woodland; also mangrove and beach forests, clumps of trees near rice-fields, fish ponds or reservoirs.

Ketupa flavipes: mountain streams in dense forest.

Like other fish-eating owls, the tawny fish owl *Ketupa flavipes* (480 to 510 mm) watches for its prey from a perch at the water's edge, then swoops to snatch it from the surface of the water, in much the same way as a fish eagle.

before dusk, and then on a dark stormy evening.

Fish owls usually hunt from a tree-stump, dead branch or some other vantage point overlooking the water's edge. They catch their prey in the same way as a fish eagle, by swooping at it, and snatching it from the surface of the water with their talons, and not by plunging bodily into the water in the manner of an osprey. The feet of fish owls are beautifully adapted to grip a wriggling, slippery, loose-scaled fish. They are devoid of feathers and covered below by numerous sharp-edged, spiky scales, while their claws are long and curved with a sharp, lower cutting edge. In fact, they are very like the feet of fish eagles and the osprey. However, although fish owls have a diet that consists primarily of fish, they will take almost any other prey that comes their way, including small mammals, birds, snakes, frogs, crayfish, crabs and sometimes insects. The mammals recorded in their diet include a small porcupine, and birds include species up to the size of junglefowl and pheasants. They also scavenge to some extent; the brown fish owl, for example, has been recorded feeding on the carcass of a crocodile. Fish owls are sometimes seen wading in shallow water. Often they are merely bathing, but not infrequently they are hunting for crayfish, crabs and other easily caught aquatic animals. Blakiston's fish owl is said to hunt regularly in this manner, and the Malaysian fish owl certainly does so occasionally, but such behaviour may be mainly incidental to bathing.

Extremely little is known about the breeding biology of fish owls. Even the most basic information is lacking from most areas for all the species, and it is not possible to do more than repeat the snippets of information that are scattered through the regional literature. All that is recorded for Blakiston's fish owl is that it nests on the ground, presumably in the northern spring and summer. The other three species use a variety of nest sites, including holes in trees and river-banks, ledges in cliffs and ruins, hollows in the forks of trees, and the old nests of crows and eagles. Clutch-sizes of from one to three eggs have been recorded for the brown fish owl, and of one egg for the Malaysian fish owl. The brown fish owl appears to breed between November and May throughout its range. In India and northern Indo-China this is the dry season, which suggests that the breeding season might be timed

The brown fish owl *Ketupa zeylonensis* (480 to 510 mm) is the most widely distributed of four species of Asian fish owls which replace each other over a large part of the continent. Fish owls differ from eagle owls, which they otherwise resemble closely, in having feet which are equipped with spiny scales as an aid to gripping fish; and less well-developed facial discs.

Ketupa zeylonensis: streams and rivers through forest and woodland.

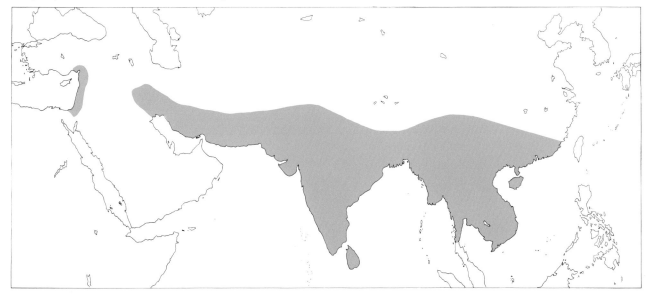

to coincide with the period when river levels are low, the water clear, and fish therefore easy to catch. Unfortunately, the same period is wet in the Middle East and a more satisfactory explanation obviously needs to be found. There are breeding records for the tawny fish owl from the Himalayas in the dry season, but they are too few to be very significant. The Malaysian fish owl breeds between December and May in Malaya and Borneo. It is the wettest time of the year in this region, but other times are only less wet, not dry. Obviously, much more information will have to be accumulated before the breeding seasonality of fish owls can be properly explained.

Like most owls, the fish owls are particularly noisy before breeding, and pairs sometimes indulge in bouts of duetting which continue for many minutes. They have a great variety of hooting and mewing calls which are probably distinctive, though descriptions in the literature are confusingly similar. The voice of the small Malaysian fish owl is perhaps the most easily recognized, for it is higher-pitched and more musical than the voices of the larger species.

Identification of the Asian fish owls is likely to be a problem only in the parts of Indo-China where the ranges of brown, Malaysian and tawny fish owls overlap. These three species are, in fact, fairly easily distinguished. The brown fish owl is large, about 480 to 510 mm long, and has fine, wavy, horizontal barring on its underparts; the tawny fish owl is also large, but lacks horizontal barring on its underparts and is a very rich rufous in colour; while the Malaysian fish owl has neither horizontal barring nor rich rufous colouring, and is relatively small, about 380 to 43 mm long.

It remains to consider the relationship between the brown fish owl and Blakiston's fish owl, for some authorities prefer to regard them as a single species. The two resemble each other, and differ from the tawny and Malaysian fish owls, in having fine, wavy, horizontal barring on their underparts. However, both species are very variable, and it is difficult to point to any differences that strongly suggest that they are really distinct. It is true that Blakiston's fish owl is generally pale in colour, and slightly larger than the brown fish owl, but these are differences that might be expected in view of its northerly distribution and, in any case, they are no greater than the differences between widespread populations of the brown fish owl. Examples of

the latter are very pale and buff in the arid areas of Palestine and Iraq, but a richer yellow brown in the humid forested areas of India and Indo-China. It is also true that Blakiston's fish owl differs from the brown fish owl, as well as the other two species, in having completely feathered tarsi, but again this difference could well be correlated with its northerly distribution. To support this idea there is the fact that the brown and Malaysian fish owls, which have tropical and equatorial distributions, resemble each other in having completely naked tarsi, while the tawny fish owl, which lives further to the north and at higher altitudes than the two latter species, is intermediate and has tarsi that are feathered to about half way down.

This dispute can be resolved only when more is known about the status of fish owls in eastern China. The brown fish owl is known to occur in Kwangsi and Kwangtung Provinces in the south, and Blakiston's fish owl in Hopei Province in the north, but it is not known for certain whether fish owls occur at all in the intervening area. If they do not, then it is entirely a matter of taste whether Blakiston's fish owl is regarded as a separate species or not. On the other hand, if there are intervening populations that intergrade with the brown fish owl in the south, and Blakiston's fish owl in the north, then all the populations must be regarded as a single species.

AFRICAN FISHING OWLS

The three African fishing owls in the genus *Scotopelia* resemble their Asian counterparts in being large and powerful, and in having similar specializations for feeding on fish; otherwise they are quite different in general appearance. They lack ear tufts, and have loose feathering on their heads which gives them a characteristic shaggy, maned look. However, in spite of their superficial dissimilarity, it is thought that the two groups have evolved from the same parent stock, and not independently on the two continents. Obviously, they must have been isolated from each other for a long time to be so different in appearance.

Even less is known about African fishing owls than about Asian species. The least poorly-known is Pel's fishing owl (*S. peli*), which is sparsely distributed throughout most of Africa south of the Sahara. It is a huge, magnificent species, a rich orange-rufous in colour, and one of the most spectacular of all the owls. It lives by rivers, lakes and marshes with forested banks, but is just as at home in riverine forest strips in desert regions as it is by rivers flowing through the great forests of the Congo. Along the Omo River in the relative arid region of south-west Ethiopia it reaches densities of up to one pair per five or six km of river, and is probably as common there as anywhere else in Africa. The other two species are more rare and much less widely distributed. The vermiculated fishing owl (*S. bouvieri*) is found mainly in riverine forest strips adjacent to the great block of continuous Congo forest, but occurs neither within the continuous forest area, nor far away from the forest edge. The rufous fishing owl (*S. ussheri*) is known only from a handful of specimens from the rainforest region between Sierra Leone and Ghana.

African fishing owls are occasionally seen in the open in the late afternoon, but they are essentially nocturnal and usually emerge from their roosts at dusk. Surprisingly, nobody seems to know how they catch their prey, though Pel's fishing owl has been seen perched on stumps overlooking the water's edge, apparently fishing, and it seems likely that they use the same technique as the Asian fish owls. They certainly resemble the Asian species in their fish-catching adaptations, for they have unfeathered feet and tarsi, similarly sharp-edged spiny scales on their feet for gripping fish, poorly developed facial discs, and a relatively noisy flight. There is little definite information about the diet of African fishing owls. Fish and frogs have been recorded in stomachs of Pel's fishing owls, and small fish, prawns and a small bird have been found in the stomachs of vermiculated fishing owls. It is probable that all three species feed primarily on fish and other aquatic animals, but that they take a wide range of other food items when opportunity offers. It is also probable that Pel's fishing owl is capable of taking larger prey than the other two species, for it is considerably bigger and more powerful, particularly in the structure of its feet.

Pel's fishing owl breeds in large stick nests, probably abandoned by eagles, and has a clutch of two to four eggs. Most clutches have been recorded during the local dry season, so it is possible that breeding is timed to coincide with the period when rivers are low and clear, and fish easier to catch. Nothing is known about the breeding biology of the other African fishing owls.

Like other fish-eating owls, the rufous fishing owl *Scotopelia ussheri* (460 to 510 mm) of West Africa has a very strong compressed bill and unfeathered legs and feet. It has been seen or collected on very few occasions and little is known about its behaviour.

Scotopelia ussheri: rainforest.

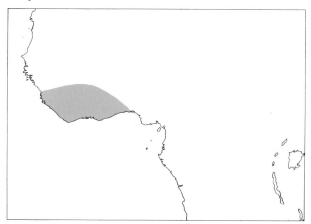

One of the best ways of locating Pel's fishing owl is to listen for it at night, for it is noisy and its calls carry for a considerable distance. Its most characteristic call is a deep, sonorous and musical double hoot which has been transcribed as 'hooomm-hut'. It is also said to have a hoot which rises to a screech and a terrifying wail. The voice of the vermiculated fishing owl has seldom been heard, but a captive individual was recorded as uttering 'either a half-dozen short "hu's" in rapid succession, or a protracted quavering hoot'. The voice of the rufous fishing owl seems to be undescribed.

Though the three African fishing owls are rather similar in general appearance and colour, they are not difficult to distinguish. Pel's fishing owl, which is the only one of the three species

Pel's fishing owl
Scotopelia peli

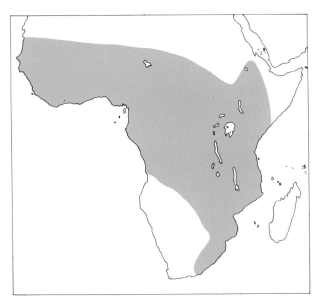

Scotopelia peli: forested banks of rivers, lakes and marshes; also riverine forest in desert areas.

Scotopelia bouvieri: riverine forest.

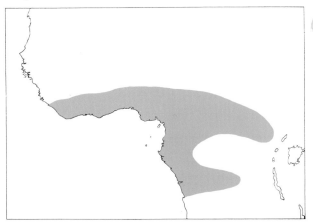

Pel's fishing owl *Scotopelia peli* (510 to 610 mm) is widely distributed in Africa, but the smaller vermiculated fishing owl *S. bouvieri* (460 to 510 mm) is confined to forest rivers in West and Central Africa. Like all fishing owls, Asian as well as African, both species are largely nocturnal.

Vermiculated fishing owl
Scotopelia bouvieri

present over most of Africa, is easily recognized by its size, for it is up to 610 mm long and one of the largest owls in the world. The two smaller species are 460 to 510 mm long and best distinguished from each other by their colour. The rufous fishing owl has bright rufous unbarred upperparts, whereas those of the vermiculated fishing owl are sandy rufous and finely vermiculated with darker brown, the general effect being much more dull. In addition, the rufous fishing owl differs from both the other species in having yellow rather than dark brown eyes, while the vermiculated fishing owl has the ground colour of its underparts white, as opposed to sienna as in Pel's fishing owl, or rufous as in the rufous fishing owl.

EAGLE OWLS

The eagle owls are among the largest and most magnificent of the owls, and are readily distinguished from all but the closely related Asian fish owls by a combination of their large size and possession of conspicuous ear tufts. They differ from the fish owls in having heavily feathered toes and tarsi, more pronounced facial discs, quieter flight and, of course, different feeding habits. As their name suggests, eagle owls are the nocturnal counterparts of such large birds of prey as the eagles and buzzards. With the exception of one apparently insectivorous species, they have a heavy, compressed, eagle-like bill and enormously powerful talons, and prey for the most part on mammals and birds up to the size of hares and game birds. Eagle owls are typical 'perch and pounce' hunters that sit and watch for their prey from a raised vantage point, and pounce on it from above. They are mainly nocturnal, depending on their acute hearing and excellent night vision to detect their prey, though they often venture forth before dusk, and even hunt in broad daylight when food is scarce, or when forced to by the short summer nights.

The consensus of opinion recognizes twelve species of *Bubo*, although there are two species with particularly well-marked races that are recognized as good species by some authorities. The races in question are discussed below. Between them, the twelve recognized species have an almost cosmopolitan distribution, their role of large nocturnal predator being taken over by owls in other genera only in Arctic regions to the north of the tree-line, where they are replaced by the snowy owl, and in Australasia

FINK/ARDEA

Populations of the Eurasian eagle owl *Bubo bubo* from southern or eastern arid regions tend to be paler, greyer and smaller than those from further north and west. This individual belongs to the race *B. b. nikolskii* (580 to 600 mm) from Transcaspia and Iran.

Above, right: The European race of the Eurasian eagle owl *B. b. bubo* (660 to 710 mm) is the largest and most powerful of all the owls. It is capable of killing young roe deer, foxes and such large game birds as capercaillie, though its normal prey consists mainly of rats and other rodents.

Bubo bubo: in Europe, forested ravines, cliffs, rocky outcrops; elsewhere a variety of habitats from rainforest to desert.

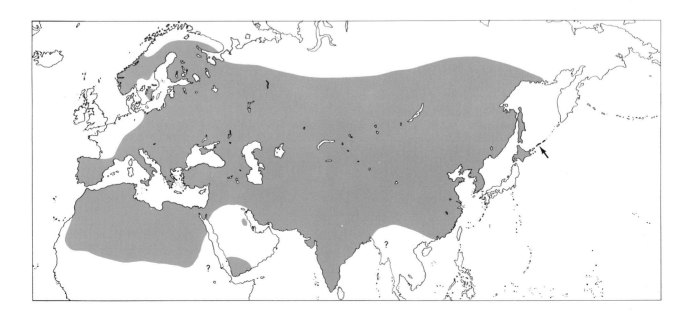

and the Pacific Islands, where they are replaced by the larger of the hawk owls. Within their enormous geographical range, the twelve eagle owls between them occupy just about all the available habitats, from equatorial rainforest and mangrove forest to boreal forest, deserts and mountain-tops, the only essential prerequisite being the presence of at least a few trees or rocky outcrops to provide cover for roosting and nesting. For the most part, eagle owls segregate ecologically in a very clear-cut way, replacing each other either geographically or in different habitats, although the extent to which continents or lesser areas are subdivided into eagle owl niches varies greatly in different parts of the world. To take two extremes, there is only one eagle owl in the whole of North and South America, compared with a total of seven in Africa, six of which are confined to the area south of the Sahara Desert.

The Eurasian eagle owl (*B. bubo*) is the best known species in the group, and also one of the most widely distributed. It ranges throughout most of Eurasia, from as far north as the Arctic Circle in Scandinavia, east across Russia to Sakhalin and the southern Kuriles, and south to

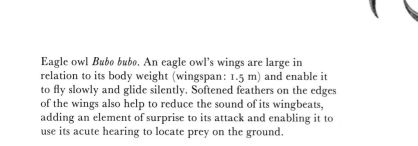

Eagle owl *Bubo bubo*. An eagle owl's wings are large in relation to its body weight (wingspan: 1.5 m) and enable it to fly slowly and glide silently. Softened feathers on the edges of the wings also help to reduce the sound of its wingbeats, adding an element of surprise to its attack and enabling it to use its acute hearing to locate prey on the ground.

the southern edge of the Sahara, to Arabia, Iran, India and southern China. As might be expected in view of its enormous range, the Eurasian eagle owl is very variable in both size and colour, the pattern of variation being similar to that of any other widely distributed Palaearctic species. Thus, it reaches its largest size, about 710 mm long, at high latitudes and altitudes, and its smallest size, about 460 mm long, at the southern limits of its range, in North Africa, the Middle East and India. Similarly, it is relatively dark and brown in humid forested areas, and pale and sandy in arid desert and semi-desert regions. The variation is typically clinal, except in the case of two very distinct populations which have sometimes been regarded as distinct species. The more distinct of the two is known as the pharaoh eagle owl (*B. b. ascalaphus*), and occupies suitable areas in the deserts of North Africa, Sinai, Arabia and the rest of the Middle East as far north and east as Lebanon, the Syrian Desert and the upper Euphrates. It is very different from accepted populations of the Eurasian eagle owl, including those with which it comes into contact in the west and east of its range. It is relatively small with weak talons, has pale plumage which is mottled rather than streaked, and is said to have a different voice. The two forms definitely interbreed to some extent in the Middle East, but the result is not primary intergradation, but rather a mixture of hybrids and typical individuals of both forms, which suggests that gene flow is very restricted. There is no recent information about the status of the two forms in northern Algeria, which is the only other area in which they are likely to come into contact, but both definitely occurred there in the last century, apparently without any sign of interbreeding. Obviously, the two forms are closely related and replace each other geographically, but it must remain largely a matter of taste whether they are regarded as separate species or not. Much the same is true of the Indian population of eagle owls that has been named *B. b. bengalensis*. It shows little sign of primary intergradation with neighbouring populations, and differs markedly from them in being smaller, darker and more richly coloured.

In Europe the Eurasian eagle owl is typically associated with forested rocky outcrops, cliffs and ravines, but elsewhere it is found in all sorts of country, including dense coniferous or broadleaved forests, light woodland, mountains up to 4500 metres, and deserts entirely devoid

LINDBLAD/COLEMAN

The Eurasian eagle owl typically nests on rocky hillsides or cliff-ledges but also makes use of the abandoned nests of buzzards and eagles. Most breeding territories hold several nest-sites which are used more or less regularly in rotation.

Right: The sole representative of the genus in North and South America, the great horned owl *Bubo virginianus* (430 to 530 mm) occupies a remarkable range of habitats, from the boreal forests of Canada and Alaska (as in the case of this individual) to tropical rainforest and mangroves.

Bubo virginianus: wide range of habitats from boreal forests in north of its range to deciduous woodland and rainforest, desert and mountainous regions.

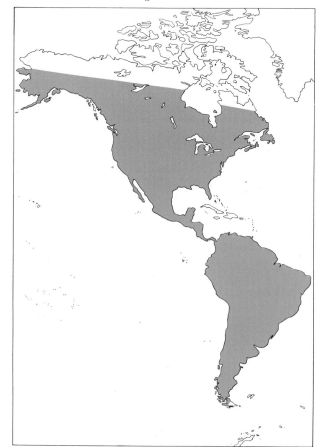

of trees. It tends to take larger prey than other owls but its diet is varied and includes mammals, birds, snakes, frogs, fish and insects; in fact, virtually anything that it comes across and can overcome. A study of the food of Eurasian eagle owls in Sweden showed 55 per cent of the prey animals to be mammals, 33 per cent birds, 11 per cent fish, and 1 per cent reptiles and amphibians, but no account was taken of insects or other invertebrates. The study showed that the most frequently recorded mammal and bird prey species were brown rats (18 per cent of the total of 484 items), assorted voles, mice and lemmings (18 per cent), hooded crows (9 per cent), assorted game birds up to the size of capercaillies (9 per cent), hedgehogs (8 per cent), red squirrels (7 per cent), assorted ducks (5 per cent) and hares (4 per cent). Like other predators, individual Eurasian eagle owls sometimes learn to specialize on particular locally abundant prey species; some concentrate on brown rats, others on hedgehogs or squirrels; there is even a record of one individual in Switzerland that specialized on frogs, a total of 2397 bones of frogs being found in pellets from its territory. On the other hand, Eurasian eagle owls are also opportunists and, being the largest and most powerful of all the owls, are capable of overcoming the most unlikely prey if they can take it by surprise. The Swedish study, for example, recorded such formidable prey items as five buzzards, three goshawks, an osprey and a wild cat, while foxes, porcupines and peregrine falcons have been recorded elsewhere. The heaviest recorded prey item is a roe deer weighing 13,000 grams. To put this in perspective, a large Eurasian eagle owl weighs little more than 3–4000 grams.

Like many other owls, the Eurasian eagle owl is resident and strongly territorial throughout the year, although some mountain populations may be forced to descend to lower ground in winter. Most breeding territories hold several nesting sites which are used more or less in rotation. The sites are usually on cliff-ledges or the floor of rocky caves, in which case the nest itself is no more than a scrape in the ground, but sometimes the old abandoned nests of eagles or buzzards are taken over. Up to six eggs are laid, three or four being the commonest number in Europe, and the clutch is usually completed early in the spring, often while there is still snow on the ground. Incubation begins with the laying of the second

LEE RUE/COLEMAN

DEANE/COLEMAN

The race of the Cape eagle owl *Bubo capensis* (460 to 480 mm) that occupies the Kenya highlands and isolated mountains south to Rhodesia is known as Mackinder's eagle owl *B. c. mackinderi*. In Kenya it is confined to areas above 2000 metres and often roosts in trees draped with picturesque *Usnea* lichens. (Above and right.)

Above left: Over most of their range great horned owls rear only one or two young per year, but in the far north they sometimes rear six or more in years when hares are very abundant.

egg, and is carried out almost entirely by the female for 35 days. The young hatch asynchronously, the later ones generally dying unless food is exceptionally abundant. The male provides all the food for the young during the early stages of their development, both parents during the later stages. The young leave the nest when they are about five weeks old, although several more weeks elapse before they are capable of flying properly, and the parents continue to feed them to some extent for several months. This prolonged period of parental care is of great importance, for it provides the young with the time in which to learn the hunting skills upon which their subsequent survival depends. It is also important that the young should have the opportunity to learn to hunt while food is abundant, and this is probably a major reason why eagle owls begin to breed so early in the spring. Early breeding ensures that the young are fledged by the end of June, leaving them several summer months in which to gain the necessary experience and skills.

In the New World the place of the Eurasian eagle owl is taken over by the great horned owl (*B. virginianus*). The two species are very closely related. In fact, they differ only in relatively minor details of plumage colour and pattern, and must have become isolated from each other in comparatively recent times. The great horned owl ranges more or less throughout North and South America, being absent only from the tundra regions of northernmost Canada and Alaska. It is difficult to think of any bird, of any group, which occupies such a wide spectrum of

Bubo capensis: montane habitats, mainly above 2000 m.

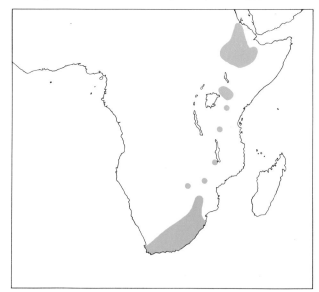

habitats, for it occurs in the boreal forests of the far north, deciduous woodlands, the rainforests of the Amazon basin and Central America, coastal mangrove forests, the desert regions of both continents, and the mountains, reaching altitudes of more than 3000 metres in the Andes of Ecuador. Like the Eurasian eagle owl, the great horned owl varies clinally in both size and colour, the variation following the usual pattern. Thus, it is largest at high latitudes and altitudes, attaining a length of 510 mm in Alaska and 530 mm in the high Andes, and smallest in tropical lowland forest and desert regions, being only about 450 mm long in much of Central America and Mexico. Similarly, it is darker and more richly coloured in humid forests than it is in deserts or areas where there is snow for most of the year. To complicate matters, the great horned owl has orange-breasted and white-breasted colour phases. However, the frequency of the two forms varies considerably from region to region, and conforms with the general pattern of colour variation. In central Canada and Alaska, for example, the white-breasted phase, which is ecologically the most appropriate, is almost totally dominant.

The feeding behaviour of the great horned owl is similar to that of the Eurasian eagle owl though, being less powerful, the maximum size of prey that it can overcome is rather smaller. The populations that live in the boreal forests of northern Canada feed mainly on varying hares. Consequently, their numbers show a regular ten-year periodicity which corresponds with the regular and well-known ten-year cycle in the numbers of the varying hare. Similar cycles in the numbers of Eurasian eagle owls have been noted in Russia, though they are less well documented. The breeding biology of the great horned owl is also similar to that of the Eurasian eagle owl, except that its clutch-size is more variable. Clutches of six eggs or more are not uncommon in the far north when hares are abundant, while clutches of one or two are the norm in tropical regions. The incubation and fledging periods are exactly the same.

Six species of eagle owls, half of the world's total, are confined to the area of Africa south of the Sahara Desert. Each of the six is much more restricted in its choice of habitat than the great horned owl, or even the Eurasian eagle owl, for they segregate by sharing out the available habitats between them, rather than by replacing

Bubo africanus: savannah and lightly wooded rocky areas.

The spotted eagle owl *Bubo africanus* (300 to 400 mm) is very variable in colour but has two main phases, the commoner being grey (left), the rarer rufous or buff (right). Being one of the smaller eagle owls, it feeds to a greater extent than most on insects, but also preys on rodents, small birds and lizards. It occurs throughout the savannah regions of Africa and in suitable areas of eastern Arabia, being most numerous in lightly wooded rocky areas.

each other in different geographical regions. One of the six species, the Cape eagle owl (*B. capensis*), is closely allied to the Eurasian eagle owl and great horned owl but, unlike them, it has a very restricted distribution, being confined to a series of isolated montane populations, some of which have been separated long enough to have evolved subspecific differences. One race is confined to the Ethiopian highlands; another, known as Mackinder's eagle owl (*B. c. mackinderi*) to the Kenya highlands, and outlying mountains as far south as Rhodesia; and a third to the South African highlands. Apart from the fact that it occurs down to sea-level in southern Cape Province, the Cape eagle owl (which might more aptly be named the mountain eagle owl) is confined to areas above about 2000 metres, where it is associated with a mosaic habitat of montane grassland mixed with evergreen forest, and Afro-alpine moorland. It occurs to at least 4000 metres on Mount Kenya. The equivalent habitats at lower altitudes are occupied by the spotted eagle owl (*B. africanus*) and milky eagle owl (*B. lacteus*). In fact, the Cape eagle owl must occasionally come into contact with the latter species at altitudes of around 1800 to 2500 metres, but its altitudinal range is basically complementary to theirs, and there can be little competition between them. The Cape eagle owl preys mainly on small rodents, but is known to take a wide variety of other food items, including hyraxes, fruit bats, birds, snakes and insects. Virtually nothing is known of its breeding biology, except that it nests on the ground, often among rocks, and has a clutch of two or three

The race of the spotted eagle owl that inhabits Africa north of the equator – *B. a. cinerascens* – differs from both the southern African race – *B. a. africanus* – and the Arabian race – *B. a. milesi* – in having dark brown rather than yellow or orange eyes.

Right: The milky eagle owl *Bubo lacteus* (530 to 610 mm) is a large, powerful species capable of killing hares, hyraxes, hedgehogs, guineafowl and francolin. By preying on relatively large animals such as these, it avoids competing with the smaller spotted eagle owl with which it coexists over much of Africa. The significance of the characteristic pink eyelids of milky eagle owls (obvious in this individual) is unknown, but they may have some signalling function.

eggs, but it is unlikely to differ much from that of the Eurasian eagle owl.

The spotted eagle owl is very widely distributed in Africa south of the Sahara and has two well-defined races which replace each other approximately along the equator. The northern form is much less spotted than the other, has greyer plumage, and brown rather than yellow eyes. The spotted eagle owl is not usually regarded as being closely allied to the Eurasian and Cape eagle owls, but the three species are superficially similar, and replace each other rather sharply in different areas and habitats. In fact, they are sufficiently similar to have been confused, even as museum specimens, in the areas in which they occur in close proximity. Spotted eagle owls have been mis-

identified as Cape eagle owls, and examples of both species from north-eastern Africa have been confused with the pharaoh eagle owl (the Saharan race of the Eurasian eagle owl). The correct identification of all three is hindered by their variability in colour and markings, but the pharaoh eagle owl is generally more buff or cinnamon in colour than the other two, while the Cape eagle owl is distinguishable from the spotted eagle owl by the heavy blotching on its chest, and much coarser barring on its abdomen. The spotted eagle owl is the smallest of the three, being 300 to 400 mm long, compared with 460 to 480 mm in the other two species. The spotted eagle owl is probably the most numerous of the African species, being common throughout the lightly wooded savannah areas, particularly

JOHNSON/NHPA

Though milky eagle owls sometimes nest in hollow trees, they more commonly take over an abandoned stick nest of a large hawk or eagle.

Bubo lacteus: riverine forest of dense woodland with open glades.

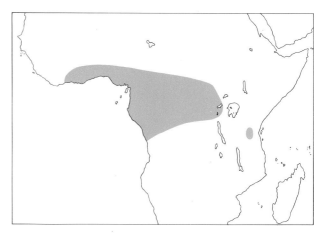

Bubo poensis: equatorial rainforest.

Left: Fraser's eagle owl *Bubo poensis* (390 to 450 mm) is one of three little known species that coexist in the equatorial rainforest of West and Central Africa. It has an isolated population in the Usumbara Mountains of Tanzania which is more commonly known as the Nduk eagle owl *B. p. vosseleri*.

Like Fraser's eagle owl, the Akun eagle owl *Bubo leucostictus* (400 to 460 mm) and Shelley's eagle owl *Bubo shelleyi* (about 610 mm) are confined to the equatorial rainforest of West and Central Africa. Shelley's eagle owl is much more powerful than either of the other species and takes correspondingly larger prey, while the Akun eagle owl has a small bill and weak feet and is probably entirely insectivorous.

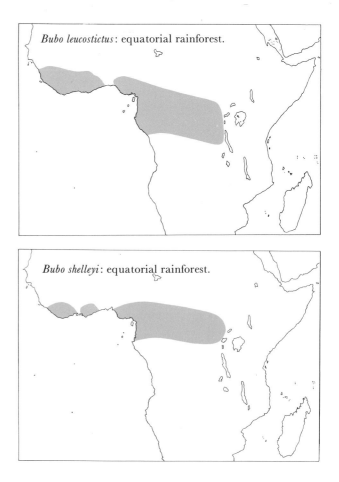

Bubo leucostictus: equatorial rainforest.

Bubo shelleyi: equatorial rainforest.

where there are small rocky hills or kopjes. It is absent from rainforest, dense woodland lacking in open spaces, and extensive areas of treeless grassland. It feeds mainly on small rodents, snakes, lizards and insects, but has been known to kill prey as formidable as a lanner falcon, and no doubt takes almost anything that it can overpower. Spotted eagle owls generally nest on the ground, often among rocks on a hill-side, but use a wide variety of other nesting sites, including holes in trees and the abandoned nests of other birds. They lay two or three eggs but, as is usual among owls, the last-hatched owlet seldom survives. They breed in the dry season, from August to October in Kenya, for example, and from December to March in the northern Congo savannahs. As a result, the young fledge at about the beginning of the rainy season and have a long period with abundant food ahead of them, during which they can learn to hunt and to fend for themselves.

The milky eagle owl (also known as Verreaux's eagle owl) is as widely distributed in Africa as the spotted eagle owl, but not quite so numerous. It is probably most abundant in riverine forest, dense woodland with open glades, and other

Shelley's eagle owl
Bubo shelleyi

Akun eagle owl
Bubo leucostictus

habitats, excluding heavy forest, that are too thickly wooded for the spotted eagle owl. However, the two species are only partially segregated by habitat, and they frequently live in close proximity in lightly wooded savannahs. Even then, there is probably little competition between them, for the milky eagle owl is a large and powerful species, 530 to 610 mm long, that is capable of feeding on correspondingly large prey. In fact, it regularly takes hyraxes, cane rats, hares, spring hares, hedgehogs, guineafowl and francolins, as well as such smaller fry as fruit bats, bush-babies, mice, snakes, frogs and insects. Milky eagle owls occasionally nest in hollow trees, but generally take over the nest of a bird of prey, sometimes forcibly. The enormous domed nests of hammerkops are also very popular, particularly after they have been abandoned by their owner and the roof has fallen in. The milky eagle owl usually lays two eggs, occasionally one or three, and resembles the spotted eagle owl in breeding during the dry season. It is said to lure predators away from its nest by means of a spectacular distraction display, in which it flops around feigning a broken wing, or even resorts to drunken flapping while hanging upside-down from a branch.

The remaining African species, Shelley's eagle owl (*B. shelleyi*), Fraser's eagle owl (*B. poensis*), and the Akun eagle owl (*B. leucostictus*), do not form a natural taxonomic group, but resemble each other in being rare, little known, and confined to dense equatorial rainforest. All three are sparsely distributed through the forest regions of West Africa and the Congo basin, while Fraser's eagle owl has an additional isolated population in the Usambara Mountains of Tanzania. The latter population is known as the Nduk eagle owl (*B. p. vosseleri*), and is regarded as a separate species by many authorities. Again, this is largely a matter of personal preference. If one is lucky enough to see them, there is little difficulty in distinguishing the three species. Shelley's eagle owl is 610 mm long and one of the largest and most powerful of all the eagle owls. It is heavily barred, both above and below, and its general colouring is very dark. Fraser's eagle owl is also strongly barred, but its general colour is more rufous, and it is small, only 390 to 450 mm long. The Akun eagle owl is about the same size as Fraser's eagle owl, but is less strongly barred and less rufous in colour. It is also distinguishable by the colour of its eyes, for they are bright

The Philippine eagle owl *Bubo philippensis* (about 400 mm) is unique among the eagle owls inhabiting tropical rainforest in having predominantly dark orange plumage.

Bubo philippensis: tropical rainforest.

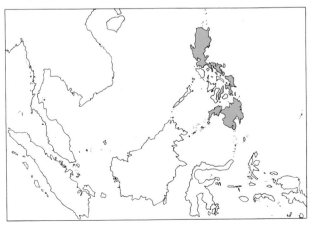

The forest eagle owl *Bubo nipalensis* (510 to 610 mm) is a powerful species capable of killing fawns, jackals and large gamebirds, as well as the smaller rodents and birds which form the bulk of its prey.

Bubo nipalensis: high rainfall forested areas.

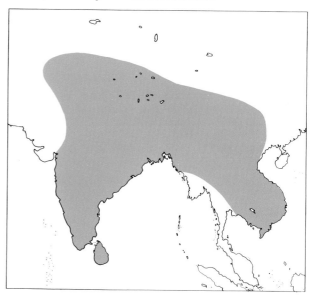

yellow, while those of Shelley's and Fraser's eagle owls are brown. What little is known of the feeding ecology of the three species suggests that there is little competition between them. The Akun eagle owl may be entirely insectivorous, for it has been seen hawking for insects in forest clearings, and the stomachs of eight specimens that were examined contained only insects, particularly Orthoptera and Coleoptera. It also has strikingly small, weak feet, and a small bill; in fact, it seems to occupy a niche comparable to that of the African cuckoo-falcon among the diurnal birds of prey. Less is known about the prey taken by the other two species, but they probably take as wide a range of items as other eagle owls, with Shelley's eagle owl taking larger prey in view of its larger size. Fraser's eagle owl is known to take bush-babies, fruit bats, squirrels, mice, small birds, frogs and insects. It is likely that Shelley's eagle owl takes similar items, together with bigger prey, such as small forest antelopes and forest guineafowl.

The eagle owl species in India and South-east Asia show some similarity to the African species in the way that they share out the resources of the region. Thus, the small, well-differentiated, Indian race of the Eurasian eagle owl occurs in lightly-wooded rocky country, and is very similar in its general appearance and ecology to the African spotted eagle owl; the dusky eagle owl (*B. coromandus*) occurs in forest patches, riverine forest and groves of cultivated trees, and is more or less the equivalent of the African milky eagle owl; and there are three species that are confined to heavy rainforest, just as there are in Africa. In fact, the parallel can be taken even further, for the high altitude Himalayan population of the Eurasian eagle owl can be considered as the ecological equivalent of the African Cape eagle owl. As in the case of the equivalent African species, the Indian race of the Eurasian eagle owl and the dusky eagle owl occur in close proximity over much of their range, though they generally remain segregated into their respective habitats. The two species are about the same size and catch very similar prey, notably rats, mice, lizards and insects. In addition, the dusky eagle owl has a reputation for raiding birds' nests, and also for specializing in catching crows, parakeets and other birds at roost. The three Asian forest species, the forest eagle owl (*B. nipalensis*), Malaysian eagle owl (*B. sumatrana*) and Philippine eagle owl (*B. philippensis*), are confined to the high

rainfall forested region of the Himalayas, Indo-China, Malaysia and the Philippines. In contrast to the three African species, which coexist but take mainly different prey, these three species replace each other in different geographical parts of the region, as is clearly shown on the distribution maps. This is in spite of the fact that the two species that occur on the Asian mainland differ greatly in size, the forest eagle owl being large and powerful, 510 to 610 mm long, and the Malaysian eagle owl relatively small and slight, 400 to 460 mm long. They might have been expected to coexist. Not much is known about the breeding biology of the Asian eagle owls, though the details that are available are in good agreement with those for other species, and need not be repeated. It should perhaps be mentioned, however, that the Indian eagle owls resemble the African species in breeding during the dry season, and presumably do so for the same reason.

So far no mention has been made of the calls of eagle owls, mainly because they are confusingly similar, and difficult to describe adequately. In fact, most species have a very varied repertoire of hoots, grunts, moans and clicks, while some

The dusky eagle owl *Bubo coromandus* (430 to 480 mm) of India and Indo-China has a reputation for specializing at catching crows and parakeets as they fly into roosts.

Bubo coromandus: riverine forest, patches of forest and groves of cultivated trees.

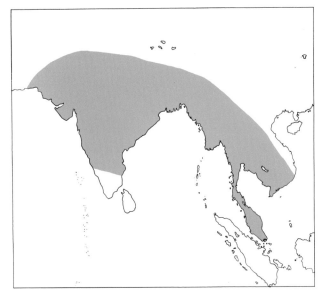

are said to emit blood-curdling shrieks and screams. There is no doubt that eagle owls are noisiest prior to the breeding season, and that many of their calls are to do with maintenance of territory and courtship, but the precise significance of most is almost totally unknown.

THE SNOWY OWL

Though the snowy owl (*Nyctea scandiaca*) is in a different genus from the eagle owls, and very different in appearance, it is quite closely related, and replaces them ecologically in the tundra regions to the north of the tree-line. It has a circumpolar distribution, breeding as far to the north as there is land that is not perpetually covered by ice and snow. It is, however, very dependent on lemmings during the breeding season, and does not often occur on many of the Arctic islands, such as Jan Mayen and Franz Josef Land, from which lemmings are absent; at best it is rare on such islands, as it is on Iceland and Spitzbergen. Snowy owls are mainly sedentary, their wintering range in most years extending only a short distance to the south of their breeding range. However, once every four or five years they irrupt well to the south of their normal wintering range, occasionally reaching as far as southern Europe, the Balkans, northern India and China, the southern United States, and Bermuda.

The basis for the irruptions of the snowy owl is the regular periodicity in the abundance of their main prey species, particularly lemmings and Arctic hares. Populations of lemmings, for example, rapidly increase when tundra conditions are good, only to crash when they eat out their food supply after four or five years. Arctic hares fluctuate in abundance in a similar way, though they reproduce more slowly than lemmings, and have a longer cycle with a periodicity of about ten years. Populations of predators respond in turn, increasing and decreasing together with their prey. It is a decline in the availability of prey, at a time when their own numbers are at a peak, that is the cause of snowy owl irruptions. The irruptions are particularly spectacular when

The Malaysian eagle owl *Bubo sumatrana* (400 to 460 mm) is a small, distinctive species with particularly long ear tufts. It is the only representative of the genus in Malaysia and is relatively common throughout its range.

Bubo sumatrana: high rainfall forest areas.

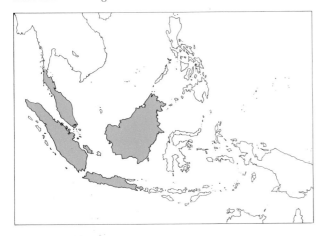

The snowy owl *Nyctea scandiaca* (530 to 660 mm) replaces the eagle owls in Arctic tundra regions north of the tree-line. Every four years or so, when populations of lemmings crash, snowy owls irrupt southwards well outside their normal range.

lemmings and hares crash together over extensive areas. However, the diet of snowy owls is by no means confined to lemmings and Arctic hares. Like eagle owls, they are large, powerful, opportunistic predators, and are capable of taking a wide variety of other prey, including ground squirrels, ducks, gamebirds, and even seabirds in coastal areas. They are crepuscular by choice, but are forced to hunt in daylight during the Arctic summer, when darkness is almost non-existent.

Snowy owls breed more or less throughout the tundra region, though they particularly favour areas where there are numerous rocky ridges, outcrops or small hillocks, to provide suitable sites for nesting, and vantage points from which to hunt for prey. Their density varies considerably from year to year, but in suitable terrain, and in years when lemmings are abundant, there may be as many as one pair per nine or ten square km. Snowy owls lay their eggs in a scrape in the ground, usually at the base of a rock, but sometimes completely in the open. Like Eurasian eagle owls, and presumably for the same reason, they lay very early, often in mid-May while there is still snow on the ground.

Nyctea scandiaca: Arctic tundra north of the tree-line.

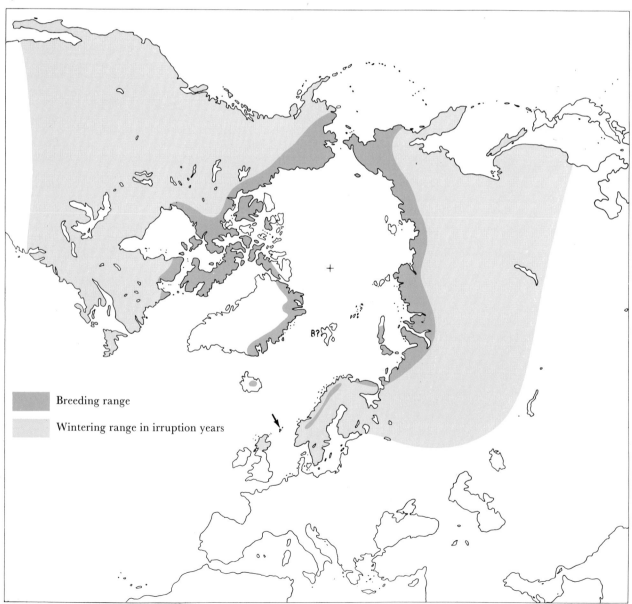

Breeding range

Wintering range in irruption years

The clutch-size is very variable and depends on the abundance of lemmings and Arctic hares; between five and eight eggs is probably normal, but between three and thirteen not unknown. Eggs tend to be laid every other day, but sometimes at longer and more irregular intervals, and large clutches often take three weeks or more to complete. Incubation, which is by the female, begins when the first egg is laid, so that a brood eventually consists of young of very different ages and sizes. However, the younger and smaller owlets soon die if there is insufficient food to go round, which ensures that the brood is quickly adjusted to the optimum size for the prevailing conditions. The actual incubation period per egg is 32 to 34 days, and the young fledge when they are about 51 to 57 days old, but the incubation and fledging period for the brood as a whole is, of course, much longer. Very few of the young survive, for predation by foxes and skuas is heavy, in spite of vigorous protection from the adults. There is also heavy mortality of the young when they attain independence, for the short Arctic summer gives them little time to learn the hunting skills that are so essential, particularly when food is scarce.

Male snowy owls attempt to divert the attention of intruders from their nest with spectacular distraction displays. They also help the breeding effort by feeding the incubating female, and later the young, but take no part in incubation.

CHAPTER SIX

Scops and Screech owls

Otus, Lophostrix

The screech and scops owls of the genus *Otus* form a widespread group of about forty species, many of which, however, can be assembled into superspecies groups. They are nocturnal and eat mainly insects, the larger species also taking rodents and small birds, particularly in winter. Most live in the tropical regions of the world, except in Australasia where the genus is replaced by the hawk owls, *Ninox*, but there are a few in temperate regions, including the common screech owls (*O. asio* and *O. kennicotti*) of North America and the common scops owls (*O. scops* and *O. sunia*) of Europe and Asia. These four species have all been well studied but there are many whose habits are almost unknown.

In general, the *Otus* owls are small, ranging from starling to pigeon-size. They have tufts which may be large, as in the white-faced scops owl (*O. leucotis*) or almost indistinguishable, as in the Palau scops owl (*O. podarginus*) and the bare-shanked screech owl (*O. clarkii*). The facial disc is generally not as conspicuous as in other owls, and they lack the distinctly bristled toes of *Ninox* and the silky chestnut and grey feather patterns of *Glaucidium*. *Otus* seems the least specialized of all owl genera. The more widely distributed species may be divided into a number of races of which the most isolated are often regarded as full species. Many species occur in two distinct colour phases, grey and rufous, broadleaf forest species having the most prominent colour differences. The general effect of the plumage is cryptic, as in other owls, and each phase seems to select a roost to match its colouring. Rufous phase owls roost in foliage and grey

phase owls roost against the bark of a tree trunk. In the northern U.S.A., grey eastern screech owls are replacing rufous where conifer plantations are succeeding deciduous forests and rufous phase owls are almost absent from the mesquite woods of the central prairies, except where broadleaved trees have been planted around human settlements.

The name 'scops' is derived from the Greek *scopus*, 'see'. This was a general name for owls, not necessarily given to the Eurasian species. 'Screech owl' relates to the call of the eastern screech owl (*O. asio*). A distinction can be made based on the calls: screech owls utter extended trills, while scops owls have simple, monotonous calls consisting of a series of short accented notes with a distinct interval between each. Using this distinction, at least one Old World species, the white-faced scops owl (*O. leucotis*) has a 'screech owl' voice, and one New World species, the flammulated owl (*O. flammeolus*) has a 'scops' voice.

Because there is little morphological variation among scops and screech owls, identification by plumage is not particularly easy and depends on finer points of patterning, especially where the ranges of two or more species overlap.

As with some of the warblers, identification is often most readily confirmed by the voice, although the calls of a few species have still to be recorded and convergent song styles cause further difficulties. Within the basic scops and screech types of call there are many variations. In America the songs of screech owls increase in both length and strength from the tropics to the Poles, even varying within a single species from the southern to northern extremes of its range. It

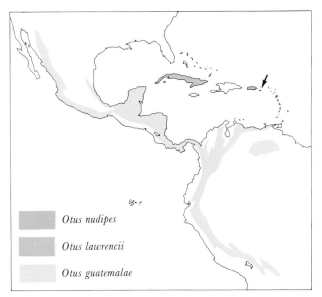

Otus nudipes

Otus lawrencii

Otus guatemalae

Otus guatemalae: submontane woodland and forest.
O. lawrencii: Cuban forest.
O. nudipes: submontane woodland and forest.

Following page: There are a great many species of *Otus* in the New World, most of which are closely related and replace each other either geographically or in different habitats. All of them are about the same size, in the region of 190 to 230 mm long. The vermiculated screech owl *O. guatemalae*, Puerto Rican screech owl *O. nudipes*, Santa Barbara screech owl *O. barbarus*, spotted screech owl *O. trichopsis* and long-tufted screech owl *O. atricapillus* (together with the white-throated and tawny-bellied screech owls) are forest species, while the Pacific screech owl *O. cooperi*, roborate screech owl *O. roboratus* and western screech owl *O. kennicotti* (together with the tropical and eastern screech owls) are woodland or open country species. The rufescent screech owl *O. ingens* (together with the bare-shanked screech owl) is somewhat intermediate between the two main groups.

The Cuban screech owl *Otus lawrencii* (200 to 230 mm) has some features, including its relatively long, bare, yellow legs, in common with the burrowing owl; it is often put into a separate monotypic genus – *Gymnoglaux*.

is thought that the increase in length and strength of call with latitude is correlated with the larger territories that are needed as food supply decreases polewards: louder and longer songs carry further. Similarly in the Old World, the length of the accented songs of scops owls becomes progressively shorter across Asia to Africa and Europe.

Many restricted populations of screech and scops owls are now endangered species. Some could be easily eliminated by the felling of forests and some populations of the Puerto Rican screech owl (*O. nudipes*) may have already been destroyed by the extensive felling that has taken place there since the arrival of Europeans. Although the insectivorous habits of these owls are, if anything, beneficial to man, many are shot and those that escape are liable to die of poisoning from pesticide-contaminated insects.

SCREECH OWLS OF THE NEW WORLD FORESTS
One of the widely-distributed *Otus* owls is the vermiculated screech owl (*O. guatemalae*) which forms a superspecies with the Puerto Rican screech owl. It has an extensive range from Bolivia and Venezuela through Central America to Yucatan and Sinaloa in central Mexico occurring in the upper tropical and subtropical forest zone in foothills and mountains. Continental birds have yellow eyes, those in Puerto Rica have hazel-brown eyes. Within this area the vermiculated screech owl is divided into five distinct groups of fifteen subspecies, some of which are so isolated and differing in plumage details that some authors treat them as full

Santa Barbara screech owl
Otus barbarus

Black-capped screech owl
Otus atricapillus

Rufescent screech owl
Otus ingens

Puerto Rican screech owl
Otus nudipes

Pacific screech owl
Otus cooperi

Roborate screech owl
Otus roboratus

Vermiculated screech owl
Otus guatemalae

Western screech owl
Otus kennicotti

Spotted screech owl
Otus trichopsis

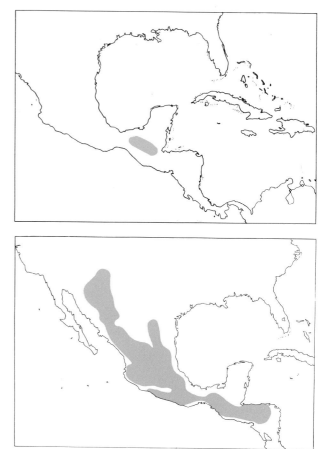

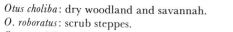

Otus cooperi

Otus roboratus

Otus choliba

Otus choliba: dry woodland and savannah.
O. roboratus: scrub steppes.
O. cooperi (including *O. seductus*): low scrub and mangrove.

Otus atricapillus: lowland tropical forest; partially also in
lower subtropical deciduous forest. The *sanctaecatharinae*
group: subtropical dry forest of southern Brazilian
mountains. Becoming isolated in area indicated.
O. watsonii: Amazonian and Guyanan forests; in central
Brazil, in remnant forests along rivers.
O. ingens: Andean forest, 1800 to 2500 m.
O. clarkii: Andean forest, 1000 to 1800 m.

Otus trichopsis: 'islands' of dry montane forest.

Top: *Otus barbarus*: high mountain forest.

As its name suggests, the bare-shanked screech owl *Otus
clarkii* (190 to 230 mm) is one of a number of species that
have more or less unfeathered tarsi. It also has less well
developed ear tufts than most members of the genus.

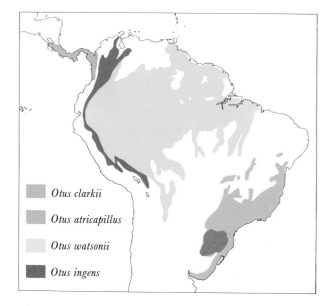

Otus clarkii

Otus atricapillus

Otus watsonii

Otus ingens

O'NEILL

98

species (*O.g. cassini*, *hastatus* and *vermiculatus*). Each subspecies has both rufous and grey phases.

On the edges of its range the vermiculated screech owl overlaps with other species, the western screech owl in Mexico and the rufescent screech owl (*O. ingens*) in the Andean region from Colombia to central Bolivia. Though examination of the distribution maps shows that these owls have overlapping ranges, the species do not mix. Rather, the ranges can be thought of as interlocking like the parts of a jigsaw puzzle, each preferring a specific niche in these forests. This is a good example of the principle of competitive exclusion: two populations occupying the same ecological niche cannot live in the same place.

The vermiculated screech owl inhabits dense submontane forests, but not lowland rain forest and mountain cloud forest. In Mexico it is replaced by the common screech owls where the forests thin out while in the south the rufescent screech owl inhabits the densest forests and the vermiculated screech owl occupies drier, more open woodlands. Another related species, the Santa Barbara screech owl (*O. barbarus*), is found in the high mountain forests of northern Guatemala and the adjacent part of Chiapas (Mexico). The vermiculated screech owl lives in the lower forests around it, so there is an altitudinal segregation of the two species. Another, less closely related species, the spotted screech owl (*O. trichopsis*), lives in 'islands' of dry mountain forest from Arizona to Nicaragua.

The Cuban screech owl (*O. lawrencii*) is often placed in a genus of its own (*Gymnoglaux*) because of its mottled appearance and lack of tufts. It breeds in cavities and trees in dense forests in limestone country, and is rather like the burrowing owl (*Speotyto cunicularia*) in appearance.

BLACK-CAPPED SCREECH OWLS
Six other species are found in South American forest habitats. The superspecies group *O. atricapillus* inhabits tropical forests, being found also in lower subtropical deciduous forests. The superspecies is composed of three groups, now more or less isolated, but a few centuries ago probably still interbreeding. The tawny-bellied screech owl (*O. watsonii*) is found in Amazonian and Guyanan forest areas and, in central Brazil, in remnant forests along rivers. The black-capped screech owl (*O. atricapillus*) inhabits upper tropical dry and deciduous forest from

Bahia to the Rio dela Plata, while the third group, a large form of the black-capped screech owl, thought by some authors to be a separate species (*O. sanctaecatharinae*) is found in sub-tropical dry forests south of the Brazilian mountains. The *sanctaecatharinae* group has a less distinct 'cap' than the *atricapillus* group, and a more freckled plumage pattern. Nothing is known of its breeding biology or its voice.

The rufescent screech owl (*O. ingens*) and the bare-shanked screech owl (*O. clarkii*) closely resembles the *sanctaecatharinae* race of black-capped screech owls. They are found in Andean forest habitats, the rufescent screech owl between 1800 and 2500 m and the bare-shanked screech owl between 1000 and 1800 m. Both species have yellow eyes and a variegated plumage pattern, but the bare-shanked screech owl has developed farther away from the common features shared by the black-capped and rufescent screech owls. There is in fact a gradual reduction of facial tufts and discs, feathers on toes and nuchal collar in the following sequence: tawny-bellied, black-capped, *sanctaecatharinae*, rufescent and bare-legged screech owls.

The white-throated screech owl (*O. albogularis*) is also a mountain species, occurring in temperate forests in the Andes above 2500 m. This dark-looking species has often been regarded as a separate monotypic genus, *Macabra*, but it has sufficient similarities with the black-capped, rufescent and bare-shanked screech owl complex, and with the vermiculated screech owl for it to be regarded as an *Otus*.

SCREECH OWLS OF OPEN WOODLAND
There is a group of New World screech owls that lives in open woodland, savannah and even cactus desert regions. They have a generally paler and greyer plumage than the forest dwellers, in accordance with their drier habitat. The pale facial disc surrounded by a dark rim contrasts particularly with the dark faces of the forest species. There is a collar around the nape, the tarsi are well feathered and the tail is short. Tail feathers tend to be longer in the forest species, to give them greater manœuvrability among dense vegetation. Together the open country screech owls form a superspecies ranging from Alaska to Argentina and include the eastern and western screech owls, sometimes considered together as the common screech owl of North America.

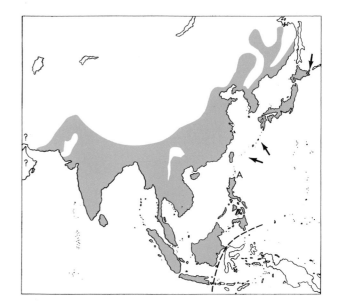

The collared scops owl *Otus bakkamoena* (190 to 230 mm) is a widely distributed Asiatic species of light woodlands, savannah-like habitats and even suburban gardens. As a result of forest clearing, its range is expanding rapidly in South-east Asia, but only at the expense of forest representatives of the genus.

The reddish scops owl *Otus rufescens* (150 to 180 mm) of Malaysia is strictly confined to lowland primary rainforest, being replaced by the collared scops owl in secondary forest, scrub and gardens and by the spotted scops owl at altitudes above 1000 metres.

Otus bakkamoena: light woodland and savannah, parks and gardens. A = *megalotis* group.

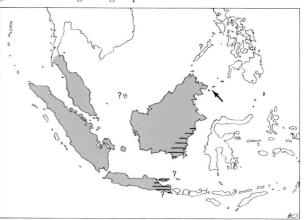

Otus rufescens: lowland primary forest.

Otus albogularis: temperate forest.

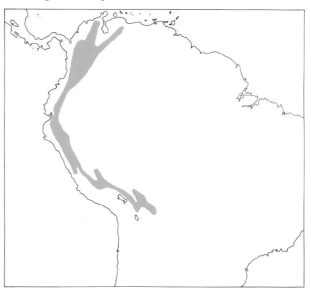

O'NEILL

The tawny-bellied screech owl *Otus watsonii* (190 to 230 mm) is one of several little known members of the genus that live in South American lowland rainforest.

The white-throated screech owl *Otus albogularis* (190 to 230 mm) is the Andean montane forest representative of the genus, occurring in forests above 2500 m.

O'NEILL

The eastern and western screech owls have been extremely well studied. They live well in captivity and will sometimes nest or roost in boxes. The eastern screech owl lives to the east of the Rocky Mountains in mixed woodland and is replaced to the west of the Rockies and in Mexico by the western species, which lives in cactus desert, riverside woodland and mesquite scrub. The two overlap geographically and ecologically in the Big Bend of the Rio Grande where mixed pairs produce hybrid offspring. For convenience, their habits will be described under the name of common screech owl.

Insects form the main diet of these owls. They are taken in the air with a loud snap of the bill or seized on the ground or on a branch with the feet. Insect-eaters are often migratory when they live outside the tropics but the common screech owl is essentially non-migratory although there is a downward movement from the mountains to the plains in winter. In this, it differs from the partially migratory European scops owl. In Canada, screech owls become inactive in bad weather and survive on an accumulation of fat laid down in the autumn. Surplus food is cached in winter roosting cavities. Winter is also the period when most non-insect food is taken. Small mammals, including flying squirrels and bats, birds, frogs, reptiles and invertebrates have been found in screech owl stomachs and ducks and poultry are sometimes attacked.

Male screech owls maintain their territories for about ten months of the year. The size of the territories varies and there is usually neutral ground between them. The males are probably solitary from September through the winter. They start calling in February, the courtship notes being heard most frequently within 20 to 30 minutes after sunset. The male flies about his territory, settling on branches to call and peer about but, if no female appears, he starts to hunt. Late in February, or in early March, the females appear in the territories. The male attempts to approach the female, courting her by running up and down a branch, crouching and uttering rasping calls. When the pair has formed, these calls and the initial courtship call cease. A couple of weeks later the female selects one of the winter roosting cavities as a nest site. The pair may leave the territory for a while, presumably to concentrate on feeding and the male also feeds the female, to help provide material for the developing eggs. They keep in touch while hunting with a duet, the male uttering a tremolo and the female replying at a lower pitch. Eventually she gives up hunting and the male feeds her throughout the 26 days that she is incubating the three to seven white eggs.

When brooding is finished, the female helps the male to feed the owlets. Small items of food are placed directly in the owlets' bills but large prey is thrown into the nest for the young to tear to pieces. The owlets leave the nest when four weeks old but for another five or six weeks they continue to receive food from their parents. From this stage the young utter guttural calls, while until the silent month of January the adults' 'whinny' or scream, a tremulous whistle, can be heard.

Screech owls defend their nests vigorously. They will attack and kill animals larger than themselves, earning the description of 'feathered wild cats'. Human intruders are sometimes attacked near the nest. The owls swoop down, striking the head, while uttering hollow sounds and snapping the bill. Roosting owls 'play possum' when disturbed, becoming motionless, as if mesmerized. One wild owl was weighed while in this state, lifted off its perch with a spring balance hooked under its bill. When alarmed, screech owls assume a concealment posture in which the ear tufts are raised and the facial disc and eye slits are arranged so as to distort the usual outline and pattern of the owl. This posture is adopted when a flock of sparrows approaches, presumably to avoid being mobbed.

Also in the common screech owl superspecies are the Choliba screech owl (*O. choliba*) of dry woodlands and savannahs from Buenos Aires to Costa Rica, the roborate screech owl (*O. roboratus*) of the scrub steppes in the Upper Maranon Valley, Peru and the Pacific screech owl (*O. cooperi* including *O. seductus*) of low scrub and mangrove on the Pacific coast from Costa Rica to Mexico. The Choliba screech owl inhabits rather more dense woodland than the others and has slightly longer tail feathers. The songs of these owls are good examples of the variation in length from tropics to temperate regions described earlier.

POSSIBLE OLD WORLD SCREECH OWLS
In forest and savannahs of the Old World there are three species that could be considered screech owls. Unfortunately, little is known of their biology and voices. During the Pleistocene, the changing heights of mountainous tableland in

FINK/ARDEA

The eastern screech owl *Otus asio* (190 to 230 mm) is widely distributed in North American woodland east of the Rocky Mountains. Its relatively short wings (right) give it considerable manoevrability in dense woodland.

Otus asio: mixed woodland, east of Rocky Mountains.
O. kennicotti: cactus desert, riverside woodland and mesquite scrub, west of Rocky Mountains. The two species overlap and interbreed in the Big Bend of the Rio Grande. A vinaceous group is found in the area shown by dotted line.

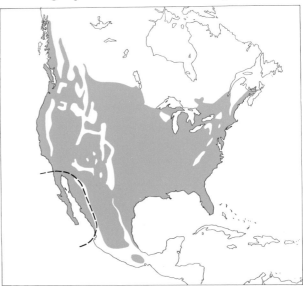

LEE RUE/COLEMAN

Africa and Oriental Asia caused impressive changes to entire forest and savannah landscapes. The great number of isolated species, often with limited distributions, are remnants of what were formerly widespread fauna elements. The giant scops owl (*O. gurneyi*), the white-faced scops owl (*O. leucotis*) and the white-fronted scops owl (*O. sagittatus*) can be considered as such old isolates, reflecting no doubt different early stages in the complicated evolution of the screech and scops owls, and perhaps also having links to the evolution of *Lophostrix* owls (see below). The white-fronted scops owl, particularly, resembles a small-sized crested owl (*L. cristata*). All these species lack a collar on the neck, have long tufts and a distinct facial disc with a black rim.

The white-faced scops owl (*O. leucotis*), sometimes also named the African screech owl, has two song races, one of which strikingly resembles the South American Choliba screech owl. It often breeds on the ground in open savannah. The heavily banded plumage, aberrant wing formula, orange-red eyes and slightly diurnal habits, have led some authorities to regard it as a separate, monotypic genus, *Ptilopsis*.

SCOPS OWLS

In the Old World the scops owls have evolved along similar lines as the American screech owls, to fill similar ecological niches in both forest and open country. Geographical and climatic changes have left isolated species with restricted distributions over Africa and the Orient. They are the remnants of once more widely spread populations and their affinities are obscure. Many of the species live on the oceanic islands off Oriental Asia where populations have been isolated and developed into many different species and subspecies. The taxonomic situation is complicated by the lack of knowledge about some species. For a few, neither breeding season, food nor even voice are known.

The greatest ecological differentiation is seen in South-east Asia where the ranges of the collared (*O. bakkamoena*), reddish (*O. rufescens*) and spotted (*O. spilocephalus*) scops owls overlap. The collared scops owl, which has only very minor morphal differences in shades of brown rather than grey and rufous phases, ranges from Pakistan and India across to southern China and Japan and down to Malaysia and the Philippines. Its habitat is open country, including towns and gardens. It is probable that its natural habitat in South-east Asia is the open savannah-like grassland and mangrove swamps of the coasts. In the forests of Malaysia the collared scops owl is replaced by the forest-dwelling reddish scops owl and, further up in the mountains, by the spotted scops owl; but through the felling and opening of the primary forest, the collared scops owl is spreading inland at the expense of the others.

The collared scops owl nests in hollow trees, rocks, old buildings and the disused nests of other birds. It lays four or five eggs in the north of its range where it nests in spring but lays only three or four eggs in the south where it breeds during the period of maximum rainfall. In the northern parts of its range, it has denser plumage on its tarsi and, in Japan and China, even the toes are well feathered.

Unlike their New World counterparts, the common screech owls, which are split up from north to south into six species (see above), the collared scops owls form one huge interbreeding species from the tropical woodlands of Java to the temperate valleys of eastern Siberia. On northern Luzon, a rather larger race, *megalotis*, is often regarded as a separate species.

The collared scops owl is unusual amongst

The Choliba or tropical screech owl *Otus choliba* (190 to 230 mm) is closely related to the eastern and western screech owls, replacing them ecologically in the dry woodlands and savannahs of Central and South America. See distribution map on page 98.

Below, right: *Otus flammeolus*: woodland.

Otus scops: woodland, parks, gardens; in north also birch and conifer forest. In Africa, savannahs and dry woodland.

Like other members of the genus, the European scops owl is largely nocturnal and spends the day roosting against the trunk of a tree where it is well camouflaged.

Above, right: The Oriental scops owl *Otus sunia* (160 to 180 mm) and flammulated scops owl *O. flammeolus* (160 to 170 mm) are geographical representatives of the European scops owl in Asia and North America respectively. In the Middle East, where the European and Oriental scops owls overlap in range, the European species prefers mountain woodland, the Oriental species riverine woodland.

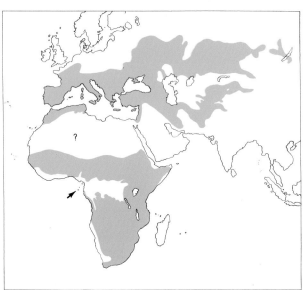

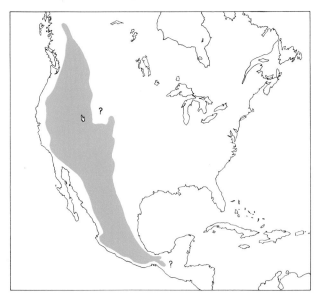

Flammulated owl
Otus flammeolus

Oriental scops owl
Otus sunia

Otus sunia: western populations (*O.s.brucei*), riverside woodland; eastern populations, savannahs, parks and dry woods.
Dotted line shows probable limit of distribution.

owls, and other birds of prey, in that it is used for human consumption. At one time Chinese doctors recommended owl soup for consumptive and rheumatic patients. The collared scops owl formed the main ingredient.

Related to the collared scops owl are the lesser Sunda scops owl (*O. silvicolus*) from the coastal forests of Flores and Rajah's collared scops owl (*O. brookii*) from the subtropical zones of Java, Sumatra and Borneo. The latter is named after Rajah Brooke, one of the White Rajahs in Sarawak. A rare and attractive bird, with striking orange eyes, little is known about it except that it feeds on insects and frogs.

THE OCEANIC SCOPS OWLS

This is a group of owls on islands off the continental shelf (beyond the 200m depth line). The best known of these is the Celebes scops owl (*O. manadensis*) of Celebes, Lesser Sunda islands, Moluccas and Philippines. The Celebes screech owl has three songs. When the breeding season is over, at the start of the monsoon, the mournful 'ploo-ek-oo-ek-oo-ek-' can be heard on moonlit nights. This call is said to be a good omen, but another call 'kiek-kok-kok-' is a bad omen for house-building or travelling. A third phrase 'oi-oi-oi-oi' is sometimes intermingled.

On the other side of the Indian Ocean there is a group of scops owls centred around Madagascar. The typical form of the Madagascan scops owl *O. rutilus* is found on Madagascar, with subspecies on Pemba (*pembaensis*, usually regarded as a separate species), the Seychelles (*insularis*, also often treated as a separate species) and the Comoros (*capnodes*). The Pemba population is known to nest near the ground on heaps of dead material. It seems that the Madagascar and Celebes scops owls are related even though they are now well separated by the expanse of the Indian Ocean. They probably had a common ancestor on the Asian mainland.

THE COMMON SCOPS OWLS

The Oriental scops owl (*O. sunia*) which is often considered to belong to the same species as the European scops owl (*O. scops*), occurs in Asia. It lives in riverside woodland from Palestine to the Aral Sea, Iran, and Turkestan and is found again in India, southern China, eastern Siberia to Japan and the Philippine islands of Mindanao and Mindoro, where the habitat is savannahs, parks and dry woods. The western and eastern populations are roughly separated by the Sind desert in India. The western group is more commonly known as *O. brucei*, but it probably interbreeds with the eastern population of the oriental scops owl in the upper Indus region. Populations living north of the January 0°C isotherm are migratory. The western population migrates to the Indus Valley and the Bombay region while the northern part of the eastern population flies to southern China and Indo-China. From Asia Minor to Baluchistan, the Aral Sea and Lake Balkhash, the European and Oriental scops owls overlap. Oriental scops owls arrive at the breeding grounds towards the end of March, one month earlier than the European birds. They take up residence in riverside woodland whereas the European species prefers mountain woods and apple orchards. The two can be distinguished by their calls. There are also small differences in plumage.

The southern, non-migratory races of the Oriental scops owl (Philippines to Arabia and Socotra) start to breed at the end of February. Migratory populations breed a month later. The eggs are thus hatched before the monsoons start and the owlets are flying before the rains cease; their development coincides with the maximum supply of insect food.

In Africa the common scops owl inhabits savannahs and dry woodlands. It is now thought by some authorities to be a separate species, *O. capensis* (*senegalensis*); its links with the European bird probably date from the time, a few thousand years ago, before the Sahara desert was formed, when the North African massifs were still covered with forests. Breeding dates vary north and south of the equator. In the north breeding begins in April, in the south in September. In both areas this is in advance of the wet season, so that the young are becoming independent as the rains bring out the insects.

The European scops owl (*O. scops*) lives from north Africa and Iberia across Europe and Asia Minor to the Urals, Baluchistan, the Aral Sea and Lake Balkhash. In the northern part of its range, north of the palm limit, the European scops owl is migratory, moving to spend the winter in the African savannahs between the Sahara and the rain forests. Owls from Siberia travel to Ethiopia, a distance of 7000 to 8000 km that may take two months to cover.

Unfortunately, their migration routes take them over countries where considerable numbers are

WEAVING/ARDEA

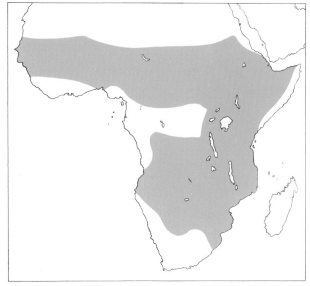

Otus leucotis: thorn scrub and savannah.

The European scops owl *Otus scops* (160 to 190 mm) ranges over most of Africa and into Asia, though African populations are sometimes separated as a distinct species – *Otus capensis*. Throughout its range it inhabits relatively open woodland and similar habitats.

Possibly the most attractive of all the owls, the white-faced scops owl *Otus leucotis* (190 to 240 mm) is an African savannah species. It usually breeds in abandoned stick nests of small hawks or plantain-eaters, but sometimes uses holes in trees or even the thorny, domed nests of buffalo weavers.

LAUBSCHER/COLEMAN

shot. Scops owls are regularly for sale in the market of Valetta, Malta. The long journey also depletes the fat reserve and pesticides that have accumulated in it from contaminated insect food pass into the nervous system and kill the bird. Non-breeding summer visitors are found in southern Scandinavia and around Moscow.

The habitat of the European scops owl is the more open country of woodland, parks, orchards and towns but in the north it also inhabits birch and conifer forests. Its food is mainly insects but it also takes lizards, small mammals and birds. The nest is built in holes in trees, in ruins, in old crow nests or occasionally on the ground. The four or five, rarely six, eggs are laid mostly in early May in southern Europe. They are incubated for 24 to 25 days by the female and the owlets leave the nest when three weeks old. The family may stay together on migration. There is a variety of calls but a characteristic evening sound of southern Europe is the short whistle, repeated at regular intervals of two seconds. Each whistle is apparently single but is, in fact, made up of a tremolo. Male and female may sing in a duet, the female's part being higher pitched and less regular. The song is by the unskilled ear sometimes confused with that of the midwife toad which also calls at night.

The flammulated owl (*O. flammeolus*) from North and Central America is closely related to the European and oriental scops owl and is sometimes combined with them as a single species or as a superspecies. It may have sprung from the small Philippine race of the Oriental scops owl. The northern population migrates

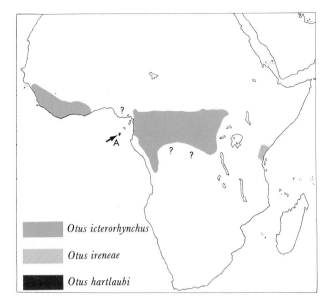

Otus icterorhynchus: tropical forest.
O. hartlaubi: highlands of São Thomé (A).
O. ireneae: coastal forest.

The largest members of the genus *Otus* are two Oriental species – the giant scops owl *O. gurneyi* (about 300 mm) and the white-fronted scops owl *O. sagittatus* (250 to 280 mm). The giant scops owl is sufficiently distinct from other scops or screech owls to be placed in a monotypic genus – *Mimizuku* – by some authors. The white-fronted scops owl, noteworthy for its unusually long tail and rufous plumage, inhabits primary forests of the Malay peninsula and possibly also northern Sumatra.

The sandy scops owl *Otus icterorhynchus* (180 to 200 mm) and the Sokoke scops owl *O. ireneae* (160 to 180 mm) are two small closely related species with forest ranges on opposite sides of Africa. The latter species must be considered endangered as it is restricted to the remnant Sokoke forest on the Kenya coast.

Otus gurneyi: forest on Phillipine islands of Marinduque and Mindanao.

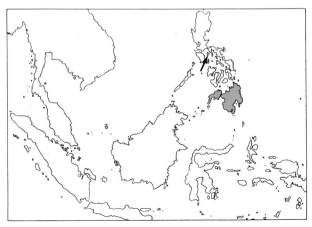

Otus sagittatus: primary tropical forest.

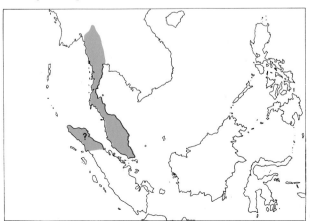

Giant scops owl
Otus gurneyi

White-fronted scops owl
Otus sagittatus

Sokoke scops owl
Otus ireneae

Sandy scops owl
Otus icterorhynchus

Andaman scops owl
Otus balli

São Thomé scops owl
Otus hartlaubi

Spotted scops owl
Otus spilocephalus

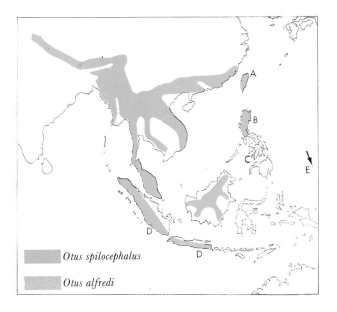

Otus spilocephalus

Otus alfredi

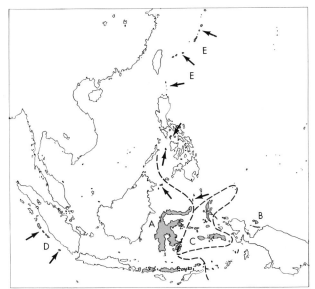

Otus manadensis: widely distributed in oceanic islands of South-east Asia. A = *O. manadensis*. B = *O.m. beccarii*. C = *O.m. magicus*. D = *O.m. mentawi*. E = *O.m. elegans*.

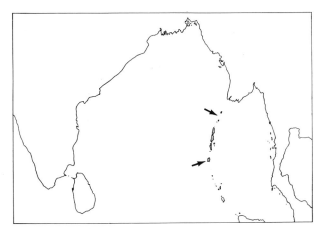

Otus balli: confined to Andaman Islands.

Top: *O. spilocephalus*: dense jungle and shaded gullies between 1000 and 3000 m. Island populations sometimes considered to be separate species: A = *O.s. hambroecki*. B = *O.s. longicornis*. C = *O.s. nigrorum*. D = *O.s. angelinae*.
Otus alfredi: mountains of Flores, over 1000 m.
O. podarginus: lowland mangrove swamps (E).

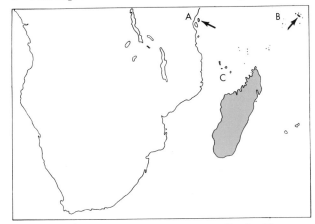

Otus rutilus: Madagascar with subspecies on Pemba (A = *O.r. pembaensis*), the Seychelles (B = *O.r. insularis*) and the Comoros (C = *O.r. capnodes*).

The spotted scops owl *Otus spilocephalus* (about 180 mm) occurs in montane forest throughout the Oriental region, from the Himalayas to Malaysia. In the Himalayas its metallic call notes have caused it to be called the Himalayan bell-bird. The Andaman scops owl *O. balli* (about 180 mm) is an island form of the spotted scops owl which has been isolated long enough to have evolved differences which earn it specific status. The São Thomé scops owl *O. hartlaubi* (160 to 190 mm) is quite different from the spotted and Andaman scops owls, being related to the European scops owl and confined to São Thomé in the Gulf of Guinea.

southwards, returning to nest one month after the southern resident population has started. Again, the palm limit forms the boundary line between migratory and sedentary populations. Three or four eggs are laid in a hollow tree or in the old nests of squirrels or flickers. Several territories may occur in a tight group, sometimes with overlapping boundaries. These groups of territories may belong to families of owls for there is usually a space between one group of territories and the next.

Throughout Africa there are isolated populations of scops owls left behind in restricted habitats as climatic change has affected vegetation. In the tropical forests there is the sandy scops owl (*O. icterorhynchus*), found in the forests of Ghana and the Cameroons, perhaps

Flores scops owl
Otus alfredi

Mentaur scops owl
Otus umbra

Palau scops owl
Otus podarginus

Celebes scops owl
Otus manadensis

Madagascan scops owl
Otus rutilus

Rajah's scops owl
Otus brookii

Lesser Sunda scops owl
Otus silvicolus

The Lesser Sunda scops owl *Otus silvicolus* (about 230 mm) from Flores, and Rajah's collared scops owl *O. brookii* (about 230 mm) from the mountains of Sumatra, Java and Borneo, are closely related and very similar to the collared scops owl.

Otus brookii: subtropical zones of Java, Sumatra and Borneo. *O. silvicolus*: coastal forest.

The Celebes scops owl *Otus manadensis* (190 to 230 mm), Palau scops owl *O. podarginus* (about 220 mm), Flores scops owl *O. alfredi* (about 190 mm) and Madagascar scops owl *O. rutilus* (190 to 230 mm) are a miscellaneous group of species which fill the scops owl niche on the islands of their name. The Mentaur scops owl *O. umbra* (about 180 mm) occupies Simalur and the Engano Islands of Java.

Otus brookii
Otus silvicolus

extending to Liberia. On the other side of the continent is the rare and recently discovered Sokoke scops owl (*O. ireneae*) of coastal Kenya. Its existence is threatened by forest clearance and bird collecting. The São Thomé scops owl (*O. hartlaubi*) is known only from the highlands of the São Thomé region in the Gulf of Guinea.

MOUNTAIN SCOPS OWLS AND RELATED SPECIES

In the oriental region are several isolated mountain populations of scops owls. They may have arrived at their restricted homes by emigration or possibly by being cut off by geographical changes. Throughout the oriental mountains, from the Himalayas to southern China, through Indo-China to Indonesia, Formosa and the Philippines, there are varied populations of which the spotted scops owl (*O. spilocephalus*) is the best known. Isolated populations on Luzon (*longicornis*), Negros (*nigrorum*), Sumatra (*vandewateri*), Java (*angelinae*) and Taiwan (*hambroecki*) are sometimes classed as distinct species, like the Andaman race (*O. balli*). The spotted scops owl resembles the Oriental scops owl but is more spotted, has a rufous face and bare lower legs. The two are separated ecologically, as the spotted scops owl prefers higher areas. It nests in dense jungles and shaded gullies between 1000 m and 3000 m and descends after breeding to the warmer lowland valleys. Its metallic notes, recalling a hammer on an anvil or mule bells have caused it to be called the 'Himalayan Bell Bird'.

There are few mountain scops owls in the southeast Asian Archipelago, east of the line of Wallace. Their taxonomy is difficult and their habits largely unknown. The Flores scops owl (*O. alfredi*) lives above 1000 m on the mountains of Flores. It is similar to the Palau scops owl (*O. podarginus*) of lowland mangrove swamps although the latter lives 2400 km. away in the Caroline Islands.

CRESTED AND MANED OWLS

The genus *Lophostrix* is considered by some to be related to *Otus* owls on one side and to the *Bubo* eagle owls on the other. Recent studies have also suggested that it may have links with *Pulsatrix* owls, the spectacled owls of South America. It contains two species, the maned owl (*L. lettii*) and the crested owl (*L. cristata*), neither of which are well known. They are intermediate

in size between *Otus* and *Bubo*, the maned owl particularly resembling a large-sized version of the white-fronted scops owl. The maned owl lives in tropical forests from Liberia to Cameroon and Northern Congo. The crested owl is American, dwelling in forests from southern Mexico to central Brazil. The two species are probably relics of a group that spread around the tropics and have only survived in the old forests that were not changed during the period of climatic cooling. About all that is known about these owls is that they eat mainly insects, but one maned owl had plant material in its stomach.

The affinities of the two rainforest species in the genus *Lophostrix* – the West African maned owl *L. lettii* (about 439 mm) (left) and the Central American crested owl *L. cristata* (about 280 mm) – are not at all clear. Some authorities consider that they are related to the wood owls, others that they form a link between the eagle owls and the scops owls.

Lophostrix lettii: old tropical forest.

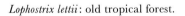

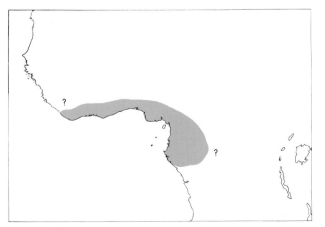

Lophostrix cristata: old tropical forest.

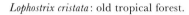

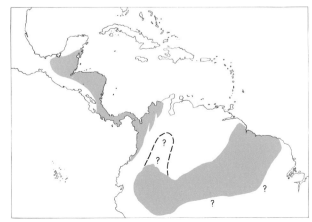

CHAPTER SEVEN

Wood owls

Pulsatrix, Ciccaba, Strix, Rhinoptynx, Asio

Because they look so much alike, and are generally forest-dwellers, owls of the genera *Pulsatrix, Ciccaba* and *Strix* are grouped under the name 'wood owls'. All are medium to large owls, with a big round head, no ear tufts, and, usually, dark eyes; exceptions are the diurnal great grey owl (*S. nebulosa*) and the spectacled owl (*P. perspicillata*) both of which have bright yellow eyes. The eleven species of *Strix* are almost world-wide in distribution, absent only from Africa south of the Sahara and from the Australian region. The genus *Ciccaba* with five species, and the genus *Pulsatrix* with three species, are more restricted: *C. woodfordii* occurs in Africa south of the Sahara, but the remaining seven species are found only in Central and South America. Because of their tropical occurrence these owls can conveniently be distinguished from *Strix* as 'tropical wood owls'. Most wood owls range in length from 300 to 500 mm: exceptions are the great grey and the Ural owl (*S. uralensis*) which, like many other birds of prey living in cold countries, are larger than related species from warm countries and have many more downy feathers. Northern wood owls are also paler than their tropical rainforest relatives, which tend generally to be dark brown.

This chapter also includes a single species of the genus *Rhinoptynx*, and five species of the genus *Asio*, most of which are also owls of woodland. The most significant difference between these and the wood owls is the presence of ear tufts. The striped owl (*R. clamator*) has ear tufts which are well developed and project to the sides of the head. In the genus

Asio, the three species of long-eared owls have conspicuous tufts placed vertically on the top of the head, while the two short-eared species have only rudimentary ear tufts. Striped and long-eared owls could be regarded as wood owls, but the two short-eared species are owls of open ground.

The hornless owls of the genus *Pulsatrix* are quite closely related to the *Ciccaba* owls of tropical America. All three *Pulsatrix* species are, however, larger and heavier than *Ciccaba* owls, and have stouter beaks and feet and more colourful plumage. All have dark faces, outlined by light 'spectacles'. Little is known about their life except that they are mostly nocturnal and prefer to live near water. They usually nest in dense tropical forests, but spectacled owls have also been seen in dry open woods. They feed on fairly large mammals (including bats), birds, and insects and also take frogs and possibly crabs. Reports indicate that they lay two eggs in tree holes; incubation and fledging periods are still unknown. The juveniles, called 'white owls' as if they were a different species, leave the nest before they are able to fly well and their conspicuous white plumage makes them easy to locate. They pass through an involved series of plumage changes which are not, however, well enough known to be described reliably.

Recent studies have suggested that *Pulsatrix* owls are closely related to the crested owl, *Lophostrix*, which shows similarities in the juvenile and adult plumage and skeleton. However there are distinct differences and there is no case for merging them. In this book *Lophostrix*

Pulsatrix perpicillata: tropical rainforest; also in dry open woodland.

The appropriately named spectacled owl *Pulsatrix perspicillata* (430 to 460 mm) inhabits dense equatorial and tropical forests in the New World and is as opportunistic in its hunting as most other owls, preying on creatures as diverse as rodents, bats, small birds, crabs and insects.

species are described in chapter 6, with scops and screech owls of the *Otus* genus, another group to which they are sometimes considered to be related.

The spectacled owl (*P. perspicillata*), a very large hornless owl, is dark brown above and light yellow-ochre below, with narrow white 'spectacles', a white patch on the front of the neck, and a dark brown belt across the breast. The large eyes are bright yellow and the tail is short. It occurs from southern Mexico to Argentina and six subspecies are recognized. One of these extends from Mexico to Panama, and the others are found in Venezuela, the Guianas, Trinidad, Brazil and Peru. In areas where the humidity and rainfall are high – for example in the tropical zone west of the Andes of Colombia and Ecuador – plumage colours are locally more intense. They are about 430 to 460 mm long and, as is usual among owls, the females are somewhat larger than the males: males weigh from 590 to 760 g, females from 765 to 980 g. The smallest birds are those found in equatorial regions, while the largest occur in regions with lower mean annual temperatures.

Because spectacled owls live in heavy tropical rainforest, we know little of their day-to-day life, their nesting habits or the prey species which they hunt. However, they do not always avoid cultivated areas, and can sometimes be found in trees shading coffee plantations. Their call has been compared to the prolonged, rapid tapping of a woodpecker – in Brazil they are known locally as 'knocking owls'. Sometimes two birds perform a duet, each bird's call having a

FREEMAN/NSP

Juvenile spectacled owls are often known as 'white owls' as if they were a different species from their parents. They take up to five years to attain fully adult plumage, moulting through a complicated series of intermediate plumages in the meantime.

slightly different tone. It is apparently not a strictly nocturnal species, but it is not yet known whether it actually hunts in daylight. Like many other owls it nests in a hole in a tree and, according to the few available records, it lays only two eggs. In Surinam a nest with eggs was recorded in August, but nestlings have been seen emerging from other nests between mid-April and mid-June. In Trinidad the breeding time is January to April. Chicks leave the nest before they can fly well, and are fed for some time by their parents before they become independent. Juveniles are white with brown wings, and have brown spectacles which contrast sharply with their white head. An owlet in captivity took five years to attain adult plumage, but a shorter time may be normal in the wild: all other wood owls attain adult plumage during their first year.

Spectacled owls feed on small mammals and insects, including grasshoppers and large caterpillars. They also take quite large mammals, including two species of spiny mice, completely covered in spines like a hedgehog. In the mangroves they are said to feed on crabs. Elsewhere birds and even bats are included in their food.

The two other *Pulsatrix* species, the rusty-barred owl (*P. melanota*) and the white-chinned owl (*P. koeniswaldiana*) are both relatively rare species about which little is known. The rusty-barred owl occurs in Ecuador and Peru. It is similar to the spectacled owl, but has white eyebrows and white tail bars, and white under-parts barred with chocolate brown. It is about 480 mm long. The white-chinned owl also has a

Pulsatrix koeniswaldiana and *P. melanota*: tropical rainforest and more open woodland.

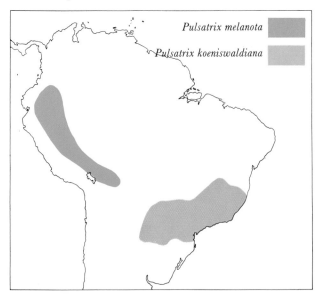

white-barred tail, but has yellow-orange on the eyebrows and underparts. It is about 430 mm long, and occurs in southern Brazil. The two species are probably similar in ecology to the spectacled owl, but their nesting and feeding habits are not well enough known to be described.

Owls of the genus *Ciccaba* largely replace those of the temperate zone genus *Strix* in the tropical forests of America and in Africa south of Sahara. Where the ranges of the two genera overlap, as they do in Mexico and southern South America, tropical *Ciccaba* owls occupy lower altitudes. Other *Ciccaba* owls are found in tropical South America, where they probably compete with the three *Pulsatrix* species, which prefer to be near water in their jungle environment. *Ciccaba* owls have a round, hornless face, with almost fully developed facial disc and conspicuous eyebrows; wings and tails are long. Almost nothing is known of their ecology, except that they are largely nocturnal, preying on insects, rodents and small birds. Like many other owls they nest in holes in trees or in abandoned nests of raptors, and they lay one or two white, rounded eggs. Like *Pulsatrix* species they have a series of juvenile plumages.

White-chinned owl
Pulsatrix koeniswaldiana

The white-chinned owl *Pulsatrix koeniswaldiana* (about 430 mm) and the rusty-barred owl *P. melanota* (about 480 mm) are poorly known species, but they are likely to resemble the spectacled owl in most aspects of their ecology.

Rusty-barred owl
Pulsatrix melanota

The mottled owl (*C. virgata*) is dark brown with light spots above, and white or tawny, heavily streaked with deep brown below. Widely distributed through the Neotropics from Mexico to north-eastern Argentina, it has many local variations of size and colour. Birds in the southern part of Tamaulipas, as well as southern Mexico, Central America and northern South America, are smaller with fine, distinct barring above; those restricted to Venezuela, northern Colombia and the extreme eastern end of the isthmus of Panama are brown, with fine light tawny barring, and those in the Amazon Valley, also finely barred, are larger and more reddish-brown with chrome-orange markings. The pale parts of the juveniles are yellow-orange, and the face is white. In captivity one chick took eight months to attain adult plumage. Adults are about 305 to 355 mm long, and weigh 176 to 248 g.

This is a nocturnal species, occurring only in heavily wooded districts, in mountains and tropical forests. Breeding starts in April or May, when two dull, white eggs are usually laid, in tree-holes or in raptors' old nests. Incubation and fledging periods are still obscure. In Mexico the call has been described as a somewhat guttural hoot but in Trinidad it is said to be a long, drawn-out single note with a rising inflection, resembling a whistled-screech. Food is reported to include small rodents, small birds, insects and reptiles.

Little is known about the three other New World *Ciccaba* species beyond their general appearance and distribution. The black and

Ciccaba virgata: tropical forest and heavily wooded areas.

Living in tropical forest from southern Mexico to northern Argentina, the mottled owl *Ciccaba virgata* (305 to 355 mm) is the most widely distributed member of this predominantly New World genus.

FINK/ARDEA

white owl (*C. nigrolineata*) is white barred with dark brown below and on the upper back, and dark brown elsewhere above. It is found from southern Mexico to western Ecuador, usually near forest borders, where it becomes active at dusk. Its length varies from 330 to 380 mm, and body weight from 440 to 500 g. The bulk of its food consists of large insects, including beetles, tettigoniids, and cicadids. The stomach of one owl that was examined contained the remains of a bat.

The black-banded owl (*C. huhula*) is an Amazonian forest species with a total length of about 305 to 355 mm, and is quite common in banana and coffee plantations. It is mainly dark brown, but barred with white above and below; birds living in south-eastern Brazil have darker

The black and white owl *Ciccaba nigrolineata* (330 to 380 mm) is more a species of forest borders and clearings than its close relatives.

Ciccaba nigrolineata: forest borders.

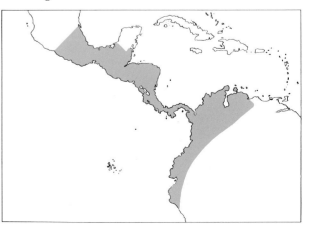

bars. The rufous-banded owl (*C. albitarsus*) lives in the humid temperate forest of the Andes from Venezuela to Ecuador, up to 3700 metres. It is about 305 mm long, with brown upperparts and breast, barred with chrome-orange, and a belly spotted boldly with white.

The African wood owl (*C. woodfordii*) is the only member of the genus *Ciccaba* in the Old World. Its foreparts above and below are very dark brown, lightly spotted with white and there are a few large white spots on the shoulders and inner parts of the wing. The belly is pale buff, heavily streaked with white and dark brown; the face is dark, with conspicuous white *lores* and eyebrows.

This owl is found in forests and woodlands over most of Africa south of the Sahara. At least two races are recognized; one is chocolate-brown and the other rufous-brown. The highland forms have slightly more feathering on the toes than the others, and those in the rainforest are redder, their colour ranging from sienna to sienna brown. In the Congo juveniles are tawny above, barred with white, and white barred with tawny on the breast. They are comparable to the New World *Ciccaba* species in length, being about 305 to 355 mm long. African wood owls frequent forest edges, and woods and dense bushes along the banks of streams, sometimes coming close to villages. By night they hunt mice and other small mammals, small birds, reptiles and insects; by day they sit motionless on tree branches, and are not easily disturbed. Several calls have been described, apparently showing considerable geographical variation. Ordinarily they nest in the open hollow of a tree, but sometimes they use a raptor's old nest, (for example an African goshawk's). One egg is the usual clutch. In South Africa their most active breeding time is known to be November.

The eleven species of owls of the genus *Strix* are represented in every continent of the world except Australia. They are easily recognizable by their disproportionately large, round head, with its particularly well-defined facial disc; they have no ear tufts. The wings are wide and rounded, and the longish tail is also rounded. With one exception they are nocturnal birds of forest and woodland. The exception is the great grey owl (*S. nebulosa*) which is also the only member of the genus to be found in both Old and New Worlds. Prey consists mainly of small mammals, which are captured on the ground, and, according to the locality, small

Ciccaba huhula: rainforest; also coffee and banana plantations.

Ciccaba albitarsus: humid temperate forest to 3700 m.

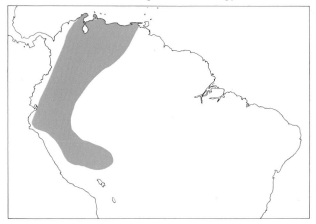

birds, bats, fish, amphibians, molluscs, worms, insects and other invertebrates supplement this staple diet.

Eggs are commonly laid in tree hollows and in the old nests of large hawks. No nest material is added. Nearly all the species nest at times in tree stumps or on the ground, though tawny and Ural owls (*S. aluco* and *S. uralensis*) occasionally forsake woodlands for buildings. A clutch of two or three eggs is common for the barred owl (*S. varia*) and the spotted owl (*S. occidentalis*) in North America, as well as for the tawny owl in India. In Europe tawny and Ural owls lay two or four, other *Strix* species one or two, eggs, while the circumpolar great grey owl lays four.

Rufous-banded owl
Ciccaba albitarsus

Black-banded owl
Ciccaba huhula

(Tropical owls normally lay smaller clutches than more northerly species; the average clutch-size in equatorial Africa is 2.5, as opposed to 4.6 in mid-Europe). Incubation, by the female alone, lasts 26 to 30 days. The interval between eggs is normally from two to seven days, but there is a record of a great grey owl laying at twelve-day intervals. Incubation starts with the first egg, and the young are brooded for about three weeks, while the male provides food for both female and chicks. The owlets leave the nest when they are five to six weeks old, remaining with their parents and usually being fed by them for the rest of the summer. Great grey owls, barred owls, and Ural owls always attack animals or people who

Though basically an Amazon forest species, the black-banded owl *Ciccaba huhula* (305 to 355 mm) nowadays exploits banana and coffee plantations. The closely related rufous-banded owl *C. albitarsus* (about 305 mm) represents the genus in the high altitude forests of the Andes.

AUSTING/LANE

The barred owl *Strix varia* (405 to 610 mm) is the New World ecological equivalent of the Old World Ural owl. Like a number of other thoroughly nocturnal owls, it is capable of catching its prey in total darkness, locating it by sound alone. However, in most normal conditions it also makes use of its keen night vision.

Right: The African wood owl *Ciccaba woodfordii* (305 to 355 mm) is the only non-American member of the genus. Like the American species, it is a largely nocturnal species that preys on rodents, small birds and insects.

Strix varia: coniferous or mixed woods in north; denser forests near swamps and streams in south.

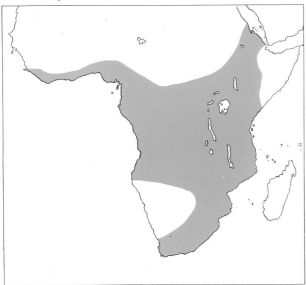

Ciccaba woodfordii: forest and woodland.

approach their fledglings or nest. They strike and lacerate the scalp and face with their sharp talons: at least five people are known to have lost an eye in this way. Tawny owls, too, have been known to attack intruders.

The barred owl is a largish brown and white, nocturnal, round-headed owl, without ear tufts, but with black eyes, a barred breast, and a striped abdomen. It resembles both the great grey and the spotted owl. Its barred breast, black eyes, and smaller size distinguish it from the former, its striped abdomen and paler colouration from the latter. Body length is 405 to 610 mm; males weigh from 468 to 774 g, females, usually larger, from 610 to 1051 g. Its range extends from Canada to Guatemala. Throughout the mountains of central Mexico these owls are larger and darker, barred in dark brown and pale off-white. Guatemalan birds are smaller (about 350 mm long), also darker, and heavily tinted with medium yellow-orange. Juveniles are sienna-brown to cinnamon-brown, barred above and below with pale yellow-orange and white. In the temperate zone forests of the New World, the barred owl largely replaces the Ural owl. In Canada and the north-eastern United States it is a bird of coniferous or mixed woods, rather than of deciduous forests, but in the southern part of its range it seems to prefer denser, darker forests, with mature trees, especially those near swamps and streams. However, it is often seen hunting away from these forests in open country and around farms. Barred owls sometimes hunt and even hoot during the day-time, especially in cloudy weather. Best known of its hoots is the sound described as 'who cooks for you, who cooks for you all', but it can also sound like the barking of a dog – and spit like a bobcat. It nests in early spring, starting to lay in January in Florida and in April in eastern Canada. It prefers to nest in the hollow of a tree, but suitable hollows are scarce and the owls are more often forced to appropriate an old nest of some other species. Sometimes it has been found nesting on the ground, in a hollow it has dug itself. The owls do not bring any new material to the nest. Favoured holes may be used for many breeding seasons – even for 20 to 25 years, if the tree remains standing long enough. The usual clutch is of two or three eggs, though up to five have been recorded, and incubation, by the female alone, lasts about 28 days. The young are brooded for about three weeks, while the male provides food, and the owlets take about six weeks to fledge. It is some time, however, before they reach full independence.

Barred owls feed mainly upon mammals such as mice, squirrels, hares and shrews, with smaller numbers of fish, amphibians, reptiles, and birds. Insects are only rarely eaten. In the southern United States, where the favoured habitat is swampy woodland, crayfish, frogs, and various kinds of fish are the most important food items. Laboratory experiments have demonstrated that barred owls can capture live deer-mice in complete darkness on a bare floor, locating quarry by sound alone. But if the prey suddenly becomes stationary or silent, they hunt by sight instead. They can locate dead prey at a distance of 2 metres when the illumination is as little as 0.00000073 foot candles. Its sight in darkness is a hundred times better than man's.

Barred owls remain within the breeding range in winter, though the more northerly breeders tend to move south. In seasons of deep snow, when mice are difficult to uncover, great flights of barred owls move from the north to New England and further south to areas where prey is more easily available.

The spotted owl (*S. occidentalis*) a largish, hornless, round-headed owl with black eyes, is the other species of *Strix* which occurs only in North America. It closely resembles the barred owl but is on average slightly smaller; it is a much darker and richer brown, the top of its head and hind-neck are spotted with white, and its abdomen is barred instead of striped. About 405 to 480 mm long, males weigh 518 to 694 g and females 548 to 760 g. This rather rare bird is permanently resident from south-western British Columbia to central Mexico. Its favourite habitats are dense, mainly coniferous, forests and wooded ravines. It nests in tree cavities, the old nests of hawks, or in crevices in cliffs. Spotted owls lay two or three eggs, usually only two, and very rarely four. Very little seems to be known about the development and behaviour of the young. This owl takes a wide variety of prey including flying squirrels, deer mice, wood rats, bats, shrews and moles, small birds and small owls, amphibians, and such insects as crickets, cockroaches and beetles. Its voice is a high-pitched hooting, like the barking of a small dog, calls being usually made in groups of three to five hoots. The spotted owl is a decidedly nocturnal species, seldom moving about in the

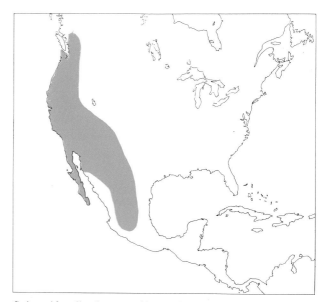

Strix occidentalis: dense coniferous forest and wooded ravines.

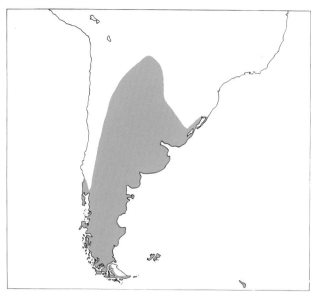

Strix rufipes: Argentina to Tierra del Fuego, also occasionally on Falkland Islands and South Georgia.

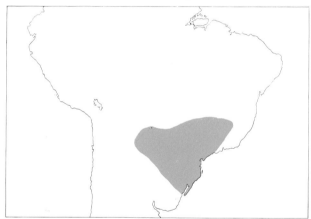

Strix hylophila: found only in Brazil.

Rusty-barred owl
Strix hylophila

Rufous-legged owl
Strix rufipes

The Brazilian owl *Strix hylophila* (about 355 mm) and the rufous-legged owl *S. rufipes* (330 to 380 mm) are two South American species whose systematic position is rather obscure, though they are retained in the genus *Strix* by most authors.

Rather similar to the barred owl in appearance, the North American spotted owl *Strix occidentalis* (405 to 480 mm) is a rather rare species that favours dense coniferous forests and wooded ravines in rocky mountainous country.

day-time unless it is disturbed at its roost.

The two exclusively South American *Strix* species, the Brazilian owl (*S. hylophila*) and the rufous-legged owl (*S. rufipes*) have not so far been studied in detail. The Brazilian owl occurs, as its vernacular name suggests, in Brazil. It is about 355 mm long, barred in dark brown and white, with the breast heavily tinged in medium yellow-orange. The rufous-legged owl is sepia above, with fine white barring and patches of yellow-orange all over and evenly barred underparts. Its length is 330 to 380 mm. It occurs from Argentina in the north to Tierra del Fuego in the south and is also a rare breeder in the Falkland Islands. In northern Chile the facial discs appear to be strongly barred in dark brown and white, while in southern Chile they are dark orange. The nesting and feeding habits, even the systematic position of these owls are still obscure.

Found mainly in the north of both Europe and North America, the great grey owl (*S. nebulosa*) is one of the most elusive birds of the taiga, able to vanish easily in the damp, mossy pine forests. It has the largest and most perfectly circular facial disc of all the owls, possibly indicating an advanced sense of hearing, which it shares with other *Strix* owls. Its massive head may be as much as 510 mm in circumference. The fierce-looking yellow eyes are noticeably small (12.5 mm in diameter compared with those of, for example, a tawny owl which are 16 to 17 mm). Plumage is dusky grey, irregularly marked with dark and white on the upperparts and broadly streaked below. In flight it shows distinctive orange-buff patches on the wings, and the long feathers of the head and neck give it a rather cylindrical appearance. Great grey owls of northern Europe and Asia tend to be lighter and more finely barred on the belly than North American ones, and also seem to be more completely streaked below. Juveniles are olive-brown, darkly barred as well as spotted with white above, and completely barred below; broad black face-markings extend from the eyes to the ear coverts. The owlets attain their adult plumage in less than five months.

The great grey owl is one of the largest of all owls, varying from 610 to 840 mm (Europe 610 to 710 mm, N. America 635 to 840 mm). However the volume of its feathers, which provide insulation from the cold conditions in which it lives make it appear much larger than it really is and, whereas female eagle owls weigh up to 4000 g,

male great grey owls weigh only 535 to 1100 g and females no more than 1900 g.

Great grey owls are found mainly in the northern coniferous forests on both sides of the Atlantic, but in many areas, e.g. central Europe, they are scarce and unevenly distributed. The southernmost nest ever found in Europe was in the forest of Bielowieza in Poland, where this owl was last reported in 1955. It is said to be the rarest owl in Europe, but so many have been recorded in northern Europe during the last ten years, that this is hard to believe.

In northern Europe great grey owls nest in thick spruce and pine forests, but they have also been recorded in pinewood in the middle of a marsh, and occasionally in birchwood. It seems likely that the suitability of the nesting site is more important than the biotope. Though it is usually thought of as an inhabitant of the wilds, it is also found breeding near farmhouses. Great grey owl territories are probably very small, since two nests have often been found close together – in Sweden as little as 100 metres apart. In Finland three nests were found within 400 metres of one another. Within their small territories great grey owls tolerate the presence of other birds of prey; Ural owls, hawk owls and Tengmalm's owls have nested undisturbed near great grey owls, though all compete with the great grey for voles.

In northern Europe great grey owls regularly make their homes in the old nests of goshawks, buzzards, or even golden eagles. Nests have been recorded at least ten times on the top of stumps and once in a hollow dug by the bird on level ground. Many investigators have claimed that the great grey owl builds its own nest, but no kind of nest-building activity was seen at any of 130 nests that were studied. Like the Ural owl the great grey owl does not bring any new material to the nest, but merely deepens it. In hawks' nests the twigs which it moves from the middle of the nest accumulate at the brim and these may be misinterpreted as an addition of the owl's. Sometimes the owl may excavate a thin hawk's nest too deeply, and the bottom may drop out. The great grey owl has never been known to nest in a hole, although holes or crevices are typical nest sites for other *Strix* owls.

In Finland great grey owls have been heard calling as early as mid-February. The call is a deep-toned, booming sequence of notes, 'hoo-hoo-hoo', often rising, and repeated at regular

HEDVALL

The great grey owl *Strix nebulosa* (610 to 840 mm) generally breeds in the abandoned nests of diurnal birds of prey. Though it is such a large species, it is relatively conservative in its hunting behaviour, preying almost entirely on voles and shrews. Being so dependent on voles, it is forced to irrupt well outside its normal range whenever vole populations crash and northern populations move south even in normal years.

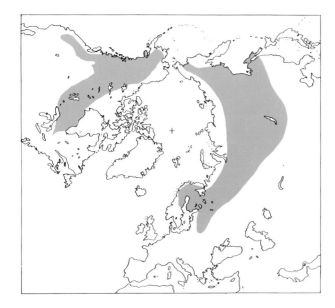

Strix nebulosa: northern coniferous forests.

intervals. The voice is, however, very weak, and its carrying power is only about 500 metres. They often snap their mandibles together to produce a loud noise – probably a stylized biting movement given as a warning, as it seems to occur in situations where a bird is on the defensive.

Dates of egg-laying vary from mid-April to mid-May. Of 122 clutches recorded in northern Europe, clutch-size varied from one to nine, with an average of 4.2. Clutch-size fluctuates in accordance with vole populations (see below). It is interesting that the great grey owl, nesting in open sites, has more oval-shaped eggs than its hole-nesting cousins the Ural and tawny owls. The female incubates for about 30 days, during which time the male brings her food. The female will attack intruders near the nest, particularly after the chicks have hatched. Chicks hatch at intervals of two or three days and leave the nest at the age of three weeks. They are reluctant fliers and spend a long time simply moving about in the branches of the nest tree. Even after six to eight weeks they are usually found near the nest, and they keep together and may stay within the territory for several months, while the female keeps constant watch.

The male alone hunts during breeding and, as long as the nestlings are small, the female tears the prey he brings to pieces before feeding them. Hunting may occur at any time of the day, but seems to be less successful in strong sunshine and during the middle of the night: at least the feeding frequency is then at its lowest. Prey is located mainly by hearing, from a suitable

perch, usually a small tree. Great grey owls favour open country such as marsh and cleared forest for hunting. They feed on small voles and shrews, occasionally taking frogs and birds ranging in size from finches to jays. Many hunters have claimed that in winter they feed on larger animals, such as hares and big game birds, but in fact small mammals are always the most common food. Great greys seem reluctant to change from small voles and shrews to other foods, and for this reason they do not normally stay in their territory all winter, unless voles are very numerous. Usually they lead a nomadic life, irrupting through the coniferous zone eastwards and westwards as well as to the north and south in response to food availability. The greatest invasions of these owls into northern Europe always occur when vole populations are at their lowest in northern Russia. They may migrate as far as southern Sweden and Germany and, if there are plenty of voles available for food, then the owls remain to breed in Finland and Sweden. When voles become scarce, the owls move back to the east again.

The Ural owl (*S. uralensis*) is rather like a large, pale, long-tailed tawny owl, with greyish-white to brownish-white plumage, boldly streaked with dark brown. The streaks are particularly long and well-defined on the underparts. The long tail is noticeably barred, and is tipped with white. As the bird flies along it gives an impression of ghostly near-whiteness. The facial disc, which forms an almost perfect circle on the round head, is off-white and unmarked, making it easy to distinguish the Ural owl from the great

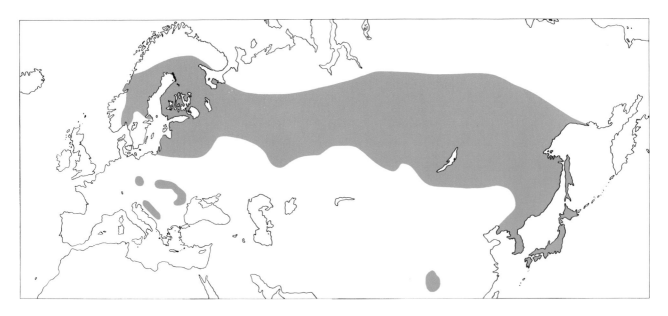

HEDVALL

Like most other members of the genus, the Ural owl *Strix uralensis* (about 585 mm) defends its nest fiercely against intruders. The habit has earned this species the name *slaguggla* (meaning attacking owl) in Sweden.

The Ural owl takes a greater range of prey items, including more large species, such as hares and game birds, than its close relative the great grey owl. As a result, it is able to remain on its territory throughout the year.

LINDBLAD/COLEMAN

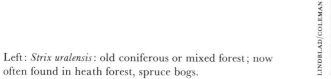

Left: *Strix uralensis*: old coniferous or mixed forest; now often found in heath forest, spruce bogs.

grey owl with its lined face. The blackish-brown eyes are not as big as those of some of the other *Strix* species, for the Ural owl is less completely nocturnal. It is about 585 mm long, the female weighing 520 to 1020 g and the male 451 to 825 g.

Ural owls are distributed over a large area of Europe and Asia. Some populations are geographically isolated, and between nine and eleven subspecies are recognized. The very isolated Chinese subspecies is the darkest of all, with blackish-brown markings. In general, the populations in Europe and Asia are darker than those in the middle of the range. The Ural owl population has recently increased in northern Europe, and the increase has produced change and variety in the owl's choice of nest sites and habitats. The most common nesting habitat used to be old coniferous or mixed forests, far from human habitation. In the last twenty years, however, the nesting habitat has become more varied. Damp heath forests are now the most common habitat, though the species also nests regularly in dry heath forests and in spruce bogs. In Finland the first nests near civilization were found in the 1950s and about thirty nests in buildings or holes near houses are known to the author. Until the end of the 1950s stumps and holes in trees seem to have been the preferred nesting sites and, until the beginning of the 1960s, old twig nests of other large birds were becoming more and more common. In 1960 the widespread use of boxes began, and since the mid-1960s nestboxes have been used more often than any other type of nest site, although occasionally buildings, flat ground and rock faces are chosen. Like the great grey owl, the Ural owl does not bring any new twigs to the nest, but merely rearranges the material it finds there to make the nest deeper.

The Ural owl feeds mainly on small mammals, such as bank, field and water voles, but it also takes squirrels, weasels and even hares, frogs and beetles and a variety of birds. Finches, thrushes and even such game birds as hazel hens and black grouse have been recorded. Its ability to change over to food other than small mammals is greater than for instance that of the great grey owl, and it is therefore able to remain in its territory during the whole year.

The breeding season is variable, and is mainly controlled by the severity of winter. In northern Europe spring hooting and duetting may begin from early March. The two-part call of the Ural owl has a barking quality. The female has a variety of calls at the nest, including a barking note of warning to the young, and various gobbling, chuckling and hissing calls. They signal aggression by snapping their bills loudly. The number of eggs varies from two to six. The average clutch-size in Finland is three, and seems only slightly influenced by the number of voles that are available. Eggs appear between late March and mid-May. Incubation lasts 27 to 28 days and the young fledge in about five or six weeks. The Ural owl is called *slaguggla* in Swedish, which means attacking owl, because of its habit of attacking intruders at the nest.

The tawny owl *S. aluco* is a moderately large, mottled brown bird with a large head. It is usually rufous brown above, mottled and streaked with dark brown, with conspicuous whitish patches on shoulders and wings. The underparts are buff, broadly streaked and faintly barred with dark brown, while wings and tail are barred. In Europe there is also a grey adult phase of plumage, although this is rare in Britain. The tawny owl is 355 to 460 mm long. As with most owls, the female is larger than the male, although they look similar. Females weigh 410 to 800 g and males 410 to 550 g.

The tawny owl is one of the most common owls in Eurasia and north-west Africa. In Europe it is usually found in broadleaved forests and open parklands, although it also occasionally lives in coniferous woods (particularly in Spain); in the Himalayas and in the Burmese and Chinese mountains it is characteristic of tall coniferous

Top right: The tawny owl *Strix aluco* (355 to 460 mm) is the commonest and most familiar owl over most of Europe. Though woodland is its preferred habitat, it is very adaptable and has even colonized the centre of cities such as London, where there are large wooded parks and gardens.

Strix aluco: in Europe broadleaved forest and parkland; in eastern mountains tall coniferous forest up to 300 m.

forests up to about 3000 metres. Tawny owls have such a wide choice of food, and are so tolerant of man, that they have been able to maintain and even increase their numbers in a changing environment. Some have even colonized the centres of large cities such as London. In Finland tawny owl nests are typically found near civilization.

The tawny owl has been described as the most musical of all the European owls. Its prolonged hooting call can be heard all through the year, but especially in autumn and winter. It is hard to see how this beautiful quavering song has been converted into the popular 'tu-whit tu-whoo' so often quoted as the typical owl call. It is perhaps interesting to note here that owls which inhabit thick woodland areas are, on the whole, much more vocal than open-country owls.

In Europe, breeding usually begins in mid-March. The owl chooses a hole or a nestbox in a tree, but occasionally uses the old nest of a crow, magpie, sparrowhawk or heron. There are even records of tawny owls rearing chicks on the ground or in rabbit burrows – a curious choice for such a traditionally tree-based species.

Like great grey owls, tawny owls vary their clutch-size according to vole abundance. In Finland the clutch-size in 188 nests averaged 3.3. The number of eggs varied from one to six, and two nests with eight eggs have been recorded. Incubation, by the female alone, starts with the first egg; food is brought to the nest by the male. There may be an interval of 48 hours to a week between the laying of each egg, which is

Tawny owls are among the most nocturnal of owls and feed mainly on woodmice and voles, which they detect while perched quietly on a branch, watching and listening. This individual is carrying a woodmouse to its young.

The very rarely recorded Hume's tawny owl *Strix butleri* (about 330 mm) may well be no more than a pale desert race of the tawny owl.

Map. *Strix butleri*: palm groves and rocky outcrops in desert.

incubated for 27 to 28 days. The young are brooded for about three weeks, the male again providing food. A thoroughly nocturnal species, the tawny owl rarely becomes active before dusk, and most of its hunting is done at night. When there are young in the nest, however, it may catch some of its food early in the morning.

The tawny owl usually hunts by waiting quietly on a perch, watching and listening. Its sight in darkness is far better than man's, and it can catch mice in very dark conditions, although in total darkness it catches its prey entirely by sound. Its large ear openings and the difference in the shape and size of the two ears probably help it to find its prey, which is usually small mammals, birds, frogs, earthworms and insects. Occasionally it will snatch fish from streams,

ponds – even from ornamental goldfish ponds. Tawny owls are very adaptable feeders and during bad vole years they change their diet to include many more birds. They are thus able to spread into densely built-up areas, where mammals are scarce, and can live in close proximity to man. Much of the new work on tawny owls has been carried out in Britain: it is discussed in some detail in Chapter 10.

Hume's tawny owl (*S. butleri*) is one of the least known owls in the world. Hume described it in 1878 in the Mekran coast of southern Baluchistan but nothing is known of its present occurrence there. It is thought that the species has not up to the present time been observed alive in the Middle East: the only three specimens recorded were taken in Sinai, Israel and western Arabia. It has lighter colouring than the tawny owl but is otherwise very similar and may, in fact, be no more than a desert form of the tawny owl with unfeathered toes. Its upperparts range from beige to dark buff, the general tint being more golden on the head and neck. The crown feathers are tipped with black, making the head look darker than the body. The back tends towards grey, while the underparts are white tinged with buff. Wings and tail are very distinctively barred rather than mottled, in brown. The facial disc is white tinged with buff, and is browner round the eyes. It is said to be about 330 mm long, and to live near palm groves and in ruins and rocks.

Three wood owls are found only in India and South-east Asia: the brown wood owl (*S. leptogrammica*), the mottled wood owl (*S. ocellata*), and the spotted wood owl (*S. seloputo*).

The brown wood owl is the largest of the three, measuring from 460 to 530 mm long, except in Indonesia, where the birds are smaller. It is rich dark brown above, darker on the head, with

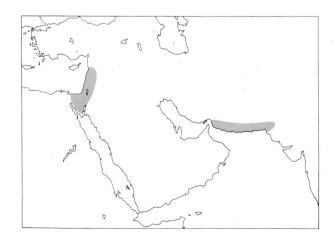

dark brown wings, faintly barred with paler brown and with a whitish patch; the throat is white, the breast washed with dark brown. The rest of the underparts are light buff, heavily barred with thin dark brown lines. Juveniles have almost completely white heads. It occurs in India east through Indo-Chinese and Malaysian subregions to southern China, Formosa and Hainan Island. It usually nests in pine, deciduous, moist temperate, and evergreen forest from the plains to 2800 metres but it has been recorded up to 4300 metres. In Borneo it inhabits lowland primary forest. Brown wood owls prey not only on the smaller mammals and birds, but also on pheasants, jungle fowl, larger squirrels, and monitor lizards. In Ceylon it is semi-diurnal and also eats fish. In Borneo and possibly elsewhere birds nest in December–January.

Patches of dark orange and white spotting on the head and mantle, as well as on the upper breast, are peculiar to the mottled wood owl. Its back, wings, and tail are mottled brown and white, the facial disc is strongly barred, the throat white and the underparts barred. There are three races, which occur in India and Arakan. Varying in length from 380 to 460 mm. it lives in open, semi-cultivated areas, and in tamarind groves from the plains up to an altitude of 830 metres.

The spotted wood owl of Malaysia, is also 380 to 475 mm long, and may be distinguished from the brown wood owl by its dark grey-brown colouring, the white spots on the forehead, crown, and mantle and the very sparse, broken white barring on the back. Distinct white patches on the wing coverts are barred in grey-brown. The face is tawny and there is a white patch at the throat; the underparts vary from white to tawny, with widely spaced brown barring. Strictly nocturnal, it feeds mainly on large beetles. Spotted wood owls are not rare, but are of more frequent occurrence in the north than in the south of Malaysia. This is a lowland bird usually met in pairs. Nesting has been recorded, but details of clutch-size or incubation are not available.

The genus *Rhinoptynx*, contains the single species of striped owl, *R. clamator*. It appears to form a link between the two modern families of owl: a barn owl (Tytonidae) crossed in captivity with a striped owl (Strigidae) produced fertile eggs.

The striped owl ranges from Mexico to Bolivia and Brazil. Its upperparts are tawny-ochre,

FINK/ARDEA

The brown wood owl *Strix leptogrammica* (460 to 530 mm) is the South-east Asian representative of the genus. Like other large wood owls, it feeds on a great variety of prey items up to the size of large rodents and small game birds.

The mottled wood owl *Strix ocellata* (380 to 460 mm) and the spotted wood owl *S. seloputo* (380 to 475 mm) are lowland species that inhabit relatively open and semi-cultivated areas, the one in India, the other in Burma and parts of Malaysia.
Strix leptogrammica: deciduous moist temperate and evergreen forest to 2800 m; in Borneo, lowland primary forest.

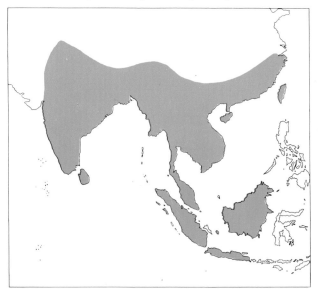

Spotted wood owl
Strix seloputo

Mottled wood owl
Strix ocellata

boldly striped with sooty brown, while below it is white or buff, with narrow brown streaks. It has short wings and a long tail, the flight feathers and tail being barred with sooty brown. It is usually between 305 to 355 mm long and one weighed 385 g, but larger birds, 330 to 380 mm long, occur on the island of Tobago. Its striped underparts and white face and throat, as well as its larger, stouter grey beak and feet, distinguish tufted owls of this genus from other long-eared owls (*Asio*) found in tropical America.

These owls are found in deciduous seasonal forest and lowland seasonal forest, and are known to eat small mammals. They often roost in groups and apparently nest on the ground. The only nest that appears to have been found was merely a beaten place in the grass of a Panama citrus orchard: it contained two unfledged young.

The five owls of the genus *Asio* fall into two widespread, but usually ecologically distinct, groups: long-eared owls, distributed throughout the temperate zones of the northern hemisphere, in tropical America, and locally in Africa and Madagascar, are dark, nocturnal owls of woodland; short-eared owls, which are found at one season or another nearly everywhere in cold

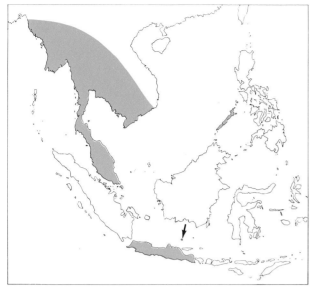

Strix seloputo: lowlands of Malaysia.

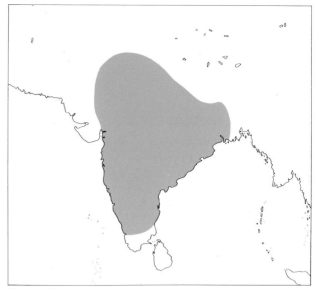

Strix ocellata: open semi-cultivated areas and tamarind groves up to 830 m.

Ranging from Mexico to Bolivia and Brazil, the striped owl *Rhinoptynx clamator* (305 to 380 mm) is a little known species that has sometimes been included in the genus *Asio* with the long- and short-eared owls which it strongly resembles.

Right: like many other owls, the long-eared owl *Asio otus* (280 to 405 mm) breeds in the abandoned nests of other birds, particularly those of corvids and small diurnal birds of prey. Its breeding success is very variable and depends largely on the abundance of voles, which form a staple part of its prey in the breeding season.

Rhinoptynx clamator: deciduous and lowland seasonal forest.

and temperate regions, are pale of plumage, predominantly diurnal, and inhabit open country.

Long-eared and short-eared owls are among our most effective mousers; meadow mice, voles and other small mammals top the list of prey species taken, supplemented by birds, insects and occasionally frogs and fish. Long-eared owls usually nest in an abandoned nest of another large bird, such as a heron, crow or hawk. Mountain birds frequently nest on the ground. They lay four to five eggs, in peak vole years eight to ten. Short-eared owls nest in a slight hollow on the ground near a clump of vegetation in marsh or meadow, laying two or four eggs in Africa, four to seven in other parts of the world: during years of vole abundance the number increases, with nine, thirteen and even fourteen eggs recorded in a single clutch. Both long- and short-eared owls normally raise one brood, but produce a second in response to a plentiful supply of food, for example when rodents are abundant. Females alone incubate, starting when the first egg is laid. Incubation takes about 26 days; long-eared owl chicks leave the nest at 23 or 24 days, short-eared at 12 to 17 days. Both are migratory, especially the most northerly breeding

birds. They have relatively longer wings than sedentary species, which no doubt help them in their long annual journeys to the breeding grounds.

The long-eared owl (*Asio otus*) is distributed in a belt right round the northern hemisphere, including many of the larger islands, between latitudes 30° and 65°N, at heights up to and sometimes exceeding 2300 metres. It is also found in Africa, where it is sometimes separated into a distinct species (*A. abyssinicus*). Very like the short-eared owl (*A. flammeus*) although less stocky and with much longer ear tufts, its upperparts are freckled and mottled with buff and grey-brown, and its buff underparts boldly marked with dark streaks and fine cross-barring. It is 280 to 405 mm long, and body weights of male and female vary from 245 to 400 gms. The long-eared owl shows tremendous colour variation, not only over its considerable world range, but also in local populations, and varies from a deep chestnut brown nearing black to a fairly pale fawn. Island forms from the Canaries and Madeira are darker than Eurasian birds.

Long-eared owls are found in light broad-leaved and coniferous forests, riverine forests with

Asio otus: light broadleaved and coniferous forest, riverine forest, trees in cultivated land.

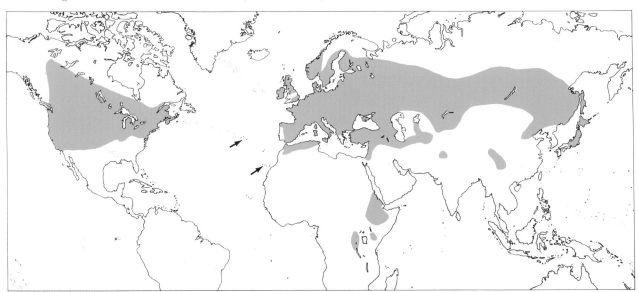

willows and poplars, copses and clumps of trees in natural and cultivated steppes, and also in parks and large gardens – though it rarely breeds in large towns. Like many other species, it nests in twig nests made and abandoned by other birds of prey. Nesting begins in March or early April, and four to six eggs are generally laid. (In Finland the average clutch-size is 5.4.) Incubation begins with the first egg and usually lasts about 26 to 28 days. The young leave the nest when they are 23 or 24 days old. Breeding success is dependent on the availability of voles, which affects the number of pairs which breed, the number of clutches produced, the number of eggs laid and the survival of the owlets. Peak vole years seem to occur every four years.

The long-eared owl is one of the most nocturnal owls in the world. During the day it sleeps in dark places close to tree trunks, preferably in conifers. Its food, predominantly voles, mice and rats, is caught in open, grassy places and along forest edges; it also takes small birds, numerous other species of small mammals, and large insects. As is well known, these owls have remarkably good eyesight at night and they are able to catch rodents in total darkness. But even more remarkable is their precise three-dimensional hearing, based on a facial disc shaped to trap sound, and asymmetrical ears located in different positions on either side of the head. Their completely noiseless flight makes it possible for them to take the unsuspecting animal by surprise. Long-eared owls are mainly sedentary, but in general the northern populations move south or west in winter.

The Madagascar long-eared owl (*A. madagascariensis*) is very similar to other long-eared owls but has always been treated as a separate species on morphological grounds. It is slightly smaller (330 mm) and darker than the long-eared owl and has more orange-yellow in the plumage. Its distribution is apparently confined to the humid forests of eastern Madagascar and to an area around Sambrino.

The stygian owl (*A. stygius*) is a large, dark owl with prominent ear tufts, found in forests and often in mountains from Mexico to northern Argentina. Like the Madagascan long-eared owl it may be very closely related to the long-eared owl. Its upperparts are sooty black, more or less mottled with white or buff; underparts are buff to yellow-buff, heavily spotted and streaked with sooty black. It varies in size from 380 to 460 mm. In Mexico it nests in trees like the long-eared owl, but in Cuba it is said to lay its two white eggs on the bare ground like the short-eared owl. Such adaptability has, of course, tremendous survival value for this owl, because it may well be able to live and breed successfully in open areas if its wooded habitat is threatened.

The short-eared owl (*A. flammeus*) is a very widely distributed species, breeding throughout the Old and New Worlds between latitudes 40°N and 70°N, as well as in the southern half of South America, in Hawaii, the Galapagos, the West Indies, the northern end of the Andes, and the mouth of the Orinoco in Venezuela. Over the main European, Asian and North American parts of the range there is only one subspecies, but seven different subspecies are described from other areas.

Short-eared owls have rather longer wings than other medium-sized owls, with a dark patch at the 'wrist' on both the upper and the lower surface of the wings. The body is pale below, boldly streaked with dark brown – except for the lava-coloured Galapagos race, which is streaked and barred below like a long-eared owl. The back is boldly mottled in pale buff and dark brown. The brilliant, lemon-yellow eyes are surrounded by dark-tipped feathers, in pale facial discs. Size varies from 330 to 430 mm, the body weight of females from 280 to 390 g, and that of males from 200 to 360 g. All short-eared owls display much smaller ear tufts than their close relatives the long-eared owls. They are always birds of open country and it is possible that they do not need special 'outline' recognition signals as much as their woodland-living relatives do.

The nest is invariably built of grasses on the ground near marshy areas. Their territories have been calculated to be 15 to 20 hectares or larger in size, which means that there may be up to five to seven pairs per square kilometre. Incubation begins with the first egg, which is normally laid in late April or early May. The eggs are laid at intervals of 24 hours and, on average, incubation lasts for about 26 days. The young leave the nest when they are 12 to 17 days old.

The short-eared owl is to some extent able to

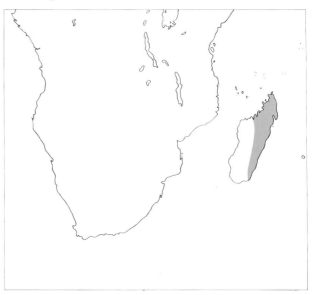

The stygian owl *Asio stygius* (380 to 460 mm) is a large dark version of the long-eared owl, to which it is closely related. It shows remarkable variability in its breeding behaviour, nesting in old nests in trees in Central America and on the ground in Cuba. Map. *Asio stygius*: forests, often mountains.

As its name suggests, the Madagascar long-eared owl *Asio madagascariensis* (about 320 mm) is little more than an island race of the long-eared owl, though it is usually given specific status.
Asio madagascariensis: humid forest.

GILLSATER/COLEMAN

The short-eared owl *Asio flammeus* (330 to 430 mm) has an immense range and has even colonized remote oceanic islands. The Galapagos Islands have a distinct race *A. f. galapagensis* which is as tame as most of the other birds of the Archipelago.

regulate its nesting to meet its prospective food supply. In a study of this species in Finland, an area of 20 square kilometres supported 40 pairs, which on average laid 7.3 eggs (range from 4 to 9); 4.7 owlets per nest reached adult age. From these territories about 300 pellets were collected and over 600 prey animals identified. On the basis of this material it was possible to calculate how much the population of 40 owl families ate during the breeding season. The owls stayed in the area between 15 April and 31 July: from 5 June onward 40 pairs fed 4.7 young per nest. One short-eared owl ate, on average, 80 gms in a day, and produced a pellet for every 30 to 90 gms of food taken. The population as a whole needed about 1500 kg for the period 15/4 to 31/7 for their living, which was divided between different groups of prey as follows:

field and bank voles	41,988 individuals
shrews	4241 individuals
mice and rats	2706 individuals
water voles and squirrels	261 individuals
small birds	690 individuals
owlets	85 individuals

The owls thus ate over 41,000 voles and altogether around 50,000 small mammals. Feeding mainly on harmful rodents, they are indeed good friends to the farmer: the short-eared owl is the best mousetrap.

Although the year of this study was a remarkable year for voles, the owls ate in addition almost 700 small birds: similarly the number of owl chicks eaten, 85, seems high. These were the one to three chicks which disappeared from each nest: the strongest young eat the weakest, ensuring that at least some of the brood survive. It is not surprising that such an opportunist species has spread widely over the temperate land masses, and even succeeded on remote oceanic islands.

The African marsh owl (*A. capensis*) is a uniform earthy colour without markings on the upperparts. The underparts are pale and faintly barred. The pale patch on the wing is a conspicuous feature in flight. It is difficult to

PATON

In the northern parts of its range, the clutch-size and breeding success of the short-eared owl is correlated with the four year cycle of abundance of voles. This clutch is about average. Note the egg-tooth on the bill tip of this newly hatched chick; it is shed soon after it has been used to break out of the egg-shell.

The short-eared owl coexists with the closely related long-eared owl over much of Eurasia. Both species hunt over open country, preying largely on voles, but the short-eared owl differs from the long-eared owl in being mainly diurnal and in roosting and nesting on the ground.

separate this species from the short-eared owl, although it differs in having uniform colouration and a darker face. The ear tufts are short but more visible than in the short-eared owl. Body length is 305 to 380 mm.

The African marsh owl nests on the ground, in a tunnel which it forces through ground vegetation, or in a well sheltered hollow under a large tuft; occasionally it uses an old crow's nest in a tree. In April (Morocco) or during the last three months of the year (Nigeria), it lays a clutch of two or four white eggs, sometimes up to six. The eggs hatch at two-day intervals. The young spend two or three weeks in the nest, then leave the nest and are probably fed nearby for another two or three weeks. It is similar in habits to the short-eared owl, but lives mainly on large insects. Like the long-eared owl it prefers hunting by night, but also shows itself during the day. Its call, a deep 'kaaa', rather like a frog's croak, is uttered on the ground; it also calls in flight. A sedentary species, it is said to be tame and sometimes gregarious.

Closely related species usually manage to avoid competition, either by living in different areas, or by occupying different parts of the environ-

Table I. Calculation of the quantity of prey taken by one Tawny, Ural, and Great Grey owl during six months.

Food taken in a period of six months	Tawny 18 kg	Ural 23 kg	Great Grey 27 kg
Moles, shrews and bats	34	22	25
Field and bank voles	174	201	654
Water voles	16	43	11
Squirrels and weasels	1	7	1
Mice and rats	23	18	12
Hares	—	1	—
Game birds	1	3	1
Jays	1	2	1
Thrushes	57	24	2
Small birds	54	5	5
Frogs and fishes	28	13	3
Total number of prey	389	339	715

Asio flammeus: open country.

ment, or adopting different ways of life, in the same area. Thus two closely related species in the same area may have different hunting techniques and so avoid competition. For some years a study was made of the ecology of the three *Strix* species, the tawny, Ural and great grey owl in Finland.

It was formerly believed that these three species occupied different geographical ranges without overlap, and so did not enter into competition with each other. In Finland, however, this is not true: the three species may nest quite close to each other. It was therefore of interest to see how much similar species in such close proximity avoided competition. The conclusions which were drawn may help to illustrate how such problems of co-existence are resolved.
From studying the feeding biology of these owls, the half-yearly food consumption of each species was estimated. In six months a tawny owl requires about 18 kg, a Ural owl about 23 kg and a great grey owl about 27 kg of food. Thus the amount eaten is directly proportional to the weight of the bird. While it might seem efficient for the largest bird to take the largest

prey, almost the reverse is true. The great grey owl, which is the largest, takes only small mammals (for example in the study period more than 650 field and bank voles but only 11 of the much larger water voles), while Ural and tawny owls take fewer of the smaller species and more of the larger. In addition, the smaller Ural owl took more larger mammals (including a hare) and more game birds, and both Ural and tawny owls took more mice, rats, frogs and fish. Great grey owls took fewer birds – many fewer than tawny owls, which were particularly severe predators of thrushes and small birds.

Although they take the same foods, these three closely related species apparently show quite distinct food preferences. The great grey owl stands out as a predator of small mammals. Its lightly-built skeleton and long, rather slender claws, which spread widely on the ground, seem well adapted for capturing voles and other small, fast moving creatures on the ground. The short, strongly curved claws of the tawny on the other hand seem well fitted for grasping birds in the air, and the strong thick claws of the Ural owl are appropriate for its role as a predator of larger mammals.

The African marsh owl *Asio capensis* (305 to 380 mm) is an ecological equivalent of the short-eared owl, living in similar open grassy or marshy habitats and differing only in being rather more nocturnal.

Asio capensis: open grassy or marshy habitats.

The three species also to some degree avoid competition by hunting at different times. Activity studies during the breeding season showed that the tawny owl is the most nocturnal of the three, hunting almost exclusively at night until the young are big and hungry, when they also bring food home in the day-time. The great grey owl is the most diurnal. The peaks of its activity happen to be the early morning and late evening hours, but they only cease feeding the young at noon. The Ural owl fits between the other two, hunting mainly at night but also remaining active in day-time. Where Ural and tawny owls overlap in range, the problem of competition for food and nest sites is solved by the Ural owls killing and eating any tawnies which come into their territory. Great grey owls nest peacefully alongside either of their congeners: neither Ural nor tawny owls try to drive away a species which is so obviously bigger than they are. While Ural and tawny owls compete for nest sites in hollow trees (which are nowadays scarce), great grey owls are satisfied with old open nests, tree stumps or even the bare ground.

Similar isolating mechanisms have been noted between short-eared and long-eared owls (*Asio* species) in Finland. The two species may nest as little as 30 metres apart without hurting or disturbing each other, and may even hunt for the same kind of prey without apparently interfering with each other's success. Short-eared owls are diurnal, long-eared owls nocturnal and thus in a neat way replace each other, exploiting the habitat without competition throughout the whole of every twenty-four hours.

CHAPTER EIGHT

Hawk owls

Ninox, Sceloglaux, Uroglaux, Nesasio, Surnia

The name 'hawk owl' has been given both to a group of southern hemisphere owls of the genera *Ninox*, *Uroglaux* and *Sceloglaux*, and to a single, unrelated northern genus, *Surnia*. As the name implies, species of these genera are more hawk-like than other owls: some have longer or narrower wings and longer tails, which give them a hawk-like silhouette. But the main difference appears to be some reduction in the size of the stiff discs of feathers around the eyes, which are the main distinguishing features of the owls. In the southern group of species it is possible that the distinctive facial feathering was never developed, suggesting that these genera have not evolved so far as other owls from the ancestral condition. Lacking facial discs, the head is proportionally smaller and more rounded in smaller species, strong-browed and more aquiline in a very large one, with the eyes and bill appearing more prominent. In the small species of the genus *Ninox* these modifications are to some extent reduced by the presence of short, stiff feathers which form a pair of prominent 'eyebrow' ridges over the eyes.

Apparently associated with the simple, reduced facial discs are small, symmetrical ear-openings. The very nocturnal owls with elaborate facial discs usually also possess specialized, asymmetrical ear-openings which enable them to pin-point the position of their prey in conditions where sight cannot be used. As the hawk owls lack this special adaptation they must presumably rely almost entirely on sight for their successful hunting.

The single species of northern hawk owl (*Surnia ulula*) ranges right around the northern hemisphere through the great coniferous forests of the temperate to sub-arctic zones. Only remotely related to its southern counterparts, the modifications which it shows are almost certainly adaptations evolved to fit a particular niche in the ecology of these regions, rather than ancestral characters retained. Characters shown by the hawk owls in general are not peculiar to them alone, for they are shared in varying degrees by other species too. The name 'hawk owl' is due to an accident of resemblance which occurred to the person who first gave them the name, but does not necessarily indicate a real and consistent difference setting them apart from other owls.

The southern hawk owl complex consists of eighteen species. Its distribution suggests that the group may once have been dispersed more widely over the earth's surface, but has now been displaced elsewhere and is successful only where competitors are few. These species provide most of the medium-sized owls of the Indonesian and Australasian regions, existing side by side with the larger owls of the genus *Strix*, barn owls (*Tyto*) and small owls of the genus *Otus*. In Australasia, where *Strix* and *Otus* are absent, hawk owls produce a wider range of species to take advantage of the wider range of vacant ecological niches.

Over much of their range the species of hawk owl replace each other geographically with little overlap. In the main, species occupy large single islands or groups of smaller islands. The Oriental hawk owl, *N. scutulata*, is an exception, with an extensive distribution on the Asiatic mainland from Sakhalin to India and Malaysia. Migratory, it has spread also to the Andaman and Nicobar Islands where its resident range overlaps that of

The boobook owl *Ninox novaeseelandiae* (about 350 mm) occupies a wide range of habitats in Australia and New Zealand. Both boobook and an alternative name – morepork – are phonetic renderings of its clear disyllabic repeated call.

The boobook owl nests in tree cavities and feeds its young mainly on insects, but to a lesser extent on small rodents, birds and lizards. Like other hawk owls, it is largely nocturnal, in spite of having a reduced facial disc and hunting mainly by sight.

Ninox novaeseelandiae: thick forests, also open areas with sparse trees or rocks.

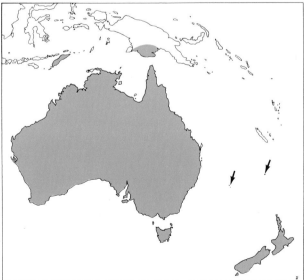

BESTE/ARDEA

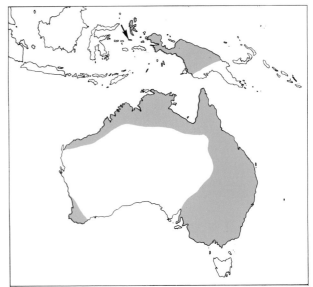

Ninox connivens: forest, particularly savannah forest.

With its very reduced facial disc and long tail, the barking owl *Ninox connivens* (380 to 430 mm) is particularly hawk-like. Being larger than the boobook owl, with which it coexists in many areas, it feeds mainly on larger prey, such as rabbits and birds up to the size of crows.

several other small species of *Ninox*. Celebes has two similar sized species of hawk owl with similar ranges which differ in ecological preferences (p. 156).

The most complex situation occurs in Australasia. Here the hawk owls are unchallenged by other genera, and in some regions three different species co-exist. They provide a good example of the more general rule that where several closely-related species share the same geographical range they tend to evolve size differences which enable them to concentrate in the main on a different range of prey, or to exploit different parts of the environment, so that they do not normally compete with each other.

Through most of Australia and New Zealand the small boobook or morepork owl (*Ninox novaeseelandiae*) is present. It occurs also in one corner of southern New Guinea, although in lowland areas there it is largely replaced by the similar-sized sooty-backed hawk owl (*N. theomacha*). A rare forest species, the small Papuan hawk owl (*Uroglaux dimorpha*) is also present to some extent. In north and east Australia, eastern New Guinea and the Moluccas, the larger barking owl (*N. connivens*) occurs in the same range as these smaller birds. In south-eastern Australia a

third, larger species, the powerful owl (*N. strenua*) occurs with the other two types, replaced in northern Australia and in New Guinea by the almost equally large rufous owl (*N. rufa*). In New Zealand the laughing owl (*Sceloglaux albifacies*) was a similar large bird which co-existed with the boobook owl.

Within the main genus, *Ninox*, the best-known species are the three southern Australian owls. The study of these species by David Fleay has provided a good background to the life and habits of the whole group. One interesting fact that one might have suspected from their lack of specialization of hearing (see above) is that, although these birds usually roost by day among branches or in cavities they are capable of hunting by day and use sight in catching their prey. Smallest of the three is the boobook owl, *N. novaeseelandiae*, which is about 380 mm long. It is the most widely distributed, occurring in a wide range of habitats from thick forest to arid, open areas of sparse trees, or in open places where there are caves or rock crevices to roost in. It has also moved into urban areas where trees are present. More like typical owls than the other two species, its wings and tail are not markedly long, the head is relatively

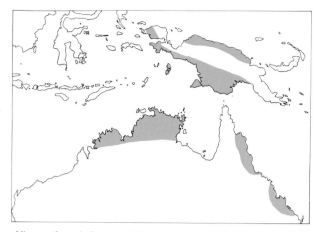

Ninox rufa: rainforest, thick savannah woodland, particularly near watercourses.

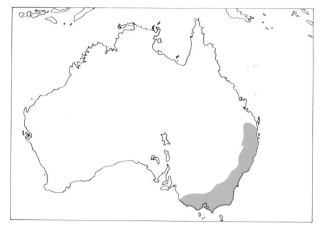

Ninox strenua: forested gullies.

large and rounded, the facial disc is fairly well-developed, and it has prominent brows of whitish feathers. Its eyes are large, with pale greenish-yellow irides.

The boobook owl's plumage is patterned with whitish spots along the edges of the mantle and on the wing coverts; wings and tail are barred, and there are dark irregular streaks on the breast. Its plumage varies in intensity of colour and markings from pale reddish-brown to deep rufous, with yellowish-buff on paler parts. Its facial disc is dark, its legs long, slender and downy. The boobook owl is best known for its clear disyllabic call of 'morepork', a call that in the earlier days of settlement was attributed to a member of the nightjar order, the tawny frogmouth. In addition, the owl may use a staccato, rapid low note in 'conversation' between individuals, and it also has a cat-like repeated yowling call. Young birds have a shrill, trilling whistle.

These owls feed very extensively on insects, but they also take mice, small birds and similar small creatures. They nest and roost in tree cavities. They will also roost in the foliage of trees, but are vulnerable to mobbing, particularly by the various honeyeaters. Sometimes it is only a noisy little band of honeyeaters, taking it in turns to peer into a hollow branch, that betrays the presence of an owl. The clutch is usually of three or, rarely, four eggs. The male prepares the nest-hollow, but the eggs are incubated by the female for about 33 days, the male bringing her food while she is on the nest and remaining nearby at other times. The young are downy and white. The first plumage is white around the face and on the underside, with dark facial discs. They leave the nest after about six weeks and moult into adult plumage at about three months.

The barking owl, sometimes called the winking owl and therefore having the Latin name *N. connivens*, is at 380 to 430 mm long, the next largest of the group. Wing, tail and legs are all fairly long, but its most striking feature is the reduced facial disc which is often barely apparent: it is less conspicuously developed than on some of the harriers and other hawk species. Its head is rounded and its large eyes with their yellow irides appear rather close together on either side of a prominent bill. The plumage pattern is similar to that of the boobook owl but without the facial and mantle markings, with few wing spots, and with heavily striated underparts. As with the boobook owl, the intensity of plumage colour varies considerably throughout the range.

Barking owls are sparsely distributed and, being birds of forest, particularly savannah forest, they have a more limited range than the boobook. They frequently roost on branches of trees, probably having less to fear from mobbing than the smaller boobook, and they may hunt by day. In most owls the female is bigger than the male, but in these larger hawk owls, the male is bigger than the female.

The species gets its popular name from its disyllabic call, an abrupt dog-like double bark, higher-pitched in the female. It also produces the long-drawn strangled scream, like a frightened woman, which has sometimes been attributed to various other species.

As with the boobook owl the male prepares the

The powerful owl *Ninox strenua* (630 to 650 mm) and the rufous owl *N. rufa* (400 to 500 mm) are the largest of the hawk owls; they are the Australasian ecological equivalents of large wood owls and replace each other in different parts of the region.

Rufous owl
Ninox rufa

Powerful owl
Ninox strenua

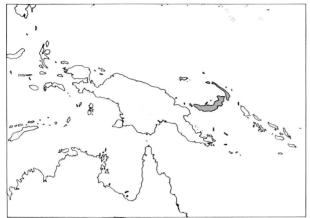

Ninox solomonis: found not on Solomon Islands but on New Britain and New Ireland.

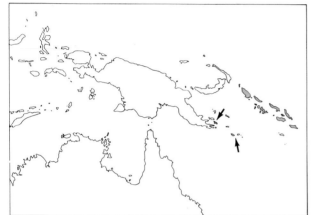

Ninox jacquinoti: Solomon islands.

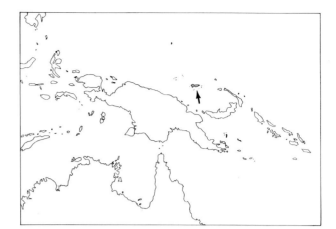

Ninox meeki: confined to Admiralty Islands.

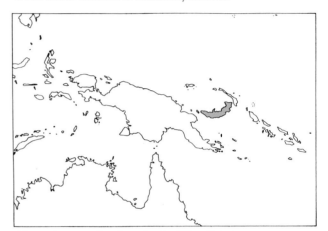

Ninox odiosa: confined to island of New Britain.

The New Ireland hawk owl *Ninox solomonis* (230 to 310 mm), Admiralty Islands hawk owl *N. meeki* (200 to 250 mm), Solomon Islands hawk owl *N. jacquinoti* (230 to 310 mm) and New Britain hawk owl *N. odiosa* (200 to 230 mm) are four members of a large group of closely related hawk owls which have speciated on various of the numerous Australasian islands and archipelagos.

nest-hollow. The nest itself may be in a tree cavity at any height from the ground upwards, and the male bird prepares it by scraping and rotating on it. The female then lays her clutch, usually of three eggs, at three-day intervals. The female incubates, fed and guarded by the male, who may attack intruders. Incubation begins with the first egg and takes about 37 days, the young leaving the nest at about five weeks. In first feather they are greyish, patterned like the adults on back and head, but with a pale forehead, a white collar, white under-side with dark grey streaking and a reduced facial disc forming a narrow dark mask across their yellow-irised eyes. Barking owls feed mainly on mammals – rabbits, rats, mice, the smaller marsupials, such as opossums and gliders – but will also take birds of various species up to crow size, and

at times large insects, these appearing to be a more important prey in the northern part of the range.

The largest of the hawk owls, the great hawk or powerful owl (*N. strenua*) is 630 to 650 mm long and occurs only in south-east Australia. Probably the most hawk-like, least owl-like, of the group, its wings and tail are fairly long, and legs long and strong, with big, powerful feet. The bill is large and prominent, made more obvious by bold brows which slant back from it over the eyes, giving a low forehead and a rather flattened crown. The plumage is dark brown above, thickly barred and spotted with white. The underside is marked with dark narrow chevrons. The face is dark, and the irides yellow. As in the barking owl, the male is the larger bird. In this species the disyllabic call is a deep 'who-whoo', higher-

New Ireland hawk owl
Ninox solomonis

Admiralty Islands hawk owl
Ninox meeki

Solomon Islands hawk owl
Ninox jacquinoti

New Britain hawk owl
Ninox odiosa

153

pitched and shorter in the female. Other calls are deep, gruff contact calls used between members of a pair; and the young have a shrill whistling call.

The powerful owl occurs in the forested gullies of the south-eastern region of Australia. It roosts in trees, in a sheltered spot with a good view around. Paired birds may roost together until nesting, when the female occupies the nest-hole and the male roosts nearby. In spite of his size the male tends to be less aggressive than the smaller barking owl, although the female may attack if she considers that the young are threatened. The nest cavity, which is situated high in a large tree, is prepared by the male. The female lays two eggs only, at a four-day interval. Incubation, by the female alone, takes 35 to 36 days. During incubation, and the early period when the young are small, all food is brought by the male. Young powerful owls are white on breast and head with a few scattered dark streaks, and heavily barred in brown and white on back, wings and tail. There is a little streaking on the forehead, and the small patches of feathers that replace the facial disc form a narrow, dark mask around their yellow-irised eyes. They leave the nest at about five weeks and mature in seven to nine months. The principal food of these birds is climbing and gliding marsupials, hares, and rodents, but birds, and even large insects, are also taken.

To the north of the powerful owl's range, it is replaced by the rufous owl (*N. rufa*) a smaller species some 400 to 500 mm long. Although smaller, it appears to be a more aggressive species and, from experiments with recorded voices of both birds, it would appear that they are mutually intolerant. The plumage of the rufous owl is finely barred all over. It is dark brown with fine buffish barring above, and on the underparts it is pale buff with fine brown bars. Its forehead and throat are pale and its yellow-irised eyes are set in a dark face. With the same strong-browed appearance as the powerful owl, and a similar though softer voice, it is a bird of rainforest and the thicker savannah woodland, and within these areas is usually found close to watercourses.

The nest is a cavity high in a large tree, and the clutch is of two white eggs similar to those of the powerful owl. Like the powerful owl it appears to feed on arboreal marsupial opossums, but it will also take other smaller creatures. Rufous owls occur in the wooded areas of north and north-east Australia, and through the lowland forests of New Guinea, but neither this, nor any comparable

LINDGREN/ARDEA

The sooty-backed hawk owl *Ninox theomacha* (200 to 250 mm) replaces the closely related boobook owl in the lowland forests of New Guinea.

Ninox theomacha: lowland forest.

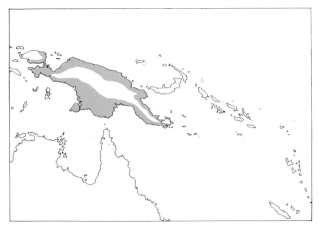

large owl of the genus *Ninox* exist in the Indonesian and Philippine regions. Their niche is apparently filled in most of these areas by the wood owl (*Strix leptogrammica*) and the spotted wood owl (*S. seloputo*) while the Solomon Islands have the fearful owl (*Nesasio solomonensis*), small in body size but with proportionately very large bill and feet.

Within the Australasian region the genus *Ninox* provides a range of species which utilize a wide food spectrum from insects to medium-sized arboreal mammals. As one begins to move northwards from this region, however, the genus provides only a series of rather similar, medium-sized owls of the boobook type. In New Guinea the boobook owl occurs in some southern savannah regions, but the typical owl of the lowland forests is the sooty-backed hawk owl (*N. theomacha*). This is 200 to 250 mm long, plain brown above and below, with blackish-brown face and yellow irides: there may be a few white spots on the scapulars. The sooty-backed hawk owl has a disyllabic call, basically similar to that of the boobook, but specifically distinct. Like the boobook it feeds mainly on insects. Its range extends to some of the islands, where it shows considerable variation. On the D'Entrecasteaux and Louisade Archipelagos, for example, the birds are a little larger and have some white markings on the underside.

These forms on the Archipelagos indicate how bird populations change when isolated on islands. Gradual differentiation from the parental form occurs and, where differences become constant in the population, taxonomists recognize them as sub-species. If isolation continues, the populations may diverge to a point where interbreeding ceases, and the island forms become a separate species. Where bird populations occur on different islands from each other it is usually difficult to say exactly when this point has been reached. But one may sometimes have the situation where an island population becomes differentiated from a parental, mainland stock and later a second invasion of the island by the parental stock occurs. By this time the two forms may have diverged to a point where they behave towards each other as separate species. The Solomon Islands hawk owl (*N jacquinoti*) is regarded as a separate species from the New Guinea bird. Within the Solomons it has begun to produce slightly different forms on each of the larger islands. It differs from the smaller sooty-backed hawk owl in being marked with transverse barring on the underside, the colour of the underside varying from one island to another.

On the island chain of the Bismarck Archipelago, adjoining both New Guinea and the Solomon Islands, several separate species have evolved. The Admiralty Islands hawk owl (*N. meeki*) is limited to this small group. It has streaking on the breast and its buffish-brown upper parts have irregular whitish barring. New Britain and New Ireland share the New Ireland hawk owl, unfortunately misnamed *N. solomonis*. This species is about 230 to 310 mm long and is also barred on the breast. New Britain has in addition its own endemic species of hawk owl, *N. odiosa*. This is a smaller species than the last, 200 to 230 mm long and more like the boobook owl in plumage, with white eyebrows and white spotting on its rufous-brown back. Its head is also spotted and the white underside is streaked and barred in brown. At the western end of New Guinea yet another form occupies the Moluccas. The Moluccan hawk owl (*N. squamipila*) has a larger size range – 250 to 360 mm – approaching that of the still larger barking owl, which is also present in the northern Moluccas. The former shows typical island variation, in colour and markings, ranging from deep brown to yellowish-brown on different islands, with the variably-barred underside white or yellowish-brown.

Further west again, Celebes has two similar small species, 200 to 260 mm long, the speckled hawk owl (*N. punctulata*) and the ochre-bellied hawk owl (*N. perversa*). The speckled hawk owl is finely spotted above, and barred on the flanks; the ochre-bellied one has only a few spots on the wing coverts and is streaked below, with a dark breast and yellow-orange belly. The speckled hawk owl is a commoner, more widely-spread bird, occurring in more open forest and in cultivated areas with some trees. It has a trisyllabic call note of two short, low-pitched notes followed by a longer high-pitched one. The ochre-bellied species is a bird of the deep virgin forests, a habitat which the speckled hawk owl seems only occasionally to penetrate. It is a scarce and little-known species.

To the north the Philippine Islands have a single species, the Philippine hawk owl (*N. philippensis*) though in winter the oriental hawk owl is a visitor to this region. The Philippine bird is small, only 150 to 200 mm long, and varies considerably from island to island, being plain or buff-spotted above, and white, with streaking, or brown, with barring, on the underside.

The Oriental hawk owl (*N. scutulata*) is a bird of the Asian mainland, which overlaps with some of the other species on its winter migrations. Between 200 to 250 mm long, it is distinguished by a uniformly dark brown back and white underparts, with heavy streaking or spotting. In the Andaman and Nicobar Islands the local subspecies is dark above and below: it overlaps in distribution with the endemic Andaman hawk owl (*N. affinis*) which is similarly marked. The Andaman hawk owl probably evolved from stocks of oriental hawk owls which invaded earlier and became genetically distinct: the local race of oriental hawk owls which at present share their habitat represents a later invasion, on which the same selection for darker plumage seems to be operating.

Oriental hawk owls are slightly better known than other hawk owls. They occur in all types of forest and also in partly cultivated or scrub areas where trees are present. In very thick forest they are usually found close to watercourses and also inhabit the mangroves of coastal zones, where they feed on small crabs in the mud as well as on a wide range of insects, amphibians, reptiles, small birds and mammals. They nest, usually, in a hole in a tree, laying a clutch of three to four eggs. Oriental hawk owls have a typical disyllabic call, rendered by a Japanese writer as 'poppow' and in India as

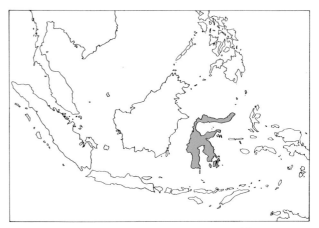

Ninox punctulata: open forest; cultivated areas with trees.
N. perversa: deep, virgin forest.

The ochre-bellied hawk owl *Ninox perversa* (200 to 260 mm) and speckled hawk owl *N. punctulata* (200 to 260 mm) represent the genus in Celebes, replacing each other respectively in rainforest and more open habitats.

Ochre-bellied hawk owl
Ninox perversa

Speckled hawk owl
Ninox punctulata

'oo-uk'; but some authors state that the Malayan race has a monosyllabic note. If so, it resembles the Andaman hawk owl, which is also said to have a monosyllabic call.

The Madagascan hawk owl (*N. superciliaris*) restricted to western Madagascar, is closely akin to the oriental hawk owl. A small species, 230 to 280 mm long, it remains well isolated from the others of its genus, and resembles owls of the northern hemisphere in having grey and brown plumage phases. It is a forest bird, roosting in trees or in small caves of rocky ravines, and sometimes flies by day. Its diet ranges from insects and reptiles to small birds and mammals.

The laughing owl (*Sceloglaux albifacies*) and the Papuan hawk owl (*Uroglaux dimorpha*) are both specialized and possibly relict forms. They are sufficiently differentiated from the other species to have been separated in special genera – of which they are the only representatives. The laughing owl is, or was, a large owl of open country and may in the past have been present over most of New Zealand. Like other species endemic to New Zealand it suffered from successive invasions of man and of new predators – possibly also diseases – which he brought with him. On the Chatham Islands, which have for long been densely occupied by man, they are known only as sub-fossil bones. On the main islands of New Zealand the species gradually decreased and was last seen in the 1930s: it may now be extinct.

The laughing owl had an overall length of 390 to 450 mm. The rounded head, with prominent eyes and bill, were typical of this group of birds, but the pale facial disc of stiff feathers seems to have been a little more strongly developed than in most of the hawk owl species. Its general plumage was yellowish-brown with darker brown streaking: wings and tail were brown with brownish-white barring, and its long legs were yellowish-buff. Its conspicuous features were whitish streaking and feather edges on wings, mantle and nape, and the whitish facial disc which accentuated the dark brown irides of the eyes. The laughing owl occurred on rocky outcrops in open places or along forest edges; the rocks provided roosts and nesting sites, and may have limited the distribution of the species. As with many other owls, their food consisted of a wide range of small creatures, including rats and mice, small birds, reptiles, insects and earthworms. The voice was varied. Harsh cacklings, strident shrieks, yelping, mewings, chucklings, and a 'cooeying' call were all noted at various times. The

The Oriental hawk owl *Ninox scutulata* (200 to 250 mm) is an Asiatic species with an extensive range from Sakhalin to India and Malaysia. Northern populations are migratory, moving south and augmenting the numbers of resident tropical populations.

Ninox scutulata: all types of forest and cultivated scrub where there are trees; in thick forest near watercourses; also in mangroves near coast.

nest, in a dry cavity under a boulder or in a rock crevice, was lined with a little dry grass and accommodated two rather rounded white eggs, with slightly roughened surfaces; there is a record of a clutch of three eggs from a captive bird. Nesting and egg-laying occurred from August to October. Incubation took about 25 days and young were reared in October to November. The female took care of most, perhaps all, of the incubation, and responsibility for the downy, yellowish-white young. The male brought food to her at the nest.

The other species of southern hawk owl, the Papuan hawk owl, is still extant, but considerably less is known about it than about the New Zealand bird. It is apparently a scarce species of lowland forest, overlapping in distribution with the sooty-

The Moluccan hawk owl *Ninox squamipila* (250 to 360 mm), Andaman hawk owl *N. affinis* (200 to 250 mm), Philippine hawk owl *N. philippensis* (150 to 200 mm) and Madagascar hawk owl *N. superciliaris* (230 to 280 mm) are more island representatives of the genus *Ninox*, the last named being the only one to occur outside the Oriental and Australasian regions.

Ninox squamipila: Moluccas and scattered islands.

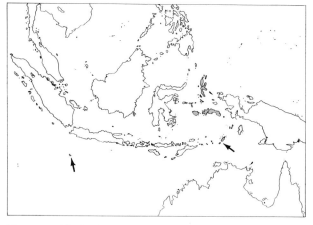

Ninox affinis: confined to Andaman Islands.

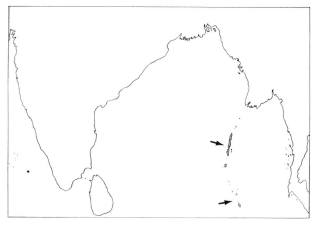

Ninox superciliaris: forest.

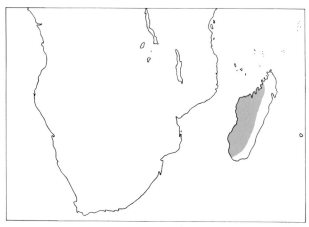

Ninox philippensis: confined to Philippine Islands.

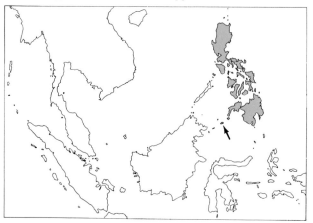

Moluccan hawk owl
Ninox squamipila

Andaman hawk owl
Ninox affinis

Madagascar hawk owl
Ninox superciliaris

Philippine hawk owl
Ninox philippensis

Right: The Papuan hawk owl *Uroglaux dimorpha* (300 to 330 mm) is a rare forest species about which extremely little is known. Half of its length is accounted for by its long tail and it is actually a smaller species than the sooty-backed hawk owl with which it coexists.

Though relatively small in body size, the fearful owl *Nesasio solomonensis* (280 to 380 mm) of the Solomon Islands has a large bill and extremely powerful talons; it occupies a niche which is filled by large wood owls or eagle owls in other parts of the world.

backed hawk owl. Some 300 to 330 mm long, it is 50 mm longer than the sooty-backed hawk owl, but the long tail accounts for nearly half its length and it is, in fact, smaller in body size. The long tail and smallish, rounded head give the bird a hawk-like outline in flight. Upperparts, wings and tail are heavily barred in blackish and reddish-brown, the crown and nape streaked with similar colour, and the underparts buffish-white with dark longitudinal streaking. The brows are white, and the irides yellow. Almost nothing is known of its general behaviour, apart from the fact that it feeds on insects and small rodents.

Also occurring in the Australasian region is the fearful owl (*Nesasio solomonensis*) it is an odd species of uncertain affinities which has some claim to being an ecological equivalent of the eagle owls, but its true relationships with other owls are unknown. It is confined to three of the larger of the Solomon Islands, Bougainville, Choiseul and Santa Isabel, and is said to be a bird of lowland and hill forest.

Nesasio solomonis: lowland hill forest.

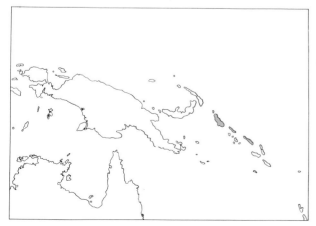

Uroglaux dimorpha: lowland forest.

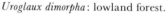
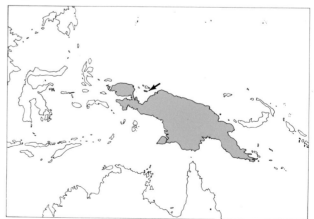

Diurnal to a considerable extent, the northern hawk owl is rather shrike-like in its appearance and behaviour, generally perching in some prominent position from which it swoops down onto its prey.

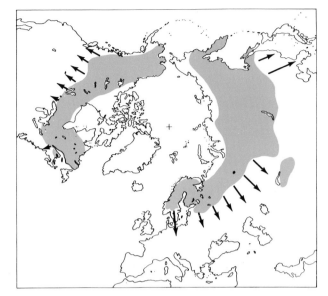

Surnia ulula: northern coniferous forest clearings or where there are mixed deciduous patches; low scrub, scattered trees and shrubs near water; lightly wooded forest-edges. Arrows show direction of migration in irruption years.

Though they share a number of hawk-like characteristics, the northern hawk owl *Surnia ulula* (360 to 410 mm) and the Oriental and Australasian hawk owls are quite different in appearance and not closely related. The northern hawk owl nests in tree cavities, often taking over large woodpecker holes.

In body size it is considerably smaller than any of the eagle owls, being only 280 to 380 mm long, but it has a beak and talons as powerful as those of the great horned owl. Its beak and talons certainly suggest that it is capable of killing relatively large prey, and it is known to take oppossums and birds, but nothing else is known of its ecology.

The hawk owl of the northern hemisphere, *Surnia ulula*, contrasts with the hawk owls of the southern regions in its bold plumage pattern and its deliberate diurnal hunting activity. Diurnal hunting is not really surprising, since the northern limits of its distribution reach the edge of the Arctic tundra: in these high latitudes there is almost continuous daylight during the summer months, and any owl of these regions must be adapted to some diurnal activity. The northern hawk owl occurs along the broad zone of the northern coniferous forests around the whole of the northern hemisphere. A bird of open places within this zone, it occurs in clearings, in open parts of forest where trees are widely spaced, or where deciduous trees give an extensive view through the forest. It is also found in low scrub, and in thinly scattered trees and shrubs along watercourses at the tundra's edge,

and extends into lightly wooded areas at the southern edge of the forest zone.

This is a medium-sized owl, about 360 to 410 mm long, with a small facial disc which extends sideways and comes down in a brow low over the eyes, to give a low-crowned, rounded profile. Its wings are large and taper to a point; its tail is long and graduated towards the tip. In combination these feathers give an outline more like that of a hawk or a small, long-tailed falcon than like an owl. Though it may perch upright, its resemblance to a hawk is often enhanced by a tendency to lean forwards and raise its tail. The eyes are relatively small, and the ears lack the specialized asymmetrical development for locating sounds seen mainly in night hunters. The plumage is boldly marked. The facial disc is greyish-white with a bold black outer edge, and its eyes have a yellow iris. The crown of its head is finely chequered in black and white, and the whole of its back is mottled and barred in brownish-black and white; wings and tail are boldly barred. The underside is covered with fine transverse black barring on white, and is palest on the upper breast.

The bird's flight is swift and direct, the pointed wings and long tail again giving a hawk-like effect.

In hunting it resembles a shrike, using a high vantage point as a look-out and swooping down on small prey, It flies fast and low near the ground, swooping up to perch at a new vantage point. Alternatively it may fly higher and more slowly, watching the ground below, hovering, and dropping when it sights a small creature.

The hawk owl's principal prey is rodents, the small mice, voles and lemmings typical of the regions in which it occurs. It will, however, take any prey that is available, including other small mammals such as squirrels or weasels, a variety of small birds, and even insects. Although a diurnal hunter, its main activity takes place at early morning or late evening and it can of course hunt during the long darkness of winter. Rodents living beneath the snow are difficult to catch and the owl may take more birds in winter. Its food supply is affected by the cycles of rodent abundance and scarcity: and in years of abundance the owls lay large clutches and rear large broods of young, while in years of scarcity the broods are smaller. In bad years, hawk owls move southwards in large numbers at the beginning of winter, appearing in regions outside their normal range of distribution. Like many birds of Arctic and sub-Arctic regions, they are often unwary of man. In their southward irruptions they allow observers to get very close.

The main calls are a soft musical hoot, uttered at about two-second intervals and apparently used as a territorial call, and a trilling whistle heard at the beginning of the breeding season. The nesting site is a natural hole or cavity. The irregular, broken top of a tall tree-stump, with a hollow in it, is a very typical site but a large woodpecker hole or the large old stick nests of rooks may also be used. Normally the nest is unlined. Breeding begins during late March and extends to early May. In poor food years clutches may be of three to four eggs, in good years of ten to twelve. Incubation, mainly by the female, begins with the first egg and lasts about four weeks. The eggs hatch over a period of several days so that the young are graded in size; the smallest one unlikely to survive if food is restricted. Downy and white, the young have a shrill, hissing call. Juvenile plumage is a grey-brown version of the adult plumage, and less fluffy than that of other owls. In most details of its life history the northern hawk owl resembles the other owls of these regions. Its main difference is in its structural and behavioural adaptation to hunting by sight, in a more hawk-like fashion, in open habitats where there is scope for such behaviour and a vacant niche exists.

CHAPTER NINE

Little, Pygmy and Elf owls

Athene, Speotyto, Micrathene, Glaucidium, Aegolius, Pseudoscops

Owls range in size from sparrow to eagle and hunt prey appropriate to their own dimensions. Among the smallest are five genera, including twenty-five species, which range across the world: the largest are pigeon-sized little owls (*Athene*), the smallest elf owls (*Micrathene*) and pygmy owls (*Glaucidium*). All feed on insects and on a fairly wide variety of small mammals, birds and reptiles. Several nest in holes, often in competition with starlings or flickers; some even nest underground in abandoned mammal burrows.

The genus *Athene* contains three closely-related species of short, plump birds known as little owls, which together cover a wide geographical range and a variety of habitats in Europe and Asia. Best known is the little owl (*A. noctua*)

of Eurasia, a species widely distributed in the Palaearctic region from about 55°N in Europe to 30°N in North Africa, slightly further south in Ethiopia and Arabia. It extends across Russia, Mongolia and China almost to the Pacific Coast of Asia, but is entirely absent from India and most of South-east Asia. Introduced into Britain after a number of attempts, little owls were first recorded breeding in Kent in 1879 and later spread rapidly throughout England and Wales.

Aptly named, this is a small, plump owl some 190 to 230 mm long with a compact, flat-headed appearance, no ear tufts of feathers, and a very short tail. The sexes are similar, mostly greyish-brown, mottled and barred with white on top, and pale with dark streaks underneath. The poorly-developed facial disc and the pale eyebrows,

Athene noctua: parklands, fields with hedges, rocky semi-desert regions and steppes.

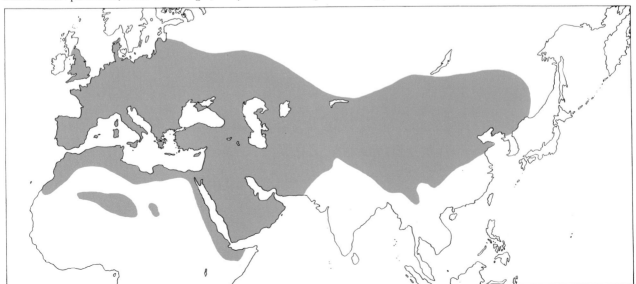

BEVAN/ARDEA

CHRISTIANSEN

Besides nesting in tree cavities, little owls make use of holes in cliffs or even burrows in the ground, particularly in desert areas.

Top left: In wooded areas the little owl *Athene noctua* (200 to 220 mm) usually nests in a tree cavity. It feeds its young on a variety of small animals, including rodents, birds, insects and even (in this case) worms.

Left: The little owl lives mainly in lightly wooded open country or rocky arid areas. It is longer-legged and more terrestrial than all but the burrowing owl and is able to run quite fast on the ground in pursuit of insects.

HOSKING

combined with the low forehead produce a frowning, disapproving expression. Perching on a tree or post, little owls often bob up and down in a comical fashion which may indicate anxiety. The wings are broad and rounded, and the flight is silent and undulating.

Little owls breed in cavities in trees, walls and cliffs, occasionally on the ground, in April and May: in Britain and western Europe most eggs appear late in April. Usually between three and five eggs are laid but clutches of seven and eight have been recorded. The eggs, matt white and elliptical, are incubated from first laying, usually by the female only. Incubation takes four weeks, and the nestlings emerge in a covering of dense, short white down. At first only the male

The spotted little owl *Athene brama* (190 to 210 mm) is ecologically similar to the little owl, replacing it in parts of the Middle East, India and Indo-China.

Athene brama: gardens, open areas with trees, rainforest to 1500 metres and desert.

feeds them, but later the female joins in, and the chicks remain in the nest for up to four weeks. Usually one brood only is attempted each year, but two have occasionally been recorded.

The food of this species is well documented in Britain. During the 1930s, when its range had spread to its maximum, it was suspected to be a wholesale destroyer of game chicks, poultry and native songbirds and the British Trust for Ornithology sponsored an inquiry into its feeding habits. The conclusions were that throughout the year little owls feed chiefly on insects, including adult and immature earwigs, craneflies, cock-chafers and other beetles. Hunting chiefly at night, they also take mammals up to the size of large rats and medium-sized rabbits. Few birds appeared in the diet, except during the breeding season when starlings, house sparrows, blackbirds and song thrushes and a very few game chicks were taken. Little owls often hunt by perching on a post or similar vantage point and watching for movement on the ground below.

This species is found in a variety of habitats, ranging from parkland, orchards and cultivated fields with hedges to rocky, semi-desert regions and steppes, but it generally shuns mountainous,

hilly or densely-wooded regions. Rather more terrestrial than most owls, little owls often settle on the ground and are able to run quite fast, while chasing prey. The voice is varied. Two calls predominate – a beautiful, plaintive 'kiew', repeated at intervals of a few seconds, and a rapidly repeated loud, yelping 'wherrow'.

Throughout their broad range, little owls are sedentary and do not undergo regular migrations, although some individuals disperse and wander outside the breeding season. Taxonomists distinguish ten subspecies or races, based mainly on differences of colour and size, although the characteristics of one race generally grade into those of neighbouring stocks. The darkest race, (*A. n. vidalii*), occurs in western Europe, including Britain; the palest, (*A. n. lilith*), inhabits the dry, sandy region at the eastern end of the Mediterranean.

In southern Iran, Baluchistan, India and parts of Indo-China, the little owl is replaced by the spotted little owl, (*A. brama*). About 190 to 210 mm long, this species is about as big as the smallest Eurasian little owls, and of similar appearance and habits. It occurs as a common and wide-spread resident in gardens, plains and open areas

GRANDJEAN

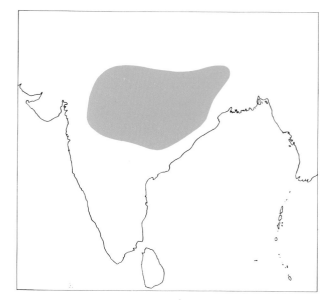

The forest little owl *Athene blewitti* (210 to 230 mm) closely resembles the other little owls, differing mainly in being darker and shorter-winged, as might be expected from its forest habitat.

Athene blewitti: dense deciduous forest.

Though superficially similar and closely related to the little owls, the burrowing owl *Speotyto cunicularia* (180 to 260 mm) is even longer-legged and much more thoroughly terrestrial. It is largely crepuscular but also hunts by day and night.

BURGESS/ARDEA

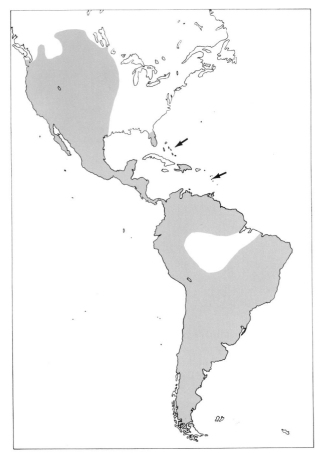

Speotyto cunicularia: terrestrial in open, treeless grassland.

As its name suggests, the burrowing owl roosts and breeds in burrows in the ground. Though capable of excavating them itself, it often takes over the abandoned burrows of such mammals as prairie dogs in North America and the plains viscacha in South America.

with scattered trees, from dry desert regions to damp rainforests, reaching an altitude of about 1500 metres in the Himalayan foothills. Like the little owl, it avoids dense forest areas. As the vernacular name suggests, it is more spotted than streaked, with underparts cross-barred. Rather more sociable than its near relative, it is often seen in pairs or family parties of three or four, and is largely active between dusk and dawn. Though quite at home in broad daylight, it generally prefers to remain concealed in a tree-hole. Like other *Athene* owls, it bobs up and down when suspicious or alarmed, has an undulating flight and hunts from posts or vantage points. It feeds on large insects, earthworms, mice, lizards and birds, which are pounced upon and carried back to the perch to be eaten.

The breeding season of spotted little owls extends from February to April; three, four or five round, white eggs are laid in a sparsely-lined hollow of a tree, wall or ruin. Unlike the little owl, male and female share incubation. The voice, which has been described as a loud, harsh, rapidly repeated 'chirurr-chirurr' interspersed with a discordant 'cheevak, cheevak', is heard especially often during the breeding season.

The forest little owl (*A. blewitti*) inhabits damp, dense deciduous forests and jungles in north-eastern and central India. Larger than *A. brama*, it is as large as eastern races of *A. noctua*, some 210 to 230 mm in length, but has shorter wings. In general appearance it closely resembles its congeners, but has more uniform, earth-brown upperparts and darker underparts, with a distinct dark bar across the throat. A rare and rather shy species, many aspects of its biology and habits remain to be discovered.

The burrowing owl (*Speotyto cunicularia*), is superficially similar to little owls both in appearance and in other respects, including its brief, undulating flights and comical bobbing behaviour when alarmed. It ranges from the plains of western North America south through Central and South America as far as Cape Horn, with isolated populations in Florida and the Caribbean and this small owl, long-legged and short-tailed, varies in colour throughout its extensive range. In southern South America, Florida and Haiti it is chocolate-coloured, heavily spotted, streaked and barred with white: in semi-desert regions, such as parts of inland Brazil, it is light sandy-brown with white markings, and in tropical forested areas of South

168

FINK/ARDEA

BARTLETT/COLEMAN

The tiny elf owl *Micrathene whitneyi* (130 to 140 mm) is one of the two smallest owls in the world. It is confined to the south-western United States and Mexico, where it is particularly associated with the giant *saguaro* cactus.

Elf owls normally breed in holes drilled in *saguaro* cacti by woodpeckers, but other suitably small cavities are sometimes used. The young are fed almost entirely on insects.

Micrathene whitneyi: dry grassy lowlands, wet savannahs, woodland, forest and cactus.

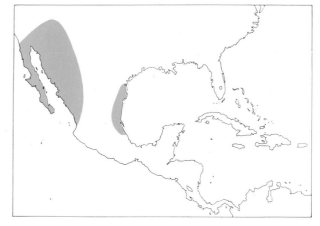

HAUTALA

Like all owlets, young boreal owls often leave their
nest some time before they are able to fly. Even after they
have learned to fly, their parents feed them for several weeks
or even months, thereby giving them plenty of time to learn
the skills involved in catching prey.

Aegolius funereus: northern coniferous forest, also mixed forest
of pine, birch and poplar.

America the pale plumage may be spotted with
orange. In length it varies from 180 to 260 mm
Andean populations being the largest.

Essentially a terrestrial species, the burrowing
owl lives mainly on open, treeless grasslands,
frequenting abandoned mammal burrows or
tunnels which it digs for itself. It breeds in loose
colonies of up to a dozen pairs, reputedly laying
two to eleven eggs in a roughly-lined chamber up
to a metre below ground, possibly at the end of
three metres of meandering burrow. Both sexes
incubate for a total of four weeks, and both help
to feed the chicks.

Food of the burrowing owl ranges from much
favoured large beetles and other insects to small
rodents, occasionally frogs and birds. During
the breeding season it gives cooing calls and a
bird disturbed in its burrow gives repeated
'cack-cack' alarm calls with a rattling hiss rather
like that of a rattle snake. Although mainly
evening hunters, burrowing owls are frequently
active by day or night.

The elf owl (*Micrathene whitneyi*) sometimes
called Whitney's elf owl, is one of the smallest
owls, with a length of 140 mm, a rounded 'earless'
head, rounded body and short tail. Throughout
the year it is confined entirely to the south-
western United States, including Texas, eastern
Mexico, and Socorro Island. Perhaps best known
for its association with the giant Saguaro cactus, the
elf owl commonly occurs also in a variety of woodlands and forests to an altitude of 2000 metres,
and on dry grassy lowlands and wet savannahs.

The preferred site for nesting is the abandoned
hole of a woodpecker or flicker, up to 10 metres
above ground in a giant cactus or tree, but any
suitable size cavity will suffice. The clutch consists
of two to five (usually three) pure white oval eggs,
which are laid on alternate days some time
during April or May. Both sexes incubate for
about two weeks before the white, downy young
hatch. The young are fed by the parents for some
time after leaving the nest-hole.

Unlike some of the other owls described in this
chapter, the elf owl is markedly nocturnal,
remaining hidden during the day in some
suitable hole or dense foliage, to emerge at dusk
and pursue the large insects which are its chief
prey. This species has an extremely loud voice for
its size; the calls most frequently heard are
rapidly repeated, high-pitched notes descending
in pitch towards the end.

The genus *Aegolius* contains four species of

LINDBLAD/COLEMAN

Tengmalm's owl *Aegolius funereus* (190 to 230 mm), better known as the boreal owl in North America, is associated with conifers throughout its range, particularly spruce in the north and various types of pine in the south. The characteristic shape of its facial disc gives it a permanently surprised expression.

small owls, of which the best known is *A. funereus* – known as Tengmalm's owl in Europe and the boreal owl in North America. The saw-whet owl (*A. acadicus*) is a common species in North America, and two other species occur more locally and are little known. The unspotted saw-whet owl (*A. ridgwayi*) occurs from parts of southern Mexico southwards to northern Costa Rica and the buff-fronted owl (*A. harrisii*) occurs in two widely spaced populations, one in extreme north-western South America and the other in southern Brazil and northern Argentina.

Tengmalm's owl is a bird of northern coniferous forests. Found especially among spruce, it occurs also in mixed forests among pine, birch and poplar. Further south, for example in central Europe, it frequents pine

forest on high ground. During the far northern summer it feeds in continous daylight, but elsewhere it is chiefly a nocturnal species, spending the day in the tops of conifers or hidden in a tree-hole. It feeds on small birds and mammals, occasionally on frogs and other small animals.

Similar in size to the little owl (190 to 230 mm long) Tengmalm's owl has a large round head with yellow bill, spotted crown, short tail, long, broad wings and well-defined facial disc without ear tufts: in many ways it resembles a small tawny owl. The legs and feet are completely covered in white feathers.

Tengmalm's owl lays its eggs in April or May, starting as early as mid-March in the south of its range or as late as June in the far north. The eggs, white and glossy, are laid at intervals of from one to three days in a hole in a tree, often in the disused nest-hole of a woodpecker. In Europe clutches of three to six are common, and up to ten have been recorded; in North America clutches are smaller. Only the female incubates, for a period approaching four weeks. Incubation starts as soon as the first egg is laid and the young hatch over a period similar to the laying period. Thus the first chick is well advanced by the time the last one hatches; should food become scarce, the smallest chicks die, leaving available supplies to be divided among a smaller number of survivors. The nestlings, which on hatching have a sparse covering of short down, develop a plumage which is buff-white above and white below, and leave the nest after about four and a half weeks.

Tengmalm's owl is a sedentary bird, with a

Aegolius acadicus: damp, dense woodland.

In its appearance and ecology the saw-whet owl *Aegolius acadicus* (170 to 190 mm) is very similar to the boreal (Tengmalm's) owl, but it is confined to North America and has a more southerly distribution. It earns its name from a very characteristic 'saw-sharpening' call which it utters mainly during the breeding season.

soft, liquid flute-like note, which it repeats at intervals of a few seconds, with alternate variations in stress. The sound has been likened to the regular dripping of water.

The saw-whet owl (*A. acadicus*) is widely distributed in damp, dense woodlands of North America, its range extending in a broad belt from south-eastern Alaska and California in the west to eastern Canada and the north-eastern United States. It extends south into Mexico, but is generally absent from the southern states. It overlaps with the boreal (Tengmalm's) owl along the Canadian border zone. In winter northern elements of the population move southward from their breeding grounds, and the population as a whole appears to shift slightly south, though much of it remains within the breeding range.

Saw-whet owls closely resemble boreal owls, but are slightly smaller (about 170 to 190 mm long), with black bill and streaked crown. Seldom seen during the day, they are largely crepuscular or nocturnal hunters, preying on small mammals and birds. Bats, frogs, even occasionally mammals and birds as large as the owls themselves, have been recorded.

These owls are most vociferous before and during the breeding season in March or April. One of their many varied calls is reminiscent of a grasshopper's stridulation; the 'saw-sharpening' call which has given the bird its vernacular name is less often heard. They nest in cavities, whose linings of moss, bark fragments, leaves, twigs and feathers are possibly left-overs from previous occupants. The most frequent

Unspotted saw-whet owl
Aegolius ridgwayi

Buff-fronted owl
Aegolius harrisii

As its name suggests, the unspotted saw-whet owl *Aegolius ridgwayi* (170 to 190 mm) differs from the saw-whet owl only in lacking prominent spots and streaks; it may be no more than a Central American race of the latter. The South American buff-fronted owl *A. harrisii* occurs in two widely separated populations, little being known about the ecology of either.

Right: *Aegolius harrisii*: habitat unknown.

Aegolius ridgwayi: S. Mexico to south-eastern Costa Rica.

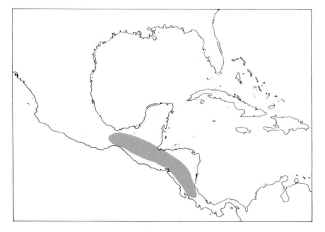

The Eurasian pygmy owl *Glaucidium passerinum* (160 to 170 mm) is more nocturnal than many members of the genus. Like most small owls, it nests in tree cavities and generally takes over holes excavated by woodpeckers.

LINDBLAD/COLEMAN

clutch-size is five or six eggs; four or seven are sometimes recorded. The eggs are pure white, of the rather oval or almost spherical shape typical of the owl family. Incubation is reported to take from 21 to 28 days, starting soon after the first egg is laid so that the nest later contains young of widely different ages. The chicks are at first white, like those of the boreal owl, but dark, chocolate brown feathers of a distinctive juvenile plumage soon grow through. The chicks fledge when they are about four weeks old.

The unspotted saw-whet owl (*A. ridgwayi*) is a central American species of limited range, occurring in a narrow belt from the extreme south of Mexico south-east to Costa Rica; it has also been recorded in Panama. Roughly the same size as the saw-whet owl, it is plain dark brown above and pale buff below, without barring or streaking. Little information is available on the ecology, behaviour or breeding biology; indeed its exact specific status seems to be in doubt; and at least one author has suggested that it may merely be a race of the southern saw-whet owl.

The buff-fronted owl (*A. harrisii*) from South America is known only from a few sightings and museum specimens; its ecology and biological characteristics have not been recorded.

The largest genus of small owls, *Glaucidium*, contains twelve species collectively called the pygmy owls. Perhaps the best known and most widespread species is the Eurasian pygmy owl, (*G. passerinum*). This lives in a broad belt 600 to 1000 kilometres wide across Europe and Asia, from western Europe and Scandinavia (excluding Denmark) through much of northern,

Glaucidium passerinum: open areas of mature coniferous or mixed forest.

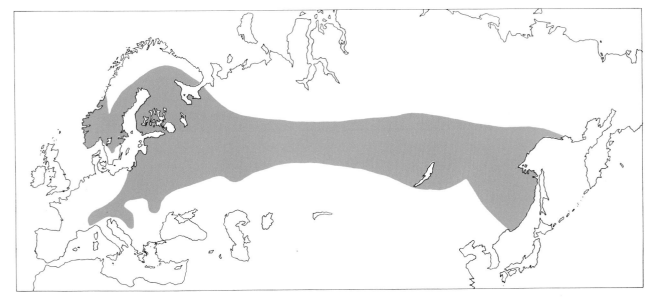

Cuban pygmy owl
Glaucidium siju

Northern pygmy owl
Glaucidium gnoma

Often considered conspecific with the Eurasian pygmy owl, the American pygmy owl *Glaucidium gnoma* (about 170 mm) ranges through open woodland from Alaska and Canada to Central America. By contrast, the Cuban pygmy owl *G. siju* (about 170 mm) is confined to Cuba and the Isle of Pines.

central and western Russia, across Siberia south of 58° to 60°N latitude, to north-eastern Mongolia, central Manchuria and the island of Sakhalin. Two subspecies or races are recognized, the eastern form of East Siberia, Manchuria and Sakhalin being, on average slightly larger, rather paler and greyer with more distinct spotting than western stocks.

The Eurasian pygmy owl is found in open areas of mature coniferous and mixed forests, where it roosts throughout the day. Though plentiful across its wide range, it is nowhere abundant, and seldom appears in daytime. Adult plumage is greyish-brown above, with light mottling and spotting and brown with streaking below. On the back of the neck is a prominent light half-collar. The head is rather small for an owl, rounded and lacking a well-defined facial disc, with no ear tufts. The wings are short and rounded, the tail is long for an owl, frequently flicked to the side when the bird is perching and on alighting cocked-up sharply like a European wren's tail. The legs and feet, which are fully feathered, are proportionally very large. Eurasian pygmy owls fly rather like shrikes, often from look-out posts on the topmost twigs of small trees.

Though only about 170 mm long, they are pugnacious predators, occasionally taking prey much larger than themselves. More usually they hunt small and medium-sized rodents, shrews, lizards or birds and insects which they catch in flight. With its wide range of food species, the Eurasian pygmy owl does not depend on any one kind of prey, and is thus buffered against sudden dramatic fluctuations in population.

Eurasian pygmy owls nest in holes and, like so many other small owls, often take over the disused holes of woodpeckers. The timing of the breeding season varies with the region; in Sweden for instance, egg-laying begins in April or May, occasionally as early as March. Three to seven eggs, sometimes eight, are laid in the tree-hole, and incubated solely by the female; incubation usually begins when the third egg is laid and lasts for twenty-eight days. Newly-hatched chicks are clad in whitish down, graduating to dark brown plumage on fledging.

On late winter and spring evenings, as the breeding season approaches, the pygmy owl utters a musical piping 'hü' call, repeated regularly every few seconds and reminiscent of the call-note of a bullfinch. When the call is

The ferruginous pygmy owl *Glaucidium brasilianum* (130 to 140 mm) is a little known and patchily distributed species of Central and South America. It is one of the more diurnal members of the genus, though its daylight activity is largely confined to the early morning and late afternoon.

Right: *Glaucidium brasilianum*: woodland along river valleys.

Glaucidium gnoma: open habitat, also mature coniferous and mixed woodland. *G. siju*: woodland.

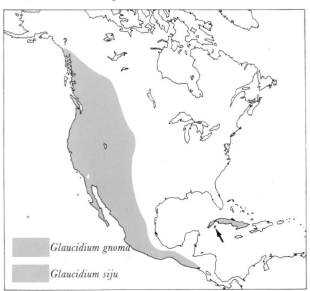

Glaucidium gnoma

Glaucidium siju

Rarely found far from trees, the ferruginous pygmy owl usually prefers woodland along river valleys.

Glaucidium minutissimum: dense tropical forest to open bush country.

The least pygmy owl *Glaucidium minutissimum* (120 to 140 mm) is about the same size as the elf owl but much less well known. These two individuals were being kept as pets by Karaja Indians in Brazil.

uttered from a perch, the sound is ventriloquial, seeming to come from different places as the bird turns its head. Occasionally members of a pair call alternatively in duet. In winter some individuals move south, usually in response to bad weather.

The American pygmy owl (*G. gnoma*) is very similar to that of Eurasia, and considered by some to be conspecific. A bird of the western Americas, it ranges from the Alaska–British Columbia border and Vancouver Island south through the Rocky Mountains, California, Arizona and New Mexico to Guatemala. Within this range, a number of geographical races have been distinguished, but they are virtually inseparable in the field. The upperparts of both sexes are greyish or reddish brown, with buff-white speckling, particularly on the head, wings and shoulders; across the back of the neck is a half-collar of black and white. Underparts are white with dark brown streaks, and the tail is dark with light bars. The most usual habitat is open but it also occurs in mature coniferous and mixed woodland.

Like many other small owls, this species nests in holes made by woodpeckers and flickers. The clutch of round, white eggs varies from two to seven, but is most usually three or four. In most aspects of its breeding and feeding biology, including its tendency to remain sedentary, the North American pygmy owl closely resembles the Eurasian form.

The ferruginous pygmy owl (*G. brasilianum*) has a rather complex and discontinuous distribution from the extreme south-western United States in Arizona and Texas, through Central America south to Southern Argentina and Chile. As the vernacular name suggests, this species is a rufous version of the North American pygmy owl. Its chief distinguishing features are rufous flanks, unspotted back, and a reddish-brown tail with dark-brown bars. However, ferruginous pygmy owls are variable, some populations being decidedly greyish, others varying considerably in the degree of barring on the tail; one form found in tropical Central America and in the eastern Andean foothills is even more rufous than the typical form. Within South America there are geographically separate populations: however only two races are generally accepted, *G. b. ridgwayi* in the northern part of the range as far south as Panama, and *G. b.*

brasilianum in the rest, to Argentina and Chile.

Very little is known about this bird's ecology. Like many of its near relatives, it frequently hunts by day, sitting on a look-out post watching for some passing rodent, bird or large insect to pounce on. Such accounts as there are suggest that in many essentials it resembles the North American pygmy owl. Rarely found far from trees, it tends to prefer woodland along river valleys. The three or four white, almost spherical eggs are laid on the floor of the nest-hole. In the north of its range, eggs are laid between March and May, but there is considerable variation in latitude. The song is a series of short whistles repeated in very rapid succession.

The least pygmy owl (*G. minutissimum*) is probably, as its name suggests, the smallest of the pygmy owls, being a mere 120 to 140 mm long. It looks like the ferruginous pygmy owls, but is smaller, with more uniform dark brown upperparts and fewer exposed white bars on the tail. It occurs from sea-level up to at least 1800 metres and ranges from Mexico and central America to Guyana, north-western Colombia, south-eastern Peru, Paraguay and the Amazon basin in Brazil, varying in habitat from dense tropical forest to open bushy country. The call is a series of four low whistles: this, or the commotion of mobbing small songbirds may be the only indication of the least pygmy owl's presence, as it tends to remain hidden.

The pygmy owl of most limited range is undoubtedly the Cuban pygmy owl (*G. siju*), which is restricted to the Caribbean islands of Cuba and the nearby Isle of Pines. Like many other owls, this 170 mm long species occurs in two colour phases, one greyish-brown and the other reddish-brown. The upperparts are dark-brown with pale mottlings, the underparts largely white with brownish markings on the throat and breast and the tail is barred with white. This is a largely diurnal species inhabiting woodland. The most usual nest is a hole in a tree, where three or four white eggs are laid. Cuban pygmy owls produce piercing series of notes rising in pitch, and a slowly repeated hooting.

In the Old World there remains a series of seven poorly known species, three from Africa and four from India and the Far East. The pearl-spotted owlet (*G. perlatum*), 170 to 180 mm long, is probably the most widespread, occurring

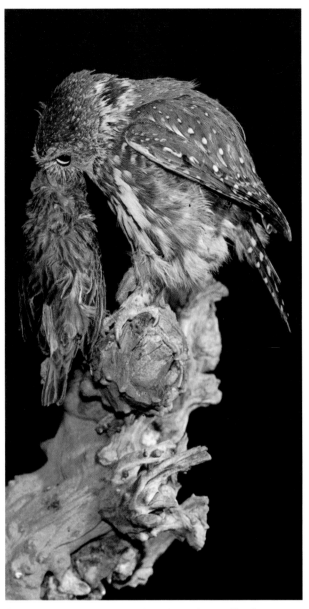

Glaucidium perlatum: savannah and acacia woodland.

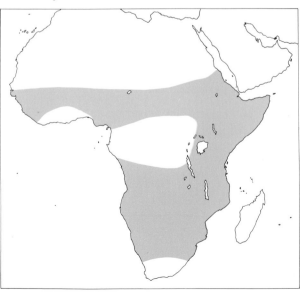

The pearl-spotted owlet *Glaucidium perlatum* (170 to 180 mm) is widely distributed in the savannah areas of Africa. Like other pygmy owls, it strongly resembles a very small sparrowhawk in flight, though it hunts in a shrike-like manner, preying on small rodents, birds, lizards and particularly insects. One of these individuals (left) is feeding on a red-billed quelea.

The red-chested owlet *Glaucidium tephronotum* (170 to 180 mm) is a little known species of African equatorial forest. It feeds largely on insects but, in common with other pygmy owls, it is very pugnacious for its size, readily tackling mammals and birds considerably bigger than itself.

Glaucidium tephronotum: dense forest.

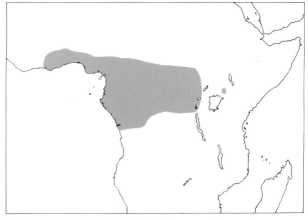

Chestnut-backed owlet
Glaucidium sjostedti

Barred owlet
Glaucidium capense

The chestnut-backed owlet *Glaucidium sjostedti* (about 250 mm), restricted to a small area of West African forest, and the barred owlet *G. capense* (210 to 220 mm), a savannah species, are two of the largest of the pygmy owls. In their respective habitats, each species coexists with a more widely distributed and slightly smaller species (the red-chested and pearl-spotted owlets) but their ecological relationships are unknown.

Right: *Glaucidium capense*: acacia bush.

Glaucidium sjostedti: tropical forest.

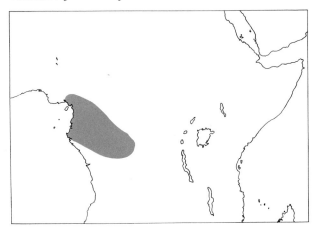

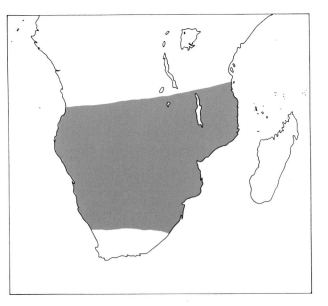

throughout large tracts of Africa south of the Sahara, particularly in the acacia woodlands but not in the equatorial forest region of West and Central Africa.

Cinnamon-brown above with copious speckles of black and white, like most of the pygmy owls it has a pale half-collar. Underparts are white with black streaking. Prey consists chiefly of large insects, but small mammals, snakes, lizards and birds are also taken. The call is distinctive, resembling a boy whistling.

The red-chested owlet (*G. tephronotum*) of tropical Africa, is dark olive-brown above with a white spotted collar and a dark brown white spotted tail. The underparts are white with dark brown spots, the sides uniform reddish-brown. This is a species of dense forest and nothing is known of its breeding biology or call.

The barred owlet (*G. capense*), 210 to 220 mm long, is large for a pygmy owl, with sepia upperparts, fine white barrings on the head and upper back, broad yellowish markings on the lower back, wings and tail. The white upperparts are thickly marked with dark brown triangular spots. This is a bird of the acacia bush, though of more limited distribution than the pearl-spotted owlet.

Even larger than the barred owlet is the chestnut-backed owlet, *G. sjöstedti*, restricted to a relatively small area of western tropical Africa. In many respects it resembles the barred owlet but differs in having yellowish orange underparts with dark yellow-brown barring on the flanks.

The barred jungle owlet (*G. radiatum*) is a bird of the Indian sub-continent, ranging from 2000 metres up in the Himalayan foothills south to Ceylon. It is a bird of damp, deciduous forest and secondary jungle, where suitable nest-holes are available.

The collared pygmy owl (*G. brodiei*) ranges from the Himalayas and Assam hills (600 to 3000 metres) to western China, the lower Yangtze Valley, Formosa, the Malay Peninsula, Sumatra and Borneo. It usually lives in evergreen or mixed deciduous-evergreen forest, among oak, rhododendron and fir, but it also occurs in forest edges and more isolated groups of trees in cultivated country. This is one of the more diurnal species of the genus, and is often seen perching and hunting in broad daylight, though it is also active at twilight and at night. In this and many other aspects of its ecology, it resembles the Eurasian pygmy owl. The call, usually consisting of four musical notes repeated at

The barred jungle owlet *Glaucidium radiatum* (about 170 mm) is widely distributed in forest and jungle on the Indian sub-continent.

Glaucidium radiatum: damp deciduous forest, secondary jungle.

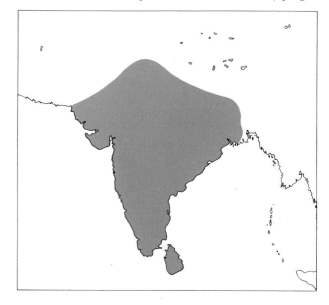

The collared pygmy owl *Glaucidium brodiei* (about 150 mm) is a bird of mountain forests throughout most of its range.

Glaucidium brodiei: evergreen or mixed deciduous forest; forest edges and groups of trees in cultivated land.

intervals and distinctively grouped has been described as 'hü hü-hü hü'.

The cuckoo owlet (*G. cuculoides*) is another of the larger species, reaching 230 mm in length. In range very similar to the collared pygmy owl, it extends further northward throughout most of China and is more restricted in south-eastern Asia, with isolated populations in Java and Bali. Like a larger version of the barred jungle owlet, it occurs in open forests of oak, rhododendron and pine at higher elevations and in tropical and sub-tropical evergreen jungle at lower altitudes. Chiefly a diurnal owl, it is an agile predator reported to catch quail in the air like a hawk; normally, however, it feeds on large insects, lizards, small birds and mice. Like other members of the family it is relentlessly mobbed by small birds and often flicks its tail from side to side – a habit of its genus. The calls are a trill and a series of harsh squawks, rising to a crescendo then ending abruptly. In the breeding season, which usually begins in April or May, a more musical and continuous bubbling whistle lasting for some seconds is uttered. Four eggs are laid in a disused hole; sometimes woodpeckers or barbets are forcibly evicted from their holes by cuckoo owlets.

Opinions differ widely as to the relationships of the Jamaican owl (*Pseudoscops grammicus*) the only member of its genus. It is among the larger of the 'small' owls – 310 mm in length, with rather short wings and tail. It is mainly dark tawny or yellowish-brown in colour, streaked and mottled with dark brown and black. The flight feathers of the tail and wings are barred irregularly with dark blackish-brown. It has a fairly well-developed facial disc, and short but conspicuous ear tufts. As its name suggests, it has been thought to be close to the scops owls – but distinct enough to warrant being placed in a separate genus. In fact it is not now generally considered to be particularly close to *Otus*; some authorities put it close to the eared owls of the genus *Asio*, while others think it is linked with the *Athene*, *Speotyto* and *Aegolius* owls.

Its range is restricted to the island of Jamaica, which means that in terms of world population it is a very rare bird. It is found in both woodland and open country, nesting in cavities in trees, though sometimes the two eggs are laid in well concealed tree-forks. It is more or less strictly nocturnal, and its voice consists of a quavering 'whoooo'.

The cuckoo owlet *Glaucidium cuculoides* (230 to 250 mm), also known as the barred pygmy owl, is one of the largest members of the genus. It is mainly diurnal and sufficiently agile on the wing to catch quail in flight, though it normally pounces on its prey from a perch.

No longer considered to be closely related to the scops owl, the Jamaican owl *Pseudoscops grammicus* (about 310 mm) is sometimes linked with the eared owls in the genus *Asio*, sometimes with the small species in the genera *Athene*, *Speotyto* and *Aegolius*.

Pseudoscops grammicus: confined to Jamaica.

Glaucidium cuculoides: open forest of oak, rhododendron and pine; tropical/sub-tropical evergreen jungle.

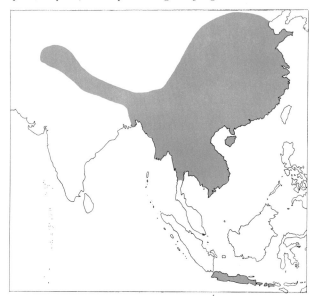

CHAPTER TEN

Conservation

Conservation is not synonymous with preservation, although it is concerned with taking measures to prevent extinction and minimize reductions in population, size or variety of the plants and animals in any defined area. It is realistic to acknowledge that changes will result from the urban and agricultural expansion necessary to cope with human population growth. Equally, conservationists must deplore the inability of man to limit his own numbers in relation to resources and support fundamental attempts to solve this basic problem. Conservation is based on ecological understanding and the planned use of land, water, air and other natural resources to prevent their destruction or waste. Sensible conservation recognizes the ecological interdependence of plants or animals on each other and it is within this broad context that the specific aspects involved in the conservation of owls must be seen. Conservation involves the management of plants and animals in both natural and man-altered environments: this management may involve rational exploitation, as in the case of game birds, attempts at control if species assume pest status, or strict protection, as when snowy owls (*Nyctea scandiaca*) nested for the first time in the Shetland Islands in 1967.

But while isolated or sensitive species may need rigorous protection from excessive disturbance, a modern understanding of bird population ecology has changed attitudes away from a negative 'leave well alone' approach. The prime objective is to ensure the provision of sufficient suitable natural habitat and given this ecological base most species can withstand considerable disturbance and will more or less look after themselves. Accordingly, two major approaches are adopted in conservation research. The first involves autecology, that is, the study of a single species as distinct from the community, in an attempt to define the habitat preferences and ecological needs of a species. Ideally such studies should reveal the factors affecting population size and the ability of the species to withstand interference.

The second aim of the conservationist is to provide a series of habitats in which as many species as possible can survive or to safeguard unique habitats even if they support relatively few species. The study of habitats involves an understanding of the physical factors (climate, hydrology and geology) as well as biotic factors (living component including the vegetation) which are responsible for the existence of a particular ecosystem. By ecosystem we mean the ecological system formed by the interaction of coacting organisms and their environment. Again the keynote must be management because many habitats of special interest are not stable climax communities and would change with time; for example, certain types of grassland are prone to revert to scrub and then woodland. The safeguarding and management of habitats which have remained virtually unaffected by man since the dawn of civilization has considerable historical and aesthetic appeal, as well as scientific value. Thus, although some species can survive, even flourish, in man-altered habitats, the need remains to manage some natural habitat for it is only in this context that the true significance of the structural and functional adaptations exhibited by the species can be understood.

We need to know much more about the factors regulating the population size of different species in order to devise sensible management programmes. Unfortunately, the field studies involved become increasingly difficult with rare species so, although we can have a reasonable knowledge of the principles involved, our knowledge has come from relatively common species rather than endangered ones. In general, birds, like all other animals, produce more young each year than are needed to replace adult losses. The excess young are available for colonizing vacant habitats but if none exists this population surplus is doomed, for the carrying capacity of the habitat limits the number of animals. In the case of small passerines, which have the potential for increasing their numbers up to eightfold in one breeding season, many of the surplus young birds provide food for predatory species. But in the absence of predators food stocks must eventually restrict numbers so that surplus individuals die of starvation and disease.

The only owl that has been studied in this respect is the tawny owl (*Strix aluco*) at Wytham Wood, Oxford, by Southern (1970). In his study area of 541 hectares the owl population was remarkably stable with about 30 pairs. It appeared that for a given habitat and range of density of prey there was a maximum density at which the owl population was regulated by territorial behaviour. The chief prey animals were woodmice (*Apodemus sylvaticus*), which varied in density from 4 to 7 per hectare, and bank voles (*Clethrionomys glareolus*) with a wide fluctuation in density of 6 to 40 per hectare. However, in some years at some seasons numbers fell below this level. The owl pairs had a territory of about 13 hectares in closed woodland and 20 hectares in mixed woodland and open ground once numbers had reached a stable level following the hard winter of 1946–7. It seems that territorial behaviour of this species living in a natural climax woodland has evolved to be on average of sufficient size to provide the adult with food. In Germany, where the food density averaged less, the mean territory size was 187 hectares per pair. Fluctuations in food resources at Oxford were first reflected in the ability of owls to lay eggs and then in their capacity to rear the chicks to fledging

The snowy owl *Nyctea scandiaca* nested in the Shetland Islands for the first time in 1967. Owl populations are regulated by the amount of prey available: in a year when plenty of food is available, all these owlets might survive.

and in the subsequent post-fledging survival of the juveniles; in 1958, when rodents were particularly scarce, all the owls failed to breed. Fluctuations in food resources did not lead to changes in the number of adult owls in the woods. Failure to breed and the laying of fewer eggs than potentially possible were the important factors influencing changes in total numbers (adults plus young) from one year to the next. The final adjustment of population size involved mortality of young in autumn and winter in almost perfect proportion to the number of birds alive (mortality was density-dependent) which led to numbers remaining virtually constant at the beginning of each breeding season. An important lesson is that there is a limit to the owl density in a given habitat, this being determined by territorial behaviour. It would be worth improving food resources if the resultant young could disperse to colonize new areas, otherwise this expediency would not make much difference to the survival prospects of the adults.

Southern was able to make predictions about tawny owl densities in other habitats and gave indications that the rate of population turnover varied according to the density of rodent prey. The tawny owl needs to acquire experience and expertise in order to hunt prey successfully in woodland, and its whole biology, including the stable territory habit, is geared to this end. Young birds remain with their parents from the time of fledging in late April/May until late July/early August during which time they learn about their surroundings and make no attempt to feed themselves. But quite the opposite applies to the moorland-dwelling short-eared owl (*Asio flammeus*) emphasizing the need to study different species on their own merit. This species alters the size of its territory from month to month according to the abundance of its main prey, the short-tailed vole (*Microtus agrestis*). If food is scarce the species becomes nomadic and seeks new hunting areas – posing quite different conservation requirements.

OWLS AND THEIR PREY

A particular habitat can support only a limited number of animals because the amount of energy available from soil nutrients and the sun determines how many simple plants and animals can exist to provide the base of the food chain. Since much energy is lost (80 to 90 per cent) at each trophic level in the food chain there are not usually more than five links before the top of the pyramid is reached and it is not surprising that these predators are vulnerable to any wastage in the exchange of energy in the ecosystem. Thus raptors and owls suffer first if the complexity of a food web becomes disturbed, for example, if the energy is channelled out of the system in the form of a game-bird crop. In this instance the problem is compounded by the activities of gamekeepers as discussed below. In general terms, natural habitats which support a complex web of life have predatory species occupying the top of the food chain, whereas man-exploited habitats do not because energy resources are deflected into other channels. The kinds of predator in any particular habitat are limited by the diversity of available prey in adequate numbers – major food items are either other birds or mammals though some owls and raptors eat large invertebrates – and these food items are diversified according to size. The raptors occupy the feeding niches available by day and the owls by night. For example, in deciduous temperate woodland foods for predators are mostly small or medium-sized birds or small mammals such as field mice, voles and shrews. By day the sparrow-hawk (*Accipiter nisus*) catches the small birds, while in suitable areas the goshawk (*A. gentilis*) favours the medium-sized birds and mammals, such as rabbits caught at the woodland edge. In these hawks the female is larger than the male so the food supply can be effectively partitioned into four size categories; in the New World three *Accipiter* hawks occur sympatrically (have the

same range) so there is a gradient of six sizes of predator. Female owls tend to be slightly bigger and heavier than the males, but the difference is by no means so great as with the *Accipiter* hawks. Perhaps the scope for partitioning prey by size is less in the case of owls which feed at night and rely to a greater extent on auditory rather than visual cues for locating prey.

The food of the tawny owl at Oxford comprised 95 per cent small and medium-sized mammals and only 4 per cent of the prey units were birds. Similar results were noted at Bookham Common, Surrey. However, in large urban areas where *Accipiter* hawks are absent tawny owls feed to a much greater extent on birds than in wood-land; at Holland Park, Kensington, in London, and in a Manchester suburb small birds contributed 93 and 89 per cent of the diet respectively. This implies an ability for flexibility which could help in the conservation of this species. In contrast, the long-eared owl does not appear to be flexible in this way. It normally feeds on a higher proportion of bird prey, about 10 to 20 per cent of all items, than the tawny owl and although a tree haunting species which can feed in open or closed woodland it also feeds over open country: woodmice and short-tailed field voles usually make up around 80 per cent of the prey. It is possible that the tawny owl competes with the long-eared owl in disturbed deciduous woodland. Certainly from being a relatively thinly but widely distributed species at the turn of the century, the long-eared owl has suffered a marked decline during the present century, particularly in Wales and southern England, having become scarce by the 1930s in many counties where it was previously well distributed. This decline occurred before toxic chemicals, suspected to have affected some species (see below), could be implicated, but when clearance of marginal land for agriculture was proceeding. In fact, several authors have commented on the fact that in various places long-eared owls have become replaced by tawny owls: in Northumberland, the Lake District, Wigtown. The long-eared owl appears not to have changed its status in Ireland where agricultural development has been slower than in Britain and where, moreover, the tawny owl is absent. This kind of situation often confronts the conservationist who discovers that a dynamic species can capitalize on the feeding opportunities (make use of the feeding niche available) in a man-altered habitat at the expense of closely related forms which are more critical in their ecological requirements. Fortunately the long-eared owl appears to be more successful than the tawny in coniferous woodland and it may prosper from the growth of coniferous forests, as has happened in Denmark. On a world basis the long-eared owl has a much wider distribution than the tawny and it also occurs in North America (page 140).

PRESERVING THE HABITAT

With flexible species like the tawny owl, conservation involves guaranteeing a number of areas of mature woodland, and is backed by the knowledge that the species will also live in sub-optimal habitats such as the very open parkland of, for example, the English farm. But how much woodland should be kept? How many tawny owls do we want? It is in making decisions of this kind that conservationists are faced with the difficult task of making value judgements rather than scientific decisions. These judgements have to reflect other requirements for land use and public needs. Fragmentation of deciduous woodland in those areas of Europe which are intensively farmed poses the problem of defining the minimum areas which can support viable populations of the woodland owls. The hunting territories of owls are so large that even in favoured woodland considerable areas are needed to hold reasonable sized populations. A reasonably sized population might be regarded as one which is self-sustaining and viable but we do not really know what is involved. It is not known over what distance sedentary species can communicate so that genetic interchange can continue. Special genetic conditions can apply in small isolated invertebrate populations but the topic is virtually unstudied so far as birds are concerned. Thus, instead of the gene frequency of the population remaining stable from one generation to the next, chance recombinations can occur which lead to local populations being formed which exhibit atypical genetic manifestations; this is known as genetic drift. So, while conservation policy must centre on safeguarding unique habitats, their size and distribution tend to reflect arbitrary factors such as what is available for sale, sympathetic land-owners, the activities of local and other conservation organizations, rather than scientific planning.

In passing, it may be noted that the first bird sanctuary established in Britain was at Walton Hall, Yorkshire, when in 1843 Charles Waterton stopped his gamekeeper from killing owls. When a species becomes very specialized conservation of course depends on protecting sufficient areas of the unique habitat. The spotted owl (*Strix occidentalis*) is a rare western counterpart of the widely distributed barred owl (*S. varia*) of North America. It inhabits heavy mature coniferous forest and wooded canyons. This habitat, particularly in Oregon, is being rapidly destroyed by modern clear-felling techniques and the species is becoming severely restricted in range, for it does not favour the new plantations which replace the old mature trees.

In the case of owls which have a cosmopolitan distribution, local scarcity can be balanced by protection in other regions. Special problems arise in the case of species formerly having a wide distribution which have become isolated in remote areas and speciated into new forms. The Seychelles owl (*Otus rutilus insularis*) was thought to be extinct but was discovered in one place in the mountains of Mahe in 1959. Unfortunately virtually nothing is known about its biology. Another owl which has significance for the study of evolution may only just be surviving today. This is the New Zealand laughing owl, (*Sceloglaux albifacies*), representative of a monotypic genus. It is a relict species which may well have survived an early colonization of New Zealand by an owl line now extinct. Only strict protection will keep the eagle owl (*Bubo bubo*) in Europe, where it has been largely exterminated by man.

The Seychelles owl *Otus rutilus insularis* was thought to be extinct, but was rediscovered in 1959 in one place in the mountains of Mahe.

SAGER

It frequents wild rocky and forested country, remote from man, and shuns cultivation. Its bulk makes it dependent on large prey, up to the size of young roe deer and foxes, so that extensive areas need to be set aside to support this kind of fauna. It has long been a practice in eastern Europe and Asia to take eagle owls as nestlings to use as decoys. Perched on a post they stimulate mobbing responses from other birds, which can be approached closely in their excitement and be killed or sometimes caught. The comments above regarding the capacity of birds to reproduce rapidly and replace themselves no longer apply when populations become fragmented and excessively disturbed. Breeding success declines and insufficient young are produced to make up for persecution, let alone colonize the places from which adults have disappeared.

Provision of reserves would in many situations be inadequate unless rigid legal protection was also afforded. In Britain, the first act for the protection of seabirds was passed in 1869, although before this time there had been a bill in 1822 protecting animals from cruelty. In 1872 an Act was passed protecting certain birds in the breeding season followed by the 'Wild Birds Protection Act 1880', which then remained the main legislation for over 75 years. This Act was spoiled by numerous orders which modified the close season locally and introduced confusion and it was only in 1954 that the 'Wild Birds Protection Act' rationalized the situation and gave full protection to owls and their eggs. This Act was modified in minor ways by the 'Protection of Birds Act 1967'. Other countries have schemes giving legal protection and have faced in various ways the problem of enacting legislation which can be effectively enforced. In many countries, bird protection is the responsibility of government departments concerned with agriculture and tends to favour game-preservation interests and the farmer. The Council (previously International Committee) for Bird Preservation was founded in 1922 by ornithological representatives from the U.S.A., Britain, France and Holland. It now covers over 60 countries, co-ordinates the needs of bird protection throughout the world and reviews the status of endangered species. It is an effective lobby in persuading governments to take remedial action when avifaunas become threatened.

Sometimes a new habitat can be created intentionally or otherwise which favours a particular species. The little owl (*Athene noctua*) was artificially introduced to Britain, particularly Kent and Northampton, late in the nineteenth century and spread to almost all England and Wales by 1925. It is a species well suited to farmland for its habits are more terrestrial than the other owls and it preys extensively on beetles and other large insects and earthworms. Numerous plantings of coniferous forest by the Forestry Commission have provided extensive new habitats throughout Britain, particularly on marginal hill land in the north and Scotland. Although extensive blocks of exotic conifer, e.g. Sitka spruce (*Picea sitkensis*) and Norway spruce (*P. abies*) have roused the wrath of many naturalists and conservationists there is no doubt that several species have profited. During the early stages of growth when the trees are less than 2 metres high an extensive grass cover develops which harbours numerous voles. Such sites are much favoured by the short-eared owl and hen harrier (*Circus cyaneus*) and both species have expanded their range and become more numerous for this reason. As the trees develop perhaps these species will be replaced by the long-eared owl; it is evident why a dynamic attitude to conservation must be adopted.

Provision of artificial nestboxes in areas lacking natural breeding sites but which are otherwise suitable can be effective. Many of the tawny owls studied by Southern at Oxford use such boxes and this has facilitated scientific study. Since foresters aim at healthy stands of trees and in many cases deplore old and rotting wood this expediency may be very important in some woodland.

THE EFFECTS OF PESTICIDES

The position of raptors and owls at the top of the food chain has made them particularly vulnerable to poisoning by various toxic chemicals which can be accumulated in sub-lethal doses by prey species and other animals lower in the chain. This major conservation problem has resulted from an enormous post-war expansion of industry, with resultant increase in toxic waste and an intensification of agricultural dependence on insecticides and herbicides. The agents causing most damage are stable fat soluble chemicals which are not readily broken down by decay processes in the environment. In consequence, they can be stored in the fatty tissue of animals with little or no immediate detrimental effect but they become concentrated in predatory species which eat these animals and cause death or serious sub-lethal consequences. The synthetic organochlorine compounds used as insecticides, of which D.D.T., dieldrin and heptachlor are important examples, have been a major source of environmental contamination, these having been applied directly to crops. Indirect but serious contamination has also resulted from the industrial waste of compounds such as the polychlorinated biphenyls (P.C.B.s).

In Britain an unexpected and synchronous decline occurred of the peregrine falcon (*Falco peregrinus*), sparrow hawk (*Accipiter nisus*), kestrel (*F. tinnunculus*) and barn owl (*Tyto alba*), coincident in time and space with introduction of the highly toxic organochlorine seed dressings. The barn owl had suffered a widespread decrease in the nineteenth century due to human persecution but subsequently partly recovered. Numbers probably fell slightly until the late 1940s but there was a marked and widespread drop after 1955, coinciding temporarily with the loss of the peregrine and other raptors and also a decline of the little owl. A national census of barn owls was held in 1963 under the auspices of the British Trust for Ornithology and it was discovered that

Poisoned tawny owl *Strix aluco*. The position of owls and other raptors at the top of the food chain makes them especially vulnerable to poisoning by various toxic chemicals, which can be accumulated in sub-lethal doses by prey species lower in the chain.

the decline was most widespread and sudden in eastern England, where arable farming was most intense. Many bodies of birds of prey were recovered containing high residues (over 16 parts of residue per million equivalent parts of tissue) of dieldrin which appeared to be the direct cause of their death. But argument and dissention greeted the early evidence for a decline of these predatory species and the situation was complicated by sub-lethal effects. For instance, peregrines, sparrowhawks and golden eagles began breaking their eggs with unprecedented frequency about 1950, the main reasons having been a decrease in egg-shell thickness and less efficient parental behaviour. Much research has been concentrated on establishing the temporal coincidence of egg-shell thinning with the increasing use of synthetic organochlorine compounds and in showing that agents like D.D.T. and gamma B.H.C. cause detrimental physiological changes, for example, by affecting the hormonal mechanisms involved in calcium metabolism, which become manifested in egg-shell thinning and egg infertility.

The population crash of peregrine falcons noted in Europe between 1950 and 1965 also occurred in North America and stimulated an important international conference sponsored by the University of Wisconsin. Experts reviewed current knowledge about the peregrine and other raptorial birds and presented their evidence that one of the most remarkable declines to be recorded in a wild animal population in recent years resulted from the widespread use of chlorinated hydrocarbon insecticides. The proceedings of the meeting, *Peregrine Falcons, their biology and decline*, were published by the University of Wisconsin Press in 1969.

In 1964, a voluntary ban was agreed between government, industry and the farmer on most uses of aldrin, dieldrin and heptachlor and there are indications that raptors are beginning to recover from the toxic contamination prevalent in the 1950s and early 1960s. Coincident with agreement for a voluntary ban, studies of predatory birds were initiated at the Monks Wood Experimental Station of the Nature Conservancy, ready to provide further data for the Advisory Committee on Pesticides and other Toxic Chemicals when they re-examined the problem in 1967. Requests were made for dead predators to be sent to Monks Wood for post-mortem examination and, in order of occurrence, kestrel, barn owl, tawny owl and sparrowhawk headed the list. But whereas 18 per cent of the kestrels and sparrowhawks examined contained tissue residues of either dieldrin or heptachlor in excess of 10 ppm or pp'-DDE in excess of 30 ppm (these are arbitrary levels at which it is highly likely that they caused the death of the subject) only 8 per cent of barn owls were so affected. Virtually all birds examined contained some residue but this need not have caused death; indeed in many cases the subject clearly died of injury, for instance through flying into telegraph wires. To date no information has been published on the sub-lethal effects of toxic residues in owls, for example, on egg-shell thinning, and these have been neglected in favour of intensive work on the more easily studied raptors.

In some cases it is known that particularly toxic chemicals will have detrimental side-effects. When endrin was used to control voles throughout 3459 acres of south German forests in 1957, 11 barn owls, 3 long-eared owls and 1 little owl were subsequently recovered dead. But probably the biggest threat to owls and other birds of prey is still the stupid and selfish behaviour of gamekeepers acting in the interest of game preservation. The intensity of persecution on some of the favoured game estates of eastern England, where predatory species have suffered most from habitat deterioration, is obviously sufficient to tip the balance against the birds. Indeed, many more raptors and owls would again establish themselves as breeding species if allowed freedom from the gamekeeper and his pole-traps. These unpleasant devices are absolutely illegal in Britain and involve placing a gin trap on top of a pole sited at a convenient perching site in some woodland ride. The Royal Society for the Protection of Birds organized a campaign against this practice in February 1972, by which date they had investigated the alleged destruction of birds of prey on 69 estates in Britain and found over 90 pole traps. The society has taken or been involved in 13 prosecutions.

Recently population statistics for sixteen bird species in the United States, including several owls and raptors, have been analysed to test whether any differences, possibly attributable to the use of pesticides, could be detected during the periods 1925–45 and 1946–65. First, the mortality rate for each during the two periods was calculated from the recoveries of ringed birds. Second, productivity was measured in terms of the clutch-size and mean proportion of young fledged per nest, while a third parameter, the age of sexual maturity of the species, was usually already known. From these data the recruitment rate necessary for a stable population, with the birth rate equalling the death rate, could be calculated and compared with the actual situation.

In the case of the great horned owl (*Bubo virginianus*) it was estimated that 1.47 young must be fledged per nesting attempt, including unsuccessful attempts, to maintain a stable population. The observed production in different areas of the United States was in close agreement with an average of 1.44 young per successful nest. In fact, both the recruitment and mortality rate appear to have remained relatively stable for the last forty years, with about 33 per cent of the adults dying each year.

In the case of the barn owl (*Tyto alba*) it was estimated that only 43–53 per cent of the population need nest successfully each year in the north-eastern United States to maintain a stable population and even fewer in the southern states (26 to 27 per cent). The differences depend on the fact that the reproductive rate and mortality rate are correlated with latitude. Thus in the north-eastern United States 4 to 16 young are produced per nest (4.43 in Switzerland) and 3.92 in the southern states, corresponding mortality rates being 50 per cent and 35 per cent (56 per cent in Switzerland). Again no changes in recruitment or mortality rates were detectable between the periods 1926–47 and 1948–67. Indeed, for none of the species studied was there any increase in mortality rate over the years. Nor was there any change in the recruitment rate, except for declines in the case of the brown pelican (*Pelecanus occidentalis*), osprey (*Pandion haliaetus*), Cooper's hawk (*Accipiter cooperii*), red-shouldered hawk (*Buteo lineatus*), and American sparrowhawk (*Falco sparverius*). These species have all suffered population declines which other studies have attributed to pesticide use and they feed on fish, reptiles, amphibians or birds. But, a survey in 1972 found that no change in recruit-ment rate was detectable in any of the species which feed primarily on mammals and this included the owls. The indications are that, compared with certain of the raptors, the feeding habits of owls have fortunately not made them particularly vulnerable to pesticide contamination.

CHAPTER ELEVEN

Owl pellets

Bird pellets, or castings, are accumulations of the undigested portions of food items consumed by birds which are not excreted in the normal manner as faeces, but are regurgitated through the mouth in compact masses. They are usually composed of hard, not easily digested, materials of comparatively little nutritional value to birds – the bones, claws, beaks or teeth of mammals, birds, reptiles, amphibians and fishes; the headparts, thorax or wing-cases of insects; the jaws and chaetae of earthworms; seed husks and other coarse vegetable materials. These hard parts of food items are usually enclosed by softer, but indigestible, substances such as the fur of mammals, bird feathers and vegetable fibres. Thus the bird's pellet is often characteristic and provides valuable clues about the type of prey.

Pellets are often associated exclusively with the nocturnal and diurnal birds of prey but, according to a survey by the International Bird Pellet Study Group in 1969, 330 species of over 60 families produce pellets. These include common Old World birds like the robin (*Erithacus rubecula*) and starling (*Sturnus vulgaris*), waterside feeders such as the kingfisher (*Alcedo atthis*) and heron (*Ardea cinerea*), and farmland species like the rook (*Corvus frugilegus*) and tree sparrow (*Passer montanus*).

All members of the four raptor families which have been studied in detail are known to produce pellets regularly – the Tytonidae and Strigidae (owls), Accipitridae (kites, hawks, eagles, harriers) and Falconidae (falcons). The pellets form in response to a mechanical barrier posed by the small pyloric opening – an extension of the stomach – and in the absence of free acidity in the stomach digestion cannot take place and resistant materials are periodically regurgitated. These can prove extremely valuable in a study of the food habits of a species. This is particularly so in the case of the owls because their ability to digest bone is poor and consequently any pellets produced contain a good skeletal record of the prey eaten. Furthermore, unlike the diurnal raptors which have very stout beaks and strong neck muscles which enable them to tear and partially consume prey, owls generally bolt entire, suitably sized food items. As a result a careful examination of their pellets can provide an accurate record of the diet.

The identification of food traces is often a difficult and time consuming job. Certain species produce pellets that are both easy to collect and analyse, but all material is worth examining. Apart from providing valuable information about various aspects of the diet of owls – individual tastes, seasonal, regional and habitat differences etc. – they have important secondary uses. Owl pellets of many species provide rapid field indicators of the presence and often relative abundance of mammals and other animals in an area – data of value to local and national surveys. Some owls are effective samplers of small mammals, producing skeletal material in quantities that would take many hours of trapping to accumulate, and owl pellets often also include bird rings. Finally, as an educational tool, they can be used effectively to demonstrate the role of avian predators in the ecosystem, and the nature of food chains.

Pellets are found at day-time roosts and night-time feeding stations – but their accumulation varies from species to species. The habits of two of the more widely studied owls, the open country barn owl and woodland dwelling tawny owl illustrate this point. The barn owl frequents a wide variety of open habitats – pastoral, arable and mixed farmland, upland pasture, water-meadows, saltmarsh, open parkland and deciduous woodland, waste ground and the rough grassland associated with young forestry planta-tions, open downland and disused quarries. Small pellets are formed and regurgitated at night while the bird is hunting and larger second pellets are later deposited at the day-time roost or nesting site, which is often in a farm barn, disused or derelict building, haystack or hedgerow tree. Such sites quickly become littered with pellets, and sizeable samples can be collected at regular intervals. If the owls are not disturbed excessively, such sites may be frequented for months, even years. The pellets of other open country hunters such as the snowy owl, little owl, elf owl and short-eared owl can also be most profitably collected at the day-time roost or at obvious vantage points on the bird's hunting range.

In contrast, collecting tawny owl pellets (and those of other woodland owls) in quantity can prove to be a very time consuming business. The tawny owl frequents woodland, copses, well-timbered gardens, parkland, farmland and even urban areas and, though it is a strongly terri-torial and sedentary species, the nocturnal roosts and feeding stations at which it deposits pellets are usually well scattered. During the winter, when it roosts high up in trees, the falling pellets quickly become scattered and fragmented. In the summer months tawny owl pellets quickly break down among the moist ground vegetation. However, it is a species that will take fairly readily to nestboxes and, by regularly visiting the nest and locating surrounding tree roosts, useful collections of pellets and prey remains can be made.

It is often possible to identify the origin of a pellet without seeing the owl, but generally a view of the predator at the nest or roost is desirable. In general terms, the larger the owl, the larger the pellet. Those of the eagle owl are normally 70 to 110 mm in length and 30 to 40 mm in width, the long-eared owl normally 35 to 65 mm by 15 to 25 mm and the little owl's pellets 30 to 40 mm by 10 to 15 mm. Such sizes are

dependent to a degree on the hunting success of the owl, which has been shown to be affected by weather conditions in several species. Strong winds and rain affect the hunting success of open country species like the barn owl, which may produce a small pellet as a result, while wet conditions often result in tawny owls casting up fibre pellets containing the remains of earthworms, beetles, slugs, or other invertebrates, which are often easy prey in wet weather.

Methods of dissecting the pellets vary with the size of the sample and type of information required. Each sample collected should be dried and stored. In the case of small samples, each

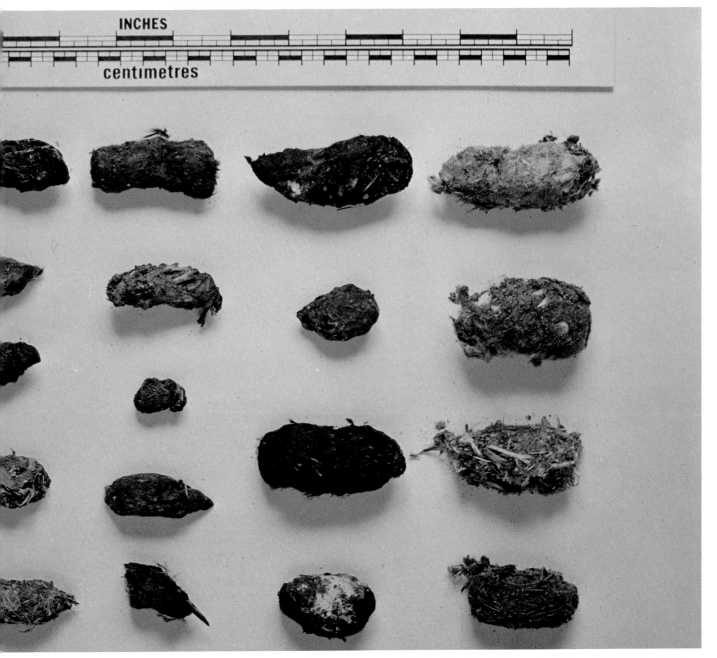

Owl pellets. Vertical rows from left to right: little owl *Athene noctua*, long-eared owl *Asio otus*, short-eared owl *Asio flammeus*, tawny owl *Strix aluco*, barn owl *Tyto alba* and snowy owl *Nyctea scandiaca*.

pellet can be placed in a separate polythene envelope containing naphthalene, and analysed separately. The insecticide is necessary because pellets form suitable repositories for insect eggs and, if these are allowed to hatch, the emerging fly, moth or beetle larvae, combined with fungal attack, will quickly reduce the pellet to a disintegrated mass of bone fragments.

After recording the dry weight and size of the pellet, it can be broken down in a dry state with dissecting needles or forceps. Where large samples are involved the pellets can be soaked in a dish of warm water and the contents separated with forceps or by a mechanical rotating paddle. The

aim is to separate the hard parts (bones and chitinous fragments) from the softer substances (fur, feathers and fibre), so that individual prey items can be examined under a good pocket lens or low power microscope. In well-studied areas, regional handbooks are sometimes available to help in identifying fragments of prey. Where problems arise, local or national museums may

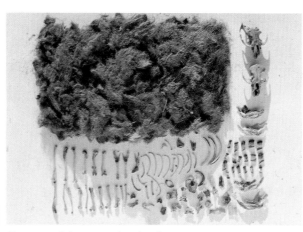

Contents of short-eared owl pellet.

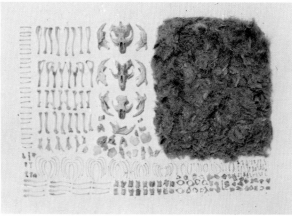

Contents of long-eared owl pellet.

Contents of snowy-owl pellet.

help. The shape, size and particularly dentition of vertebrate skulls are important in identification, as are the head-parts, wing-cases and appendages of invertebrates. It is often possible to accumulate a reference collection of prey traces quickly by storing named items in glass tubes or plastic pill boxes, or by mounting them washed and varnished on stiff board.

After analysis and identification of prey species, care is needed in drawing conclusions about diet. The pellets of some birds contain a very biased record of the birds' diet. Those of the heron, for instance, are composed of little more than a mass of clumped hair. Its digestive powers are good and only the most resistant hard parts remain – the ear-bones of fish and cheek teeth of mammals for example. Although the digestive powers of owls are poorer, the same principle applies. Soft-bodied foods, such as nestling birds and certain invertebrates, may be overlooked or not properly identified. Small mammals or birds may be decapitated or larger food items may be partially consumed (often when parent owls are feeding their young), so complicating any analysis. Similarly, the skulls of small insectivorous birds, amphibians and reptiles will frequently disintegrate, placing an emphasis on the correct identification of bones such as the pelvic girdle, sternum and synsacrum.

Batches of 20 pellets or 40 or more prey items are normally required to provide a basic indication of an owl's diet at any one time – indeed, the larger the sample the better. Invertebrate prey such as earthworms and beetles can rarely be quantified and should be expressed on a presence or absence basis. Larger food items can be added together and expressed as a percentage of the prey total, in tabular form or as pie diagrams. Listing foods in this way can, however, give a false impression of the relative nutritional value of a food item to the owl. Clearly, small animals such as pygmy shrews (*Sorex minutus*) or house sparrows (*Passer domesticus*) are of much less importance to the owl, than, for example, brown rats (*Rattus norvegicus*) or blackbirds (*Turdus merula*). Conversion factors based on the weight of prey item must be applied if nutritional values are required.

Pellets, therefore, are a useful source of data: careful searching in the field, patient analysis in the laboratory and careful interpretation of findings can provide a wealth of information about the feeding habits of the world's owls.

PART III

Check list of species

This check list is based on that of J. L. Peters (*Birds of the World*, Vol IV (1940), Harvard University Press). The sequence is basically the same as his, but where new information is available, the list has been brought up to date. This is particularly noticeable in the case of the genus *Otus*. Drs Hekstra is in the process of re-arranging the genus extensively, and the *Otus* section is based on his revisions.

CLASS: Aves
ORDER: STRIGIFORMES

FAMILY: *TYTONIDAE* (Barn and grass owls)
SUBFAMILY: *TYTONINAE*
GENUS: *TYTO*

Tyto soumagnei	Madagascar owl
T. alba	Common barn owl
T. rosenbergii	Celebes barn owl
T. inexpectata	Minahassa barn owl
T. novaehollandiae	Masked owl
T. aurantia	New Britain barn owl
T. tenebricosa	Sooty owl
T. capensis	Common grass owl
(including *T. longimembris*)	

SUBFAMILY: *PHODILINAE* (Bay owls)

Phodilus badius	Common bay owl
P. prigoginei	Congo bay owl

FAMILY: *STRIGIDAE*
SUBFAMILY: *BUBONINAE* (Typical owls)
GENUS: *OTUS*

Otus lawrencii	Cuban screech owl
O. guatemalae	Vermiculated screech owl
O. nudipes	Puerto Rican screech owl
O. barbarus	Santa Barbara screech owl
O. atricapillus	Black-capped screech owl
O. watsonii	Tawny-bellied screech owl
O. ingens	Rufescent screech owl
O. clarkii	Bare-shanked screech owl
O. albogularis	White-throated screech owl
O. choliba	Choliba screech owl
O. roboratus	Roborate screech owl
O. cooperi	Pacific screech owl
O. trichopsis	Spotted screech owl

O. asio	Eastern screech owl
O. kennicotti	Western screech owl
O. leucotis	White-faced scops owl
O. manadensis	Celebes scops owl
O. podarginus	Palau scops owl
O. alfredi	Flores scops owl
O. rutilus	Madagascan scops owl
O. sunia	Oriental scops owl
O. scops	Common scops owl
O. flammeolus	Flammulated owl
O. bakkamoena	Collared scops owl
O. brookii	Rajah's scops owl
O. silvicolus	Lesser Sunda scops owl
O. rufescens	Reddish scops owl
O. icterorhynchus	Sandy scops owl
O. ireneae	Sokoke scops owl
O. spilocephalus	Spotted scops owl
O. balli	Andaman scops owl
O. hartlaubi	São Thomé scops owl
O. sagittatus	White-fronted scops owl
O. gurneyi	Giant scops owl

GENUS: *LOPHOSTRIX*

Lophostrix lettii	Maned owl
L. cristata	Crested owl

GENUS: *BUBO*

Bubo virginianus	Great horned owl
B. bubo	Eurasian eagle owl
B. capensis	Cape eagle owl
B. africanus	Spotted eagle owl
B. poensis	Fraser's eagle owl
B. nipalensis	Forest eagle owl
B. sumatrana	Malaysian eagle owl
B. shelleyi	Shelley's eagle owl
B. lacteus	Milky eagle owl
B. coromandus	Dusky eagle owl
B. leucostictus	Akun eagle owl
B. philippensis	Philippine eagle owl

GENUS: *KETUPA*

Ketupa blakistoni	Blakiston's fish owl
K. zeylonensis	Brown fish owl
K. flavipes	Tawny fish owl
K. ketupa	Malaysian fish owl

GENUS: *SCOTOPELIA*

Scotopelia peli	Pel's fishing owl
S. ussheri	Rufous fishing owl
S. bouvieri	Vermiculated fishing owl

GENUS: *PULSATRIX*

Pulsatrix perspicillata	Spectacled owl
P. koeniswaldiana	White-chinned owl
P. melanota	Rusty-barred owl

GENUS: *NYCTEA*

Nyctea scandiaca	Snowy owl

GENUS: *SURNIA*

Surnia ulula	Hawk owl

GENUS: *GLAUCIDIUM*

Glaucidium passerinum	Eurasian pygmy owl
G. gnoma	Northern pygmy owl
G. siju	Cuban pygmy owl
G. minutissimum	Least pygmy owl
G. brasilianum	Ferruginous pygmy owl
(including *G. jardinii*)	
G. perlatum	Pearl-spotted owlet
G. tephronotum	Red-chested owlet
G. capense	Barred owlet
G. brodiei	Collared pygmy owl
G. radiatum	Barred jungle owlet
G. cuculoides	Cuckoo owlet
G. sjostedti	Chestnut-backed owlet

GENUS: *MICRATHENE*

Micrathene whitneyi	Elf owl

GENUS: *UROGLAUX*

Uroglaux dimorpha	Papuan hawk owl

GENUS: *NINOX*

Ninox rufa	Rufous owl
N. strenua	Powerful owl
N. connivens	Barking owl
N. novaeseelandiae	Boobook owl
N. scutulata	Oriental hawk owl
N. affinis	Andaman hawk owl
N. superciliaris	Madagascar hawk owl
N. philippensis	Philippine hawk owl
(including *N. spilonota*, *N. spilocephala*)	
N. perversa	Ochre-bellied hawk owl
N. squamipila	Moluccan hawk owl
N. theomacha	Sooty-backed hawk owl
N. punctulata	Speckled hawk owl
N. meeki	Admiralty Islands hawk owl
N. solomonis	New Ireland hawk owl
N. odiosa	New Britain hawk owl
N. jacquinoti	Solomon Islands hawk owl

GENUS: *SCELOGLAUX*

Sceloglaux albifacies	Laughing owl (thought to be extinct)

GENUS: *ATHENE*

Athene noctua	Little owl
A. brama	Spotted little owl
A. blewitti	Forest little owl

GENUS: *SPEOTYTO*

Speotyto cunicularia	Burrowing owl

GENUS: *CICCABA*

Ciccaba virgata	Mottled owl
C. nigrolineata	Black and white owl
C. huhula	Black-banded owl
C. albitarsus	Rufous-banded owl
C. woodfordii	African wood owl

SUBFAMILY: *STRIGINAE*

GENUS: *STRIX*

Strix butleri	Hume's wood owl
S. seloputo	Spotted wood owl
S. ocellata	Mottled wood owl
S. leptogrammica	Brown wood owl
S. aluco	Tawny owl
S. occidentalis	Spotted owl
S. varia	Barred owl
S. hylophila	Rusty-barred owl
S. rufipes	Rufous-legged owl
S. uralensis	Ural owl
(including *S. davidi*)	
S. nebulosa	Great grey owl

GENUS: *RHINOPTYNX*

Rhinoptynx clamator	Striped owl

GENUS: *ASIO*

Asio otus	Long-eared owl
(including *A. abyssinicus*)	
A. stygius	Stygian owl
A. madagascariensis	Madagascar long-eared owl
A. flammeus	Short-eared owl
A. capensis	African marsh owl

GENUS: *PSEUDOSCOPS*

Pseudoscops grammicus	Jamaican owl

GENUS: *NESASIO*

Nesasio solomonensis	Fearful owl

GENUS: *AEGOLIUS*

Aegolius funereus	Tengmalm's (Boreal) owl
A. acadicus	Saw-whet owl
A. ridgwayi	Unspotted saw-whet owl
A. harrisii	Buff-fronted owl

Owl voices

Nocturnal animals with no sense of smell depend on acoustic utterances for their communication. Most owls have, therefore, developed a great variety of vocalizations. Often very beautiful, these vocalizations make it possible to distinguish an owl species from other species living in the same area. Even very similar species may easily be told apart by listening to their songs. Allopatric species, in contrast, may have similar songs, even if they are not closely related. For instance, the beautiful monotonous 8-second trill, which is given by the Southeast Asiatic *Glaucidium cuculoides*, can also be heard from *Otus guatemalae* in Central and South America.

Although similar songs may occur in species belonging to different genera, an astonishing amount of variation is sometimes found between races of the same species. In dealing with the phenomenon of geographical variation, literature still too often refers only to morphological characters. Since the early works of Bernard Rensch and Ernst Mayr, however, we know that characters of *all* kinds may vary geographically within the same species; and song is no exception to this rule. The white-faced scops owl *Otus leucotis* from Africa and the eastern screech owl *O. asio* from North America provide striking examples of this, and geographic song variation may in fact occur in all owl species with large distributional areas.

It is difficult to deal with bird songs in a book, because they are difficult to express in syllables. Fortunately, a fair number of owls have songs of a comparatively simple nature, which can be characterized in words. The songs are presented here in Tables as often as possible, to make it easy for the reader to compare a song with the song of a related species with which he may be more familiar. Only common songs, which will normally be of a territorial nature, are given. It should be borne in mind that, in several owl species, both male and female give the territorial song, with just a difference in pitch, the female often singing higher. Tables will provide information on geographical song variation in only few species. This does not mean that such variation is absent in the remaining species, but simply that our knowledge about these is still incomplete. Of still other species, notably those from tropical rain forests, nothing is known as regards habits and song.

Problems exist in the study of owl songs not only on the descriptive level, but also on the functional level. For instance, how do some nocturnal species like the barn owl manage to live without any loud vocalization?

Explanation to Tables

The tables mainly provide information as to tempo and number of syllables of the songs. The whole scale denotes about 10 seconds but in general no absolute values are aimed at. That is, the reader should always compare a given song with a song familiar to him. The following system has been followed as to intervals and pitch:
in sequence of decreasing tempo:
huhu hu-hu hu hu hu hu etc.
in sequence of decreasing pitch: *he, hü, hu, ho*. (*ü* to be pronounced as in French *tu* or German *Glück*)
A rapid trill has been presented in the form:
h-h-h-h-h-h-h.

This system only applies to the genera *Phodilus*, *Jubula*, *Otus*, *Glaucidium*, *Bubo*, *Ciccaba* and *Strix*, the songs of which have been written down from tape-recordings (unless otherwise stated). These genera have been dealt with by Wouter van der Weyden, who also wrote the introduction. The system does not apply to the remaining genera, which have been treated by Howard Ginn, on the basis of song-descriptions in the literature.

Otus

There is a great variety of beautiful songs in the large group of scops and screech owls. A common character of their songs is the monotonous, regular repetition of short, musical notes. Differences between species mainly pertain to tempo, arrangement and pitch of the notes. Screech owls (mainly New World) usually have rapid songs, consisting of many notes. Scops owls (mainly Old World), on the contrary, have slower songs, consisting of only a few notes. Well-known examples are the rapid trill of the eastern screech owl *Otus asio* from North America, and the single, pure whistle of the European scops owl *O. scops*, respectively.

An interesting, musical song is found in the Japanese *O. sunia*. This bird gives a repetition of three notes. Not infrequently, the first note is omitted, but the bird will exactly keep time, as if it were western music or poetry: ♩♩♩ | ♩♩♩ | ♩♩ | ♩♩♩ etc. In Korea, the two songs are perhaps more distinct, since the native people ascribe different meanings to them: if the bird gives three syllables, they believe that harvest will be rich, but if only two syllables are heard, the crop will be poor.

Some *Otus* species are well known for the perseverance with which they give their monotonous notes for hours on end. They are capable of an unbelievable clockwork regularity. One specimen of the European scops owl was observed to give its whistle 120 times in succession, at intervals of $2\frac{1}{2}$–3 seconds, without aberration! Even imitation of the song will sometimes not disturb the rhythm.

SCREECH OWLS

Otus lawrencii:
Described as an accelerating *coooo-cooo-coo-cu-cu-cu*, becoming somewhat higher at the end.

O. guatemalae: Mexico
h-h-h-h-h-h-h-h-h-h-h-h-h-h-h-h-h-h-h-h-h-h-h-h-h-h-h-h-h-h-h-h-h-h-h-h-h-h-h-h-h-h-h-h-h-h-h-h-h-h-h-h, ... Pure trill of 8–9 seconds with gradual crescendo

O. guatemalae: Venezuela
h-h-h-h-h-h-h-h-h-h-h-h-h-h-h-h-h-h-h-h-h-h-h-h-h, ... Pure trill of 3–6 seconds, higher than in Mexico

O. nudipes:
h-h-h-h-h-h-h-h-h-h-h-h-h-h-h-h, ... Pure trill of 2–3 seconds, lower than in Mexico

O. barbarus: Not described

O. atricapillus: Not described

O. watsonii: Not known, but a series of 20–25 low, mellow whistles has been attributed to it: *hoo hoo hoo* etc.

O. ingens: Not known

O. clarkii: Not known

O. albogularis:
1. *huhuhuhuhuhuhuhu,* . . . . Series of 7–17 clear notes, repeated at varying intervals
2. *ko-ko-koko-koko-koko-koko-koko-koko-koko-ko-ko-ko-ko-ko-ko* . . . . Series of 15–32 notes, repeated at varying intervals

O. choliba:
1. *w-h-h-h-h-h-h-h-h-h-h-h-uu,* . . . . *w-h-h-h-h-h-h-h-h-h-h-h-uu,* . . . . . Last one or two notes accentuated; repeated at regular intervals
2. *hu-hu-hu-hu-hu-hu-hu-hu-hu,* . . . . Series of 3–16 notes, repeated at varying intervals

O. roboratus: Not described

O. cooperi:
1. *kô-kô-kô-kô-kô-kô-kô-kô-kô-kô-kô-kô-kô-kô,* . . . . Very gruff voice; repeated at varying intervals
2. *k-k-k-k-k kôkôkôkôkôkôkôkôkôkôkô,* . . . . Very gruff voice; repeated at varying intervals

O. trichopsis:
1. *hu-hu-hu-hu-hu-hu-hu-hu,* . . . . *hu-hu-hu-hu-hu-hu-hu-hu,* . . . . Series of 5–14 clear notes, sometimes slightly slowing down. Intervals not very regular
2. *hu-hu hu hu   hu-hu hu hu   hu-hu hu hu hu,* . . . . Usually a sequence of 2–5 series, normally given in duets. Also variations, like *hu-hu-hu-hu hu hu hu*

O. asio:
1. *hühühühuhuhu,* . . . . Long, decending 'whinny' with tremolo, repeated at irregular intervals. In Texas only *hüüüü*
2. *h-h-h-h-h-h-h-h-h-h-h-h-h-h-h-h-h-h-h-h-h-h-h,* . . . . 'Single trill' of 2–4 seconds' duration

O. kennicotti
1. *hu hu hu hu hu-hu-hu* . . . . Known as 'bouncing ball', because of accelerando
2. *h-h-h-h-h-h h-h-h-h-h-h-h-h-h-h-h-h,* . . . . Known as 'double trill'

O. leucotis: West Africa
ku kuoo, ... *ku kuoo,* . . . . Second note with downward inflection

O. leucotis: Southern Africa
w-h-h-h-h-h-h-h-oo, ... *w-h-h-h-h-h-h-h-oo,* . . Last note accentuated

Otus manadensis: Celebes
1. *hüee,* . . . . *hüee,* . . . .
2. *hüüü,* . . . . *hüüü,* . . . .

Otus manadensis: Halmahera
kru, ... *kru,* . . . . .   Timbre perhaps somewhat different than suggested here

O. manadensis: Ryukyu
hü kyühü, . . . *hü kyühü,* . . . *hü kyühü,* . . . *hü kyühü,* . . . *hü kyühü,* . . . *hü kyühü,* . . . *hü kyühü,* . . . etc

O. podarginus
Described as a sharp, whistled quirt, repeated at intervals of about 2 seconds.

O. alfredi: Not known

O. rutilus: Madagascar, Mayotte
hu hu hu hu hu hu hu hu, ... *hu hu hu hu hu hu hu,* . .   Series of 3–10 syllables, repeated at regular intervals

O. rutilus: Gran Comoro
hu hu hu hu hu hu hu hu hu hu hu hu hu hu hu hu hu hu hu hu hu hu hu hu hu hu hu hu hu hu etc   Timbre perhaps different; said to resemble *cho* (*o* as in *gone*)

O. rutilus: Pemba
hu hu hu hu hu hu hu hu hu hu hu hu hu hu hu hu hu hu hu hu hu hu hu hu hu hu hu hu hu hu etc   Timbre perhaps somewhat different

O. rutilus: Seychelles
Described as *toc-toc*, like knocking in of wedges by woodsman.

O. sunia: SE Asia
ku ku ku-ku, . . . *ku ku ku-ku,* . . . *ku ku ku-ku,* . . . *ku ku ku-ku,* . . . *ku ku ku-ku,* . . . *ku ku ku-ku,* etc

O. sunia: Japan and Korea
yü kyü hü, . . . *yü kyü hü,* . . . *yü kyü hü,* . . . . *kyü hü,* . . . *yü kyü hü,* . . . *yü kyü hü,* . . . etc

O. sunia: Middle East
Described as consisting of 2 syllables. Probably resembling *ku ku*.

O. scops: Southern Africa
krrr, ... *krrr,* . . . . *krrr,* . . . .   Timbre variable

O. scops: West Africa
kürürü, ... *kürürü,* . . . .   Timbre variable

O. scops: Europe to Turkestan
kyüü, ... *kyüü,* . . . . *kyüü,* . . . . *kyüü,* . . . . *kyüü,* . . . . . .   Clear bell-like whistle

O. flammeolus:
hoo, ... *hoo,* . . . . *hoo,* . . . . *hoo,* . . . .   Sometimes 2 hoots at a time: *hoo hoo*; or a few grace-notes before each hoot: *k-k hoo*

O. bakkamoena: Indo-China to Nepal
huw, ... *huw,* . . . .   With downward inflection

O. bakkamoena: Java
wuu, ... *wuu,* . . . . .   With upward inflection

O. brookii:
Said to be a clear, startling note, repeated monotonously.

O. silvicolus: Not known

O. rufescens:
hüüüü, ... *hüüüü,* . . . .

O. icterorhynchus: Not known

O. ireneae:
hü hü hü hü hü hü hü hü hü hü hü hü hü hü hü hü hü hü hü hü hü hü hü hü hü etc

O. spilocephalus:
he . . . . *he,* . . . . *he* . . . . *he,* . . . . *he* . . . *he,* . . . .   Clear whistles, sometimes sounding like *ple* . . . *ple*, . . . etc. songs of the many distinct subspecies are not described.

O. balli: Not known

O. hartlaubi: Not known

O. sagittatus: Not known

O. gurneyi: Not known

Glaucidium

Pygmy owl songs usually consist of repetitions of short, musical notes, thus resembling the songs of scops and screech owls. But prolonged mewing sounds and harsh calls occur also. *Glaucidium perlatum* from Africa gives a series of prolonged descending whistles, very characteristic, but difficult to syllabify. It is known of several species of *Glaucidium* that, if one imitates its song anywhere in its habitat, a whole army of passerine birds is attracted, searching to drive away the intruder. By giving these imitations, ornithologists are sometimes able to discover new bird species for a given area.

Glaucidium passerinum:
1. *hü, ... hü, ... hü, ... hü, ... hü, ... hü, ...*

Intervals 1–3 seconds. Sometimes double notes like *hü-hü*. Often 1–4 preceding grace notes, like: *t-t hü*

2. *hu hu hü hü hee hee . . . .*

As type 3 of *G. gnoma*

G. gnoma:
1. *hü hü hü hü hü hü hü hü hü hü hü hü hü, ...*

Series of 10–15 clear notes, given at the rate of about 3–4 notes every 2 seconds

2. *hü, ... hü, ... hü, ... hü, ... hü, ... hü, ...*
3. *hu hu hü hü hee hee . . . .*

Normally 5–8 startling notes, running up the scale

G. siju:
1. Described as a startling shrill *ku-ku-ku-se-se-si-si-si*, rising in tone.
2. Another type is described as a slowly repeated *too-too too*

G. minutissimum:
Said to consist of 4 whistling notes, with a slight pause between the first two.

G. brasilianum:
hüj hüj hüj hüj hüj hüj hüj hüj hüj hüj hüj hüj hüj hüj hüj hüj hüj hüj hüj, ...

Series 11–33 notes, each one with an upward inflection, uttered at the rate of about 5–6 notes every 2 seconds

G. perlatum:
1. *hu hu hü hü hee hee heeew heeew heeew heeew heeew heeew heeew . . . .*

The series becomes higher after the first note, then follow slower whistles, protracted and with downward inflection

2. *hü hü hü hü hü hü hü hü hü hü hü hü hü hü hü hü hü hü hü hü hü . . . .*

A series of 20–25 notes, somewhat rising in pitch and volume

G. tephronotum:
1. Described as similar to the mewing song of *G. perlatum*, though fainter.
2. Another type is described as a soft, fluting, or ringing *hoo hoo hoo*.

G. capense:
hü hü hü hü hü hü hü hü hü hü hü hü hü . . . .

A series of 10–14 clear notes, uttered at the rate of about 2 notes per second; the series shows a crescendo at the start and sometimes a diminuendo at the end; the notes may have a downward inflection

G. brodiei:
1. *hü hü-hü hü, ... hü hü-hü hü, ... hü hü-hü hü, ... hü hü-hü hü, ... hü hü-hü hü, ...*

Usually 3–4 series in succession, the initial and final series softer and incomplete

2. *klü-klü-klü-klü-klü-klü-klü-klü-klü-klü-klü-klü-klü-kü-kü ku ku ku . . . .*

A series of 13–20 clear notes. Becoming somewhat softer and slower towards the end

G. radiatum:
1. Described as: *kro kro kra kra kra kra kra*, a series of 4–8 notes.
2. Described as: *kakuk kakuk kakuk kakuk kakuk kakuk kakuk kakuk kakuk*.

G. cuculoides:
1. *h-h-h-h-h-h-h-h-h-h-h-h-h-h-h-h-h-h-h-h-h-h-h-h-h-h-h-h-h-h-h-h-h-h-h-h-h-h-h-h-h-h-h-h-h-h-h, ...*

A pure trill of 7–14 seconds' duration, sometimes less

2. A crescendo of harsh squawks, rapidly rising in pitch, to end with some hysterical cries.

G. sjöstedti: Not known

Ciccaba

Ciccaba virgata:
1. *bu bu bu bo, ...*

Repeated at intervals (long? irregular?)

2. *ho ho ho ho ho ho ho ho ho ho ho ho ho ho-ho-hoho, ...*

Series of 13–21 hoots in rising accelerando, the last hoots becoming softer and lower. Also long drawn out rising, screech-like note

C nigrolineata:
1. *hoou hoou hoou hoou hoou hoou hoou hoou hoo hoo, ...*

Series of 5–11 hoots, each hoot protracted and with upward inflection

2. *ho ho hu hu huuw huuw,* . . . . First 4 hoots rising in pitch; accent on last two

C. huhula: Not known, but if this owl is conspecific with *C. nigrolineata*, their songs will be similar.

C. albitarsus: Not known.

C. woodfordi:
1. *uwuuuw,* . . . . *uwuuuw,* . . Often in combination with type 2, especially in duets

C. woodfordi: East and South Africa
2. *hu-ho hu-hoho-hoho,* . . . . Repeated at long intervals

C. woodfordi: West Africa
2. *ho-hu ho-hu-hu-hu,* . . . . Repeated at long intervals

Strix

Strix butleri:
Described as a clear long-drawn *huu* uttered at intervals, sometimes varied by a tremulous and more throaty hoot as in *S. aluco*.

S. seloputo:
1. *hooo,* . . . . *hooo,* . . Repeated at rather long intervals

2. Also rapid or rolling series of hoots.

S. ocellata:
1. Described as a loud, quavering, eerie *chūhūa-aa*, uttered regularly.
2. Also a single, mellow, metallic hoot.

S. leptogrammica:
Described as a series of four (Thailand) or three (India/Ceylon) hoots.

S. aluco:
1. *hüüüüw* . . . . *hü hühühühü,* . . . . Characteristic pause of 3–6 seconds between first and second part. Last part a descending tremolo
2. *üwee,* . . . . Repeated at irregular intervals

S. occidentalis:
1. Described as: *ho ho-ho hoo,* . . . . A series of 3–5 hoots
2. *ho ho ho ho ho ho ho ho ho ho ho ho hu hu hu,* . . . .

S. varia:
1. *hu hu hu-hu* . . . . *hu hu hu-hu-aw,* . . . . Usually syllabified as: *who cooks for yóu, who cooks for yóu all?*
2. *ho ho hu hu hu hu hu hu hu hu hu hu-huuw,* . . . . A series of 7–15 powerful hoots

S. hylophila: Not known

S. rufipes: Not known

S. uralensis:
1. *huho* . . . . *hoho hoho,* . . . . Characteristic pause of 2–5 seconds between first and second part. The latter somewhat variable
2. *hohohohohohohohohuhuho,* . . . . Somewhat increasing in pitch and loudness, descending again at the end

S. nebulosa:
hoo   hoo   hoo   hoo   hoo   hoo   hoo   hoo   hoo   hoo   hoo   hoo, ... A series of 9–14 low hoots

Bubo

Most eagle owls give low, mournful hoots in successions of 1–10. But several species are still poorly known. Although the low hoots carry very far, they are not as terrifying as those of certain wood owls. Not many people have ever heard a hooting eagle owl in the wild, because they are very rare, at least outside Africa.

Bubo virginianus:
ho-hohoo ho ho, ... 3–8 hoots with both individual and geographical variation in number, arrangement and accent

Several variations known   *ho-ho-ho-hohoho ho ho, ho hohoho ho ho* etc.

B. bubo:
1. *huuhoo,* . . . . *huuhoo,* . . . . Each hoot protracted and with downward inflection
2. *ho-ho-ho-ho-ho-ho huuhoo,* . . . . Repeated at varying intervals; often in duets

B. capensis:
hu hu-ho, ... *hu hu-ho,* . . . . The final *ho* rather faint, and lower

B. africanus:
huhoo hoow,...huhoo hoow,..............

The *hoo* about a minor third lower than the *hu*, and the *hoow* still somewhat lower, and softer

B. poensis: Not known

B. nipalensis:
Described as a low, moaning hoot.

B. sumatrana:
Said to be a low twofold hoot *hoo hoo*, repeated at intervals, each hoot with a downward inflection.

B. shelleyi: Not known

B. lacteus:
1. *ho ho,*...*ho ho,*..........

At close distance sounding very gruff. Interval may be different

2. *ho-ho-ho-ho-ho-ho ho,*...

Repeated at varying intervals; each series starts very low, becoming higher and louder

3. A weaker whistle, repeated at intervals, seems to be common too.

B. coromandus:
Described as an accelerating *wo wo wo wo wo wo wo-wo*, getting softer and fainter at each successive note.

B. leucostictus: Not known

B. philippensis: Not known

Lophostrix

Almost nothing is known about these owls, *Lophostrix lettii* and *Lophostrix cristata*. They seem to be mobbed at by noisy passerine birds, which gives some hope that observers will discover more living birds in the wild, and learn something about their mysterious song.

Phodilus

The asiatic bay owl (*Phodilus badius*) has a very peculiar song, unique among the owls. It is a series of high whistles at varying pitches, difficult to characterize in words. A vague impression is given by the following description: *ülee-üü üwee üwee üwee üwee*. Nothing is known of the song of its African counterpart *Phodilus prigoginei* (known by only one specimen!), but it may be of a similar type.

Tyto

Tyto soumagnei:
wac-wac-wac...and another single, explosive call.

T. alba:
Described as an eerie screech, long and drawn out. Also a loud hiss and snores. In flight sometimes a *get-get*.

T. rosenbergii: Not known

T. inexpectata: Not known

T. novaehollandiae:
Described as *quair-sh-sh-sh*. Various chattering calls and quavering shrill notes also described.

T. aurantia: Not known

T. tenebricosa:
Described as between a scream and a whistle, rapidly going down the scale, like the sound of a falling bomb.

T. capensis:
Described as uttering weird screeches, similar to *T. alba*. A loud hiss.

Ketupa

Ketupa blakistoni: Not known

K. zeylonensis:
1. *boom-boom*...or *boom-o-boom*...

A deep, hollow, rather ventriloquial, humming, repeated at intervals

2. *hu-who-hu*...
3. *haw haw haw ha,*...
A cat-like mewing call is also described.

K. flavipes:
A deep *whoo-hoo* and a cat-like mewing have been described.

K. ketupa:
to-wee....to-wee,...

A soft, musical sound, in tone somewhere between a trill and a whistle

Scotopelia

Scotopelia peli:
1. *kuu-ku-ku* . . . .   A deep booming call, increasing in volume, with the last note drawn out

2. A screeching howl and a purring sound like that of a large cat such as a leopard.
3. A loud hoot rising to a screech and ending in an eerie wail which gradually dies away.

S. ussheri: Not known

S. bouvieri: Not known

Pulsatrix

Pulsatrix perspicillata:
1. Flight call is a short whistle of about ½ second duration, repeated every 5 to 10 seconds.   Two calls, differing in pitch are described

2. *hoo-hoo-hoo-hoo-hoo-hoo-hoo* . . . .   A short, rapid series of low chuckling hoots in all lasting about 1 second
Also a prolonged, tapping sound not unlike that of a woodpecker

P. koeniswaldiana: Not known

P. melanota: Not known

Nyctea

Nyctea scandiaca:
Normally silent. In flight, a loud *krow-ow* repeated several times. Also a loud *rick-rick-rick*. A further call, similar to vibrant croak of raven *Corvus corax*.

Surnia

Surnia ulula:
1. *ki-ki-ki-ki-ki-ki-* . . . .   Rather hawk-like and chattering, repeated about 12 times

2. *kiya kiya kiya kiya kiyayak* . . . .

Micrathene

Micrathene whitneyi:
1. *whi-whi-whi-whi-whi-whi-* . . . .   A rapid and high-pitched call, with a cackling quality. Often becomes higher in pitch and more excited in quality as it progresses, and descends in pitch towards the end

2. *chew-chew-chew-chew* . . . .

Uroglaux

Uroglaux dimorpha: Not known

Ninox

Ninox rufa:
Described as *woo-hoo* or *oo-hoo* or *woo-woo*. Similar to but softer than *Ninox strenua* (see below).

N. strenua:
Described as a rich *who-whoo* or *woof-woof*, not unlike the moo of a cow in tone.

N. connivens:
1. *ho-wuk-wuk* . . . . or *er-wook-wook,* . . . .   Rather a barking quality
2. *karr* . . . . *koo-wook* . . . . *koo-wook* . . . . *koo-wook* . . . . *koowook*   Male and female differ in pitch and sometimes duet. It also screams with a bloodcurdling cry like a woman calling for help

N. novaeseelandiae:
A rather high-pitched call repeated many times in quick succession. Written as *boo-book, mo-poke* or *buck-buck.* Also a cat-like mew: *ow-ow-ow* and a *cree-cree.*

N. scutulata:
1. *oo-uk* . . . . *oo-uk* . . . . *oo-uk* . . . . *oo-uk* . . . . *oo-uk* . . . . *oo-uk*   A very distinctive soft musical sound, repeated 5 to 10 times or even more at intervals of about 1 second. Birds sometimes duet

2. *hoo-hoo* . . . .*hoo-hoo* . . . . A low gentle call, repeated rapidly and regularly at intervals of about 7 seconds

N. affinis:
A loud *craw*. Also described in Japan and India as *oo-uk*.

N. superciliaris: Not known

N. philippensis: Not known

N. perversa: Not known

N. squamipila: Not known

N. theomacha: Described as a disyllabic call similar to *N. novaeseelandiae.*

N. punctulata: Described as a trisyllabic call, 2 short, low-pitched notes followed by a longer, high-pitched one.

N. meeki: Not known

N. solomonis: Not known

N. odiosa: Not known

N. jacquinoti: Not known

Sceloglaux

Sceloglaux albifacies:
A loud series of shrieks, repeated frequently. A call like a man calling *coo-eeee* . . . . . has also been described, and many varied mewing, yelping and whistling notes.

Athene

Athene noctua:
Loud *kiew, kiew* repeated monotonously, with musical, plaintive quality, at intervals of several seconds. A call of *wherrow*, uttered particularly near the nest, is also described.

A. brama:
A large variety of harsh, chattering notes are described. *chirurr . . chirurr . . chirurr* followed by or alternating with *cheevak . . cheevak . . cheevak.*
Also described: *kucha, kwachee, kwachee-kwachee-kwachee* and a double *zi-gwet.*

A. blewitti: Not known

Speotyto

Speotyto cunicularia:
A mellow *coo-c-hoo* . . . . . or *coo-hoo-.*

Rhinoptynx

Rhinoptynx clamator:
1. *ah-ah-ah-ah-ah-ah-ah-ah-ah* . . . . A series of low-pitched staccato hoots lasting in all about 1½ seconds
2. *ahoooooo* and *hoooo* . . . . Each lasting about ½ second
3. *ow-ow-ow-ow-ow-ow* . . . . A series of loud, barking sounds

Asio

Asio otus:
oo . . . oo . . . oo etc. . . . . Rather dove-like in quality, repeated every three seconds or so. Female call is higher pitched *shoo-oogh*, slurring down at end, repeated at longer intervals

A. stygius:
hu-hu . . . .

A. madagascariensis:
hak-hak-hak . . . .

A. flammeus:
1. *keaw keaw,* . . . . Rather a silent bird. A harsh flight note is also described, and a *tyak, tyarrp* call similar to calls of jackdaw *Corvus monedula*
2. *toot-toot-toot* . . . . or *boo-boo-boo* . . . . repeated 6 to 10 times at variable pace.

A. capensis:
Described as a hoarse, harsh frog-like croak.

Pseudoscops

Nesasio

Aegolius

Pseudoscops grammicus:
Described as a curious *wow* and a tremulous *whooooo*.

Nesasio solomonensis: Not known

Aegolius funereus:
1. *poo-póó-poo-póó-poo-póó* . . . .

Alternate notes are stressed. A soft, liquid call, it sounds rather like water dripping

2. *oolooooloo* . . . .

A. acadicus:
1. *too-too-too-too-too-too-too* etc. . . . .
A long series of short whistles, repeated mechanically in endless succession. As many as 100 to 120 whistles per minute:

From a distance it has a bell-like quality

2. *sa-a-ayt-sch- whet* . . . .

A weak 2-syllable call like a saw being sharpened; it has a somewhat grass-hopper-like quality

A. ridgwayi:
A series of mellow whistles, each note distinct. It somewhat resembles the song of *A. acadicus.*

A. harrisii: Not known

Glossary

allopatric   Having non-overlapping ranges.

asynchronous hatching   'Staggered' hatching of eggs. Eggs are laid over a period of days; owls, hawks, eagles and some other species begin to incubate when the first egg is laid, so eggs hatch at different times, in order of laying. The earliest hatchlings stand the best chance of survival when food supplies are limited.

binocular vision   Vision in which both eyes view the same scene from slightly different aspects: an aid to judging distance.

colour phase   Many owls have two main colour forms, rufous and grey, known as colour phases.

conspecific   Of the same species.

ear tufts   Erectile tufts of feathers above the eyes of many species. They have nothing to do with ears. Controlled by scalp muscles, they probably play a part in social communication.

facial disc   Saucer-shaped disc of feathers surrounding the eyes, which acts as a sound reflector. It varies in extent and definition from species to species, being most fully developed in those that are most nocturnal.

horns   Ear tufts.

intergradation   The way in which categories sometimes merge imperceptibly without clearly defined limits.

irruption   The movement outside their normal range which excess individuals of some species are forced to undergo in years when food supplies become limited.

isolating mechanisms   Any mechanisms that keep related species reproductively distinct (e.g. geographical isolation, variation in breeding seasons, lack of sexual attraction between different species, sterility or lack of viability of hybrids, etc.) or ecologically distinct (e.g. geographical isolation, preferences for different habitats, feeding methods and foods etc.).

lores   The sides of the head between the eyes and the bill.

mantle   The back and folded wings.

monotypic genus   A genus with only one species.

montane forest   Mountain forest.

nominate race   The race from which a species takes it name.

orbit   Eye socket.

pellet   Accumulation of undigested parts of food, regurgitated through the mouth in a compact mass.

relict form   A race or species that has become geographically isolated in a small part of its former range.

sedentary   Not migratory.

tapetum   Reflecting layer behind the retina of the eye possessed by many nocturnal animals, which enables dim light to be utilized more efficiently.

wing load   Relationship of body weight to wing area.

Books for further reading

BENT, A. C.: *Life Histories of North American Birds of Prey*
Dover Publications Inc., New York, 1958

DEMENT'EV ET AL.: *Birds of the Soviet Union*
National Science Foundation, Washington, 1966–68

DE SCHAUENSEE, R. M.: *Guide to the Birds of South America*
Oliver and Boyd, London; Livingston, New York, 1970

FLEAY, D.: *Nightwatchmen of Bush and Plain*
Jacaranda Press, Brisbane; Cowman, Tri-Ocean, New York, 1968

FISHER, J., SIMON, N. AND VINCENT, J.: *The Red Book: wildlife in danger*
Collins, London; Harper and Row, New York, 1969

GLUE, D. E.: 'Owl pellets', *Birds of the World* 5, pp. 1368–70
IPC London, 1970

GROSSMAN, M. L. AND HAMLET, J.: *Birds of Prey of the World*
Clarkson N. Potter Inc., New York, 1964

GEROUDET, P.: *Les Rapaces diurnes et nocturnes d'Europe*
Pelachaux et Niestlé, Neuchatel, 1965

HOSKING, E. AND NEWBERRY, C. W.: *Birds of the Night*
Collins, London, 1945

LLOYD, G. AND D.: *Birds of Prey*
Paul Hamlyn, Feltham, 1972; Bantam Books, New York, 1972

MACWORTH-PRAED, C. W. AND GRANT, C. H. B.: *Handbook of African Birds*
Longmans, London, 1952–73

RIPLEY, S. D. AND SALIM ALI: *Handbook of the Birds of India & Pakistan*
Oxford University Press, London; Smithsonian Institution, Washington, 1968

SPARKS, J. AND SOPER, T.: *Owls: their natural and unnatural history*
David and Charles, Devon; Taplinger, New York, 1970

VOOUS, K. H.: *Atlas of European Birds*
Nelson, London, 1960

The Authors: biographical notes

Dr Philip Burton read zoology at University College London, and received his Ph.D degree for work on the feeding behaviour and anatomy of waders. He now works in the sub-department of ornithology of the British Museum (Natural History). His main research subject is the anatomy of birds. He worked for a time at the American Museum of Natural History in New York, and recent research has taken him to both Africa and Central America.

Dr Michael Fogden trained as a zoologist at the University of Oxford and has specialized in the ecology and physiology of birds in the tropics. He spent several years working in the rainforest of Borneo, based at the Sarawak Museum, three years as a Ford Foundation Research Fellow at the Nuffield Unit of Tropical Animal Ecology in Uganda and now works in Mexico for the Centre for Overseas Pest Research. He has published scientific papers on the ecology of bats and tarsiers as well as on the ecology and physiology of birds, and popular articles on a variety of biological subjects.

Howard Ginn read zoology, botany and physiology at Cambridge. For the past five years he has been a Research officer at the British Trust for Ornithology. Before that he worked at the Game Research Association on partridge distribution and later at the Huntingdon Research Centre on the toxicity and safety evaluations of various compounds, ranging from medicinal and agricultural chemicals to cosmetics.

David Glue trained as a zoologist at London University and later joined the British Trust for Ornithology as a Research Officer in the Population section. He has been concerned with the organization and results of several bird surveys and censuses and has published papers on the breeding biology of various groups of birds, seasonal mortality and causes of death in birds of prey, and pellet analysis and food of birds of prey.

Dr Colin Harrison is a biologist, working in the sub-department of Ornithology of the British Museum (Natural History). He has studied birds in the field in many countries and worked on bird behaviour under aviary conditions. In the museum he works on the structure of systematics of birds and on their nests and eggs.

Gerrit Hekstra graduated from the Free University, Amsterdam. After teaching for several years he became Secretary of Biological Council of the Royal Netherland Academy of Sciences and now works as a biologist in charge of environmental planning at the Ministry of Public Health and Environment, the Netherlands. His thesis, on the geographic variation, ecological differentiation and species formation in the genus *Otus* is in process of being published.

Dr Heimo Mikkola worked on owls and other birds of prey from 1965–72 in the University of Oulu, and has made a special study of the great grey owl (*Strix nebulosa*). Since 1972 he has been in the Department of Zoology, University of Kuopio, completing his doctoral thesis on ecological isolation in the owls of Finland. He has written several articles for scientific journals on owls and on a variety of other zoological subjects.

Dr R. K. Murton read zoology at University College London and after graduating joined the Ministry of Agriculture, Fisheries and Food as an ornithologist employed to study biology of species harmful to agriculture and food production. He moved to the Nature Conservancy in 1970. He has produced various scientific papers in the field of bird ecology and physiology of reproduction and two books on natural history.

Ian Prestt is a Fellow of the Institute of Biology and has BSc and MSc degrees from the University of Liverpool. He has held various posts in the Nature Conservancy, at one time being particularly concerned with the conservation of British birds of prey and the effects on them of chemical pesticides. He is now Deputy Director in the Central Unit on Environmental Pollution, Department of the Environment in London.

Dr John Sparks is a zoologist who has undertaken extensive post-doctoral research into bird behaviour at London University and The Zoological Society of London. He has written a number of books on various aspects of animal life and now works for the BBC television Natural History Unit at Bristol.

Dr Bernard Stonehouse trained as a biologist at the Universities of London and Oxford. Working on animal ecology for most of his career, he has held appointments at the University of Canterbury, New Zealand, Yale University and the University of British Columbia. He is now teaching a new course in environmental science at the University of Bradford, England.

C. A. Walker is a member of the Department of Palaentology at the British Museum (Natural History), studying fossil birds and reptiles. He has written articles and papers for scientific journals and conferences on both fossil and recent birds.

Reginald Wagstaffe studied ornithology at the University of Cincinatti, Ohio. He worked as a professional zoologist and botanist in a number of museum posts, specializing in the taxonomy of birds. Now retired, he works part-time in the Zoology Museum of Cambridge University.

Wouter van der Weyden studied biology at the Free University of Amsterdam, and has made an extensive study of the songs of the scops and screech owls.

Index

Numbers in italics refer to illustrations.

A

Aegolius, 170–175, 184, 209
  acadicus, 33, 171, *172–3*, 173, 175, 209
  funereus, 33, 128, *170*, *171*, 171–173, 209
  harrisii, 171, *174*, 175, 209
  ridgwayi, 171, *174*, 175
Aegothelidae, 40
Agathokles, 22
Agrippa, death of, 24
Archaeopteryx lithographica, 30–31
Asio, 116, 137–144, 184, 208, *32, 39*
  abyssinicus included in *A. otus*
  brevipes, 32
  capensis, 143–144, *146*, 208
  flammeus, 33, 139, *139*, 141, 143, *143*, 144, *144*, 146, 187–188, 208
    galapagensis, 143
  henrici, 30
  madagascariensis, 141, *142*, 208
  otus, 33, 35, 138, 139, *140*, 141, 144, 146, 188–189, 192, 208
  pigmaeus, 32
  priscus, 33
  stygius, 33, 141, *142*, 208
Athene, 164–168, 184, 208
  blewitti, *167*, 168, 208
  brama, 166, *166*, 168, 208
  murivora, 33
  noctua, 21, 33, 164–166, *165*, 168, 190, 192, 208
    lilith, 166
    vidalii, 166
Athene, *see* deities, association with
Athens, sacred owl of, *20, 21*
attack, *see* behaviour, attacking
attitudes of public to owls, 18, 20, 21
Australian aborigines, owl man of, *19*
autecology, 186

B

Barking owl, *see Ninox connivens*
Barn owls, *see* Tytonidae
Barn owl
  African *see Tyto alba affinis*
  Andaman *see T. a. de-roepstorffi*
  Australian, *see T. a. delicatula*
  Bahama, *see T. a. lucayana*
  Canary Islands, *see T. a. gracilirostris*
  Cape Verde Islands, *see T. a. detorta*
  Celebes, *see T. a. rosenbergii*
  Common, *see T. alba*
  Cuba, *see T. a. furcata*
  Dark-breasted, *see T. a. guttata*
  Indian, *see T. a. stertens*
  Madagascar, *see T. a. hypermetra*
  Madeiran, *see T. a. schmitzi*
  Minahassa, *see T. inexpectata*
  New Britain, *see T. aurantia*

New Guinea, *see T. alba meeki*
North American, *see T. a. pratincola*
São Thomé, *see T. a. thomensis*
Savu, *see T. a. everetti*
Sumba, *see Tyto alba sumbaensis*
Barred owl, *see Strix varia*
Bay owl
  Ceylon, *see Phodilus badius assimilis*
  Common, *see P. badius*
  Congo, *see P. prigoginei*
Bay owls, *see* Phodilinae
behaviour,
  attacking, 55, 102, 123–124, 131, 132, 154, 181
  defensive, 46, 93
  predatory, 188
    Asio, 146, 149, 163, 166, 168
    Bubo, 72, 77, 88
    Glaucidium, 180, 184, 185
    Ketupa, 64, 67
    Nyctea, 92
    Otus, 94, 101
    Scotopelia, 69
    Strix, 124, 125, 126, 130
    Tyto alba, 44
  territorial
    Asio, 141, 143
    Bubo, 77
    Ketupa, 64
    Otus, 101
    Strix, 128, 132, 187
    Tyto alba, 46
Birds of the World, J. L. Peters, 47
Black and white owl, *see Ciccaba nigrolineata*
Black-banded owl, *see C. huhula*
Boobook owl, *see Ninox novaeseelandiae*
breeding, 187, 192
  Asio, 139, 141, 143–144
  Aegolius, 172, 173, 175
  Athene, 164, 165–166, 168
  Bubo, 77–78, 79, 80, 82, 88
  Ciccaba, 119, 120, 122
  Glaucidium, 176, 179, 184
  Ketupa, 67–68
  Micrathene, 170
  Ninox, 148, 150, 152, 154, 156, 158
  Nyctea, 92–93
  Otus, 101, 102, 106, 108, 111
  Phodilus, 59
  Pulsatrix, 116, 118
  Speotyto, 170
  Strix, 122–123, 125–126, 128, 130, 132, 134–135
  Surnia, 163
  Tyto, 46, 52, 54, 56
Brodkorb, *Catalogue of Fossil Birds*, 30
Bubo, 26, 32, 39, 61, 72–90, 114, 205–206
  africanus, 33, 80, *80*, *81*, 82, *82*, 88, 205
    africanus, 82
    cinerascens, 82
    milesi, 82
  binagadensis, 33
  bubo, 31, 33, *35, 38, 40*, 72, *73*, *74–75*, 76, *74*–78, 80, 82, 88, 92, 128, 189–190, 205

ascalaphus, 76
bengalensis, 76
nikolskii, 72
capensis, *78*, 79, 80, 82, 205
  mackinderi, *78*, 79, 80
coromandus, 88, *89*, 205
florianae, 32
incertus, 30
lacteus, 80, 82, *83*, 84, 86, 205
leguati, 33
leucostictus, 80, *85*, 88, 205
nipalensis, *87*, 88, 205
philippensis, *86*, 88, 205
poensis, *84*, 86, 88, 205
  vosseleri, *84*, 86
poirreiri, 30
shelleyi, *85*, 86, 88, 205
sinclairi, 33
sumatrana, 88, *90*, 205
virginianus, 26, 33, 39, 76, 77, *78*, 78–79, 192, 205
Buff-fronted owl, *see Aegolius harrisii*
Burrowing owl, *see Speotyto cunicularia*

C

cactus, Saguaro, 169, 170
caeca, intestinal, 40
Caprimulgiformes, 31, 40
carving, Palaeolithic, 18
Catalogue of Fossil Birds, Brodkorb, 30
census, *see* population survey
Ciccaba, 116, 119–122, 204–205
  albitarsus, 122, 204
  huhula, 121–122, *123*, 204
  nigrolineata, 120–121, *121*, 204–205
  virgata, 33, 120, *120*, 204
  woodfordii, 116, 122, 124, *125*, 205
competition, 86, 99, 119, 144, 145, 146, 147
conservation, 186–192
Crescens, Petrus von, 25
Crested owl, *see Lophostrix cristata*

D

death, association with, 22, 24
decoys, 25–26, 190
density, population, *see* population density
deities, association with, 21
diet, 45–196, *passim*
distribution
  geographical, 42–184 *passim*
  geological, 31–33

E

Eagle owl
  Akun, *see B. leucostictus*
  Cape, *see B. capensis*
  Dusky, *see B. coromandus*
  Eurasian, *see B. bubo*
  Forest, *see B. nipalensis*
  Fraser's, *see B. poensis*
  Mackinder's, *see B. capensis mackinderi*
  Malaysian, *see B. sumatrana*
  Milky, *see B. lacteus*
  Nduk, *see B. poensis vosseleri*
  Pharaoh, *see B. bubo ascalaphus*
  Philippine, *see B. philippensis*